"I did not think we, as a society, could agree to disagree, which makes this book incredibly powerful – and incredibly needed in our divisive times. Higdon and Huff have provided both depth and breadth to multiple areas of our mediated world and in so doing have presented readers with a cogent and incredibly valuable text that will enable readers to learn about the mass media, themselves, and concrete ways to make change."

Allison Butler, *Senior Lecturer & Director of Undergraduate Advising, Director Media Literacy Certificate Program, Department of Communication, University of Massachusetts, Amherst*

"In the age of new and powerful tools of communication, democracy has become more fragile and vulnerable to attacks by right-wing forces. What is clear is that the tools of communication, culture, literacy and critical thinking are more crucial than ever in creating both informed citizens and maintaining a substantive democracy. *Let's Agree to Disagree* is a brilliant and informative guide and analysis to the most defining features of what it means to create critically literate citizens, to enable how they might communicate constructively with each other, and what it means connect an informed public to critically engaged actions. Higdon and Huff provide a brilliant, crucial analysis of the dangers that democracy now faces; they provide an invaluable analysis of what it means to understand and engage the role of communication in fighting against the forces of civic illiteracy, and the role that citizens can play in engaging, understanding, and assessing how to think, engage, and act through an informed lens of critical thinking. *Let's Agree to Disagree* is both a primer and an invaluable resource on misinformation, critical thinking, a disregard for the truth, and what is necessary to address the new and powerful forms of communication that now shape politics, power and mass consciousness. This is a book that should be read by anyone who believes that matters of literacy, truth, rationality, and civic courage are essential to fighting for a radical democracy."

Henry Giroux, *McMaster University Professor for Scholarship in the Public Interest, Paulo Freire Distinguished Scholar in Critical Pedagogy, at McMaster University*

"*Let's Agree to Disagree* provides a comprehensive analysis of the challenges, failures, and successes of communication and critical thinking for justice and democracy. Nolan Higdon and Mickey Huff have written an essential book for all educators because dialogue and critical reflection are the heart of progressive education. The better we learn to listen, question, and respond with compassion, empathy, and respect, the more likely we will build genuine relationships of caring and critical inquiry where authentic learning occurs and social justice thrives."

Jeff Share, *Ph.D., University of California, Los Angeles*

Let's Agree to Disagree

In an age defined by divisive discourse and disinformation, democracy hangs in the balance. *Let's Agree to Disagree* seeks to reverse these trends by fostering constructive dialogue through critical thinking and critical media literacy. This transformative text introduces readers to useful theories, powerful case studies, and easily adoptable strategies for becoming sharper critical thinkers, more effective communicators, and critically media literate citizens.

Nolan Higdon is a lecturer at Merrill College and the Education Department at University of California, Santa Cruz. Higdon's areas of concentration include digital culture, news media history, and critical media literacy. Higdon is a founding member of the Critical Media Literacy Conference of the Americas. He sits on the boards of the Action Coalition for Media Education (ACME) and Northwest Alliance For Alternative Media And Education. His most recent publications include *The Anatomy of Fake News: A Critical News Literacy Education* (2020) and *The Podcaster's Dilemma: Decolonizing Podcasters in the Era of Surveillance Capitalism* (2021). He is a longtime contributor to Project Censored's annual book, *Censored*. In addition, he has been a contributor to *Truthout* and *Counter-Punch;* and a source of expertise for numerous news outlets including *The New York Times, CNBC,* and *San Francisco Chronicle.*

Mickey Huff is the director of Project Censored and president of the nonprofit Media Freedom Foundation. To date, he has co-edited 13 editions of the Project's yearbook, including most recently *Project Censored's State of the Free Press* (2022), with Andy Lee Roth. He is also co-author, with Nolan Higdon, of *United States of Distraction: Media Manipulation in Post-Truth America (and what we can do about it)* (2019). Huff received the Beverly Kees Educator Award as part of the 2019 James Madison Freedom of Information Awards from the Society of Professional Journalists, Northern California. He is professor of social science, history, and journalism at Diablo Valley College, where he co-chairs the history program and is chair of the Journalism Department. Huff is executive producer and host of The Project Censored Show, a weekly syndicated public affairs program that airs across the U.S. on Pacifica Radio. Learn more at projectcensored.org.

Let's Agree to Disagree

A Critical Thinking Guide to Communication, Conflict Management, and Critical Media Literacy

Nolan Higdon and Mickey Huff

Routledge
Taylor & Francis Group

NEW YORK AND LONDON

First published 2022
by Routledge
605 Third Avenue, New York, NY 10158

and by Routledge
4 Park Square, Milton Park, Abingdon, Oxon OX14 4RN

Routledge is an imprint of the Taylor & Francis Group, an informa business

Library of Congress Cataloging-in-Publication Data
A catalog record for this title has been requested

ISBN: 978-1-032-16904-0 (hbk)
ISBN: 978-1-032-16898-2 (pbk)
ISBN: 978-1-003-25090-6 (ebk)

DOI: 10.4324/9781003250906

Typeset in Garamond
by Taylor & Francis Books

Contents

Illustrations

Figures

Table

Acknowledgements

We are grateful to the crew at Routledge and the Taylor & Francis Group for nurturing our scholarship through a clear publication process. Much adoration and praise is owed to Dean Birkenkamp for believing in and supporting our vision for this manuscript, as well as Lakshita Joshi, Lewis Hodder, Dominic Corti, and Jeffrey Boys.

We are fortunate to collaborate with numerous transformative organizations that improve our lives and the lives of others. Much of what we lay out in this text comes from our experiences working with these groups: Action Coalition for Media Education, Behind the Headlines, Credder, Critical Media Literacy Conference of the Americas, Critical Media Project, Improve the News, Media Freedom Foundation and Project Censored, Mount Diablo Peace and Justice Center, Pacifica Radio, PropWatch, The Real News Network, and Union for Democratic Communication. The culmination of this project is due to the strength and inspiration we derive from their work and the good people associated with them.

Similarly, this project was enhanced by an incredible network of thought-provoking individuals we're honored to count as stellar colleagues and stalwart allies: Elizabeth Abrams, Mnar Muhawesh Adley, Maximillian Alvarez, Robin Andersen, Marcia Annenberg, Adam Armstrong, Sharyl Attkisson, Margli Auclair, Phil Auclair, Jorge Ayala, Nicholas Baham III, Matt Bailey, Manfred Becker, Kate Bell, Adam Bessie, Ben Boyington, Lonny Avi Brooks, Kenn Burrows, Allison Butler, Mary Cardaras, Robert Carley, Renee Childs, Jamal Cooks, John Corbally, Ian Davis, Roberto de Roock, Brian Dolber, Janice Domingo, Jessie Dubreuil, Bridget Ford, Andrea Gambino, Stephen M. Gennaro, Henry Giroux, Noah Golden, Eleanor Goldfield, Mary Grueser, Rachel Guldin, Doug Hecker, Aaron Heresco, Michael Hoechsmann, Amina Humphrey, Linda Ivey, Charlotte Katz, Josef Kay, Dorothy Kidd, Grant Kien, Dan Kovalik, Amanda Lashaw, Michael Levitin, Dylan Lazaga, Cynthia Lewis, Danielle Ligocki, Jen Lyons, Kalemba Kitzo, Steve Macek, Susan Maret, Emil Marmol, Abby Martin, Lisa Martin, Stuart McElddrey, James

McFadden, Kate McQueen, Mark Crispin Miller, Michael Nagler, Sangha Niyogi, Christopher Oscar, Chase Palmieri, Peter Phillips, Albert Ponce, Matthew Powell, Kayla Rivara, Reina Robinson, Andy Lee Roth, Greg Ruggiero, Danuta Sawka, T. M. Scruggs, Jeff Share, Lauren Shields, Phoebe Sorgen, James Stancil, Colleen Sweeney, Max Tegmark, Alison Trope, Obed Vasquez, Wanda Washington, Rob Williams, and Amber Yang. Thank you all for your insight, scholarship, advice, and most of all, thank you for your friendship and ongoing support.

A special shout out to Allison Butler, Albert Ponce, and Jeff Share for giving deep and meaningful feedback in a very short period of time. It was a lot to ask of you, yet you came through for us with sound advice and insight to improve the manuscript and help clarify our thinking. For that, we are most grateful. We are so appreciative that Michelle Ciccone produced the exemplary educator resources for this text.

We want to thank all of our students, past and present, for the feedback and opportunities they provide to us to become better teachers and critical thinkers, in and out of the classroom.

Every author needs a respite from the fog of writing and research, and some of the most memorable ones were when the animals interrupted our writing process. Thank you to our furry friends, Emma, Lemmy, Ozzy, and Vangl for helping keep things real.

Thank you to Ray McDaniel for never missing an opportunity to start a debate and say "I am a critical thinker." Those memories remain a source of humor and strength every time critical thinking is discussed.

Last, but certainly not least, to our life partners, Meg Huff (and kids!) and Kacey Van der Vorst, without your continued support of our scholarship, none of this would be possible. When you write a book, your entire family writes a book. We are so appreciative and fortunate to have you in our lives.

We hope you all remind us of the lessons and strategies we've compiled in this book the next time we get into an argument or have a rare dispute. Sometimes we can agree to disagree.

Nolan Higdon and Mickey Huff
January 2022

Introduction

Why Should We Agree to Disagree?

From a Folsom State Prison cell in 1965, American writer, activist, and early Black Panther Party member Eldridge Cleaver wrote:

> The destiny of the entire human race depends on what is going on in America today. This is a staggering reality to the rest of the world; they must feel like passengers in a supersonic jetliner who are forced to watch helplessly while a passel of drunks, hypes, freaks, and madmen fight for the controls and the pilot's seat.

Three years later, his words were published in a collection of essays titled *Soul on Ice*. Also in 1968, astronaut Frank Borman described what it was like to be on Apollo 8 and see the earth in its entirety as "You're going to get a concept that maybe this really is one world and why the hell can't we learn to live together like decent people."[1]

Borman and Cleaver's commentary noted the sense of division that proliferated throughout America at the end of the 1960s. Few events contributed to the sense of disunion more than the April 4, 1968 murder of Rev. Dr. Martin Luther King Jr. That same evening, then presidential primary candidate Robert Kennedy pleaded for national unity: "Let us dedicate ourselves to what the Greeks wrote so many years ago: to tame the savageness of man and make gentle the life of this world."[2] Two months later Kennedy would be murdered. Despite the appeals for unity, it seemed America was in a state of inescapable polarization after a decade of cascading events such as the 1967 and 1968 Detroit and Los Angeles race riots; violent clashes between police and anti-war activists, most notably at the 1968 Democratic Party Convention in Chicago; an influential 1968 presidential run by the white supremacist party of George Wallace; the deaths of innocent civilians and students at Kent State and Jackson State in 1970; the expansion of the unpopular Vietnam War; and the murder of inspirational figures such as John and Robert Kennedy, Martin Luther King Jr., Malcolm X, and Fred Hampton.[3]

DOI: 10.4324/9781003250906-1

In fact, a 1968 published report commissioned by President Lyndon Baines Johnson summed up what was all too obvious about the state of the nation: "To pursue our present course will involve the continuing polarization of the American community and, ultimately, the destruction of basic democratic values."[4] Polarization continues to be a concern for 21st century Americans after a number of macabre cases: Dylan Roof, a white supremacist, shot up a black Charleston church in 2015; James T. Hodgkinson shot a Republican congressperson and three other people at a baseball game in 2017; the anti-racist Heather Heyer was murdered at a 2017 white nationalist rally in Charlottesville, Virginia; Cesar Sayoc mailed bombs to members of the media and Democratic Party in 2018; six men sought to kidnap Michigan Governor Gretchen Whitmer in 2020 over policy disputes; and thousands of people marched on the U.S. Capital in January of 2021 causing property damage and the deaths five of people to overturn the 2020 Presidential Election results.[5] In fact, a 2021, a CBS/YouthGov poll found that over half of Americans view other Americans as the number one threat to their way of life.[6] This was true for over half of Democrats, Republicans, and independent voters.[7]

Commentators and scholars argue that the tumult of the 1960s is familiar to contemporary audiences because the U.S. has been in a cultural, political, and social malaise since the 1970s.[8] Until the1960s, the U.S. seemed to experience dramatic changes every decade or two, but since the 1970s, the U.S. has remained in stasis, having the same battles over the same issues with almost no notable progress.[9] In *The Decadent Society: America Before and After the Pandemic*, Ross Douthat contends that the decadence – a state of excessive indulgence – afforded to U.S. citizens has left them with little motivation to engage with big ideas and transformative visions of the future.[10] In Douthat's estimation, Americans are stuck in a sclerotic state, fighting the same political battles since the 1970s over taxes, abortion rights, racial justice, immigration, and foreign policy, to name a few. Meanwhile, larger issues that require collectivist solutions and a transformative response such as the climate crisis receive a tepid response, if any.

We wrote this book in the hope that it will be used to change the course of where the U.S. purported democratic republic is heading. We hope this text can play a role in helping Americans escape the torpid state of polarization and engender a renewed interest in collectivist approaches to contemporary issues. Rather than succumb to the seduction of division and abandon participatory, representative democracy, we hope readers will courageously utilize this text as a means for strengthening it. We believe, in the words of the former Prime Minister of the United Kingdom, Winston Churchill, that democracy is "the worst form of government except for all those other forms that have been tried from time to time."[11] Indeed, whether it be the failed compromises that led to the U.S. Civil War in the 19th century or the rise of fascism on the run up to the Second World War in the middle of the 20th century, history reveals that if the people have the temerity, the collective efforts of the citizenry can mobilize to save democracy.

Divided Republic

Just as it did in 1968, the hyper-partisanship of the 21st century threatens the viability of American democracy. According to Larry Diamond and Leonardo Morlino, effective democracies consist of four key elements:[12]

1   A political system for choosing and replacing individuals through free and fair elections;
2   the active civic participation among the citizens;
3   protection of the human rights of all citizens;
4   a rule of law, that is equally applied to all citizens.

The concept of democracy was cemented in Ancient Greece where the *demos,* a term in reference to the "common people," was married to *kratos,* which denoted "strength." Scholars have long argued that the strength of democracy rests upon social capital. According to political scientist Robert D. Putnam, **social capital** refers "to the social networks, norms and trust that enable people to act together effectively in the pursuit of shared objectives which is accumulated through the relationships and interactions among the electorate."[13] Social capital rests upon both constructive dialogue and a shared experience among the citizenry, both of which have been hampered by the nation's polarized politics.[14]

In recent decades, the American electorate appears to be in a vast conflagration of hyper-partisan politics. A May 2021 paper from the World Inequality Lab explains that since 1948, western democracies have seen educated elites usurp power over liberal-leaning parties and financial elites doing the same for right-leaning parties. The authors argue these multi-elite party systems avoid policies that seek to improve the material conditions of the people and amplify cultural issues that divide the electorate such as green and anti-immigration movements.[15] As a result, contemporary U.S. voters have largely bifurcated into distinct political tribes that look to party affiliation rather than policy preferences to inform their electoral participation.[16] In fact, a 2019 study from Michael Barber and Jeremy C. Pope in the *American Political Science Review* found that low-knowledge respondents, strong Republicans, Donald Trump-approving respondents, and self-described conservatives who voted for Trump, approved of whatever he said, including his support for some liberal policy measures, because they are loyal to their party not policy.[17]

As social identity theorists have long predicted,[18] party polarization results in factionalism: Party adherents political identity is limited to lauding and defending the in-group while touting hostile opinions about the out-groups.[19] For example, a 2017 study from Gregory A. Huber and Neil Malhotra in *The Journal of Politics* about online dating found that an individual's party affiliation is a decisive factor in choosing a dating partner.[20] Similarly, a 2020 Pew Research poll found that seven out of ten self-identified Democrats would not consider dating a person who voted for Trump.[21] Shanto Iyengar and Sean J. Westwood explain that partisan divides can persist because "unlike race, gender and other social divides where group-related attitudes and behaviors are constrained by social norms, there are no corresponding pressures to temper disapproval of political opponents."[22]

In addition to polling, the malignancy of hyper-partisan politics appears in voting patterns. Since the 1990s, studies have found that Americans are drifting further and further to the political extremes.[23] For example, a 2021 Pew Research study found that before the 1990s, it was common for voters to select presidential candidates and U.S. Senators from different parties in a single electoral year. However, since then it has become an almost non-existent practice in American politics as voters vote uniformly with one party or another.[24] Two years earlier, Pew concluded that "the level of division and animosity – including negative sentiments among partisans toward the members of the opposing party – has only deepened."[25]

Scholars argue that media help ossify the hyper-partisan divisions.[26] This includes the news media, social media, and entertainment media, from Madison Avenue to Netflix, Hollywood to Silicon Valley, and an endless array of television and online streaming-type programs.[27] In terms of both digital and legacy media, a handful of corporations dominate the media that Americans use.[28] Rather than unite the people in a shared experience conducive to constructive dialogue, this corporate-dominated, private for-profit media in the U.S. has sought to divide the electorate. In *Hate Inc.,* journalist Matt Taibbi notes that legacy media – such as network news, cable news, and the newspapers – abandoned the Cold War framing of news stories, which pitted the American audience against the communists, for a partisan framing that pits Democrats against Republicans.[29] This style of reporting deliberately stokes hyper-partisan fears by characterizing the opposition party and their supporters as villainous as the communists were reported to be in the mid-20th century. This milquetoast approach to reporting was borrowed from pro-wrestling, which for decades had profited from confirming audience desires to be on the side of the "good guy," by mimicking an ultimate villain, a foil, who is the "bad guy." This corrosive approach to the electorate was made worse by the advent of internet platforms such as Google, Facebook, Instagram,

TikTok, and Twitter, which all rely on a business model of data collection and analysis that feeds users information that confirms their views rather than challenges them, making users further afraid of the "other side."

Rather than reject the hyper-partisan discourses of corporate media, political campaigns amplify incandescent characterizations of political opponents. For example, in 2008, then presidential candidate Barack Obama mocked conservative voters by claiming that "they get bitter, they cling to guns or religion or antipathy to people who aren't like them or anti-immigrant sentiment or anti-trade sentiment as a way to explain their frustrations."[30] In 2012, Republican presidential candidate Mitt Romney claimed that 47 percent of voters would not vote for him "because they are dependent upon government ... believe that they are victims ... believe the government has a responsibility to care for them ... these are people who pay no income tax."[31] In 2016, candidate Hillary Clinton referred to Trump supporters as a "basket of deplorables."[32] Not to be outdone, Trump has lobbed a litany of sexist, racist, and xenophobic insults at voters, referring to those of Mexican descent as "rapists" and women as "fat pigs," "dogs," "slobs."[33] More recently, Joe Biden referred to some voters pejoratively by referring to one as "a damn liar," another as "too old to vote" for him, and even called a student a "lying, dog-faced pony soldier" (whatever that exactly means).[34] Lost in the hyper-partisan milieu of American political culture is citizens' desire to engage in constructive dialogue.

Destructive Dialogue

Despite the widespread use of so-called *social* media, the increased polarization of the U.S. reveals Americans choose to avoid or silence their political rivals rather than engage in democratic dialogue. We see it in news media with people such as Brian Seltzer of CNN arguing that deplatforming Donald Trump is acceptable because "reducing a liar's reach is not the same as censoring freedom of speech;"[35] Fox News Channel's Sean Hannity hosting and talking over New York Mayor Bill de Blasio for over 40 minutes;[36] in 2020, CNBC's Rick Santelli launching a shouting match on air where he yelled over others about COVID-19 restrictions;[37] and that same year, a journalist and a Trump campaign official yelling at each other about the official vote count from the 2020 Presidential Election on Fox News Channel.[38] The impulse to silence rather than engage in dialogue with ideological enemies runs rampant in electoral politics, such as the September 2020 Presidential debate that saw Trump interrupt his Democratic challenger Joe Biden over 50 times;[39] and Biden asking Trump, "Will you shut up, man?" at that very same debate.[40]

In fact, Americans question whether dialogue with other Americans, a necessity for the cultivation of social capital, is even worth their time. In 2020, Bahman Fozouni, a professor emeritus in the Political Science Department at California State University, Sacramento, asked "should we find ourselves in the company of the Trumpies, does it make sense to engage them in a political conversation?"[41] A year earlier, filmmaker Michael Moore argued that liberals have "all tried at Thanksgiving dinner to convince the conservative brother-in-law of the wrongness of his ways, but he's three years deep into pro-Trump. He's lost. And we have to kind of give up on them, because we don't have the time."[42] However, we're arguing here that maybe we need to take the time, and make an opportunity to engage in critical discourse through constructive communication rather than write people off because it seems easier. It is one thing to want change, but it is quite another to do the difficult work required to change minds and build alliances.

It should also be noted that assuming others are "lost" ignores the ways in which bad information can make otherwise good people do horrible things. Take the example of Ashli Babbitt, an Air Force veteran who falsely believed the 2020 election was stolen and was shot and killed while storming the Capitol building in Washington, D.C. to stop the election certification process on January 6, 2021. If the information had been factual, which it was not, Babbitt would most likely be heralded as a hero for defending the democratic process. This reveals that it was not their values – love of country and democracy – that made them act in a horrific manner, but a sensationalist and toxic media diet that fed the decision. This is all the more reason to engage in dialogue and build social capital because to dismiss or ignore those different from ourselves is to risk further damage and harm to themselves and the larger democratic society.

As conservative professor of jurisprudence and Director of the James Madison Program in American Ideals and Institutions at Princeton University, Robert P. George explains, this is a death knell for a democracy because "you cannot run a democratic republic if people are not willing to engage each other and learn from each other and treat each other respectfully—not just out of politeness but out of a desire to advance the common good."[43] Similarly, noted civil rights activist and former Harvard and Princeton scholar Cornel West reminds us that civil discourse has been lost to destructive conflict because of

> the eclipse of integrity and honesty and decency, and the normalization of corruption, deceit, and mendacity. It's all about manipulating your political opponents to diminish them and show that they have nothing to say or contribute. People no longer have dialogue. It's all monologue.[44]

The threat destructive dialogue poses to democracy has shaped recent discourses about civil war. A **civil war** refers to "an armed conflict between citizens of the same country."[45] In 2019, U.S. attorney Joseph diGenova, a Fox News regular, declared that "We are in a civil war."[46] He recognized the connection between civil war and dialogue, noting that "the suggestion that there's ever going to be civil discourse in this country for the foreseeable future is over ... It's going to be total war."[47] In the 19th century, the U.S. experienced a civil war over issues relating to slavery.[48] A civil war is anathema to a democracy because it illustrates that the democratic institutions can no longer politically and peaceably manage conflicts. Yet, by early 2021, over half of Americans surveyed,[49] up from just under one-third three years previous,[50] believed America was heading for a civil war in their lifetime. Similarly, Rep. Steve King (R-Iowa) posted a meme warning that states which typically vote for his party have "8 trillion bullets" in the event of civil war.[51] Whether or not a civil war occurs is immaterial; what does matter is that a substantial portion of Americans are so polarized that civil war is even a consideration.

The Unraveling of American Democracy

As Professors of Government at Harvard University, Steven Levitsky and Daniel Ziblatt explain in *How Democracies Die*, "one thing is clear from studying breakdowns throughout history, it's that extreme polarization can kill democracies."[52] In fact, as the U.S. became more polarized, studies began to question both the viability and existence of American democracy. In 2014, Princeton and Northwestern University political scientists Martin Gilens and Benjamin I. Page concluded that America was an oligarchy, not a democracy.[53] An **oligarchy** refers to a power structure where a few people hold the majority of power. Gilens and Page cited that the demands of poor and working class voters are addressed by the political class only on the rare occasion it overlaps with the demands of the wealthy.[54] Similarly, in 2019, the U.K.-based Economist Intelligence Unit suggested that the U.S. had fallen in international rankings on their Democracy Index to the 25th most democratic, a long way from number one.[55] They classify the U.S. as a "flawed democracy," which means that the elections are free and fair, basic civil liberties are respected, but there are underlying issues (e.g. the erosion of the free press and suppression of opposition political parties and viewpoints).[56] The political philosopher Sheldon Wolin argued that in the U.S., the strata of wealth and erosion of democracy were intrinsically linked in a system he referred to as "inverted totalitarianism." Wolin explains that 20th century totalitarian regimes utilized the state as the central location of power and domination, but:

Inverted totalitarianism, in contrast, while exploiting the authority and resources to the state, gains its dynamic by combining with other forms of power, such as Evangelical religions, and most notably by encouraging symbiotic relationship between traditional government and the system of private governance represented by modern business corporation. The result is not a system of co-determination by coequal partners who retain their distinctive identities but rather a system that represents the political coming of age of corporate power.[57]

Echoing Wolin, Johns Hopkins University's School of Advanced International Studies professor of practice, Yascha Mounk concludes that "America is not a democracy."[58] In October 2015, Matthew Yglesias writing for *Vox* declared that "American democracy is doomed."[59] In 2018, Republican speech writer David Frum wrote that the election of Trump as President of the U.S. highlighted the ways in which "democracy is a work in progress. So is democracy's undoing."[60] University of California, Irvine's Shawn Rosenberg warned in 2019 that the last vestige of "democracy is devouring itself."[61] A year later, Matthew Kroenig, a professor of government and foreign service at Georgetown University, warned that the world was revisiting an age-old battle between democracy and autocracy.[62] Similarly, in 2019, the editor of Stanford University's *Stanford Magazine*, Jill Patton, noted the litany of recent scholarship, warning that we are witnessing "an existential moment for democracy" as "autocrats are on the rise."[63]

Conflict Management, Critical Thinking, and Communication

As Ruth Ben-Ghait explains in the 2020 *Strongmen: Mussolini to the Present*:

There are two paths people can take when faced with the proliferation of polarization and hatred in their societies. They can dig their trenches deeper, or they can reach across the lines to stop a new cycle of destruction, knowing that solidarity, love, and dialogue are what the strong man most fears.[64]

Indeed, the concerns over the rise of authoritarian and oligarchic governments reveal that constructive dialogue is an exigency for 21st century democracies. Whereas autocrats and oligarchs rely on violence and other coercive measures to address conflict, democracies rely on the citizens to organize and engage in the political process. Scholars have long argued that conflict is inevitable, and democratic processes and institutions exist to peaceably resolve conflicts among competing political preferences.[65] In a democracy, the questions regarding conflict center on how citizens manage it rather than how they should eradicate it. In this text, we attempt to not only illuminate the dangers posed by destructive conflict, but to promote constructive dialogue for the purposes of managing conflict.

Constructive dialogue is civil, which means all parties involved engage in acts of reciprocity and critical thinking for the purposes of strengthening our democratic culture. We are aware that civility has been long used as tool of exclusion. However, in this text, to be civil is to be inclusive, courteous, and considerate of where people are at in terms of their knowledge and lived experience. Rather than expect or demand that everyone already share the same values, concerns, perspectives, and evidence citizens needs to assess where they are and work from there, including ascertaining how they became who they are now. This takes time and patience, even resolve, but these are necessary to mitigate the many differences that exist in a complex, multicultural society. We are also reminded of the words of Buddhist monk, Thích Nhất Hạnh, who wrote in *The Art of Communicating*, "When we say something that nourishes us and uplifts the people around us, we are feeding love and compassion. When we speak and act in a way that causes tension and anger, we are nourishing violence and suffering."[66]

This text does not just offer theoretical arguments about the relationship between democracy and dialogue. Rather, it offers real-world examples of how people have been able to use dialogue to bridge deep divides over class, race, gender, sexuality, and more. Some individuals involved in such dialogue include politicians like U.S. Representative from New York Alexandria Ocasio Cortez (AOC); activists such as Daryl Davis; scholars such as Cornel West; and sports figures such as Drew Brees.

The engagement with others in dialogue does not mean that individuals need to agree; sometimes they can agree to disagree. Richard Rorty pointed this out when discussing the debates between physical scientists and social scientists about notions of humanity, noting that they were "not issues to be resolved, only … differences to be lived with."[67] That is to say, the purpose of constructive dialogue goes beyond trying to make others agree. Instead, it is a way to share ideas and perspectives that enable us as a society to build *social capital*. Robert D. Putnam's 1993 *Making Democracy Work*, referenced earlier in this introduction, defined social capital as the "features of social organizations, such as trust, norms, and networks, that can improve the efficiency of society by facilitating coordinated actions."[68] Putnam underscored the centrality of social capital to a democracy. At a time when many Americans believe they are more divided than ever, Putnam offers wisdom that those concerned with democracy should strive to follow.

This Book

On a broader level, this text equips readers with the skills to discern fact from fiction; evaluate and construct sound arguments; and engage in constructive dialogue. The larger goal of the text is to develop readers' critical thinking and effective communication skills for the purposes of strengthening democratic discourse. The content we present for analysis is focused on mass media. As media scholars we are well aware of the influence that film, music, podcasts, news, television, streaming services, internet content, and other media have on audiences. One of our goals with this book is to have students practice critical thinking while using media.

The title of this book, *Let's Agree to Disagree*, is not an invitation to accept disagreement without engaging in constructive dialogue. Instead, we hope readers will engage with others in areas where they may disagree. Disagreement is a normal part of the human experience, one to be managed and mitigated by constructive communication and critical discourse. Disagreement does not mean one accepts oppression or inequity. In fact, the text discusses the importance of communicating boundaries. The challenge for democratic societies is how to manage such conflicts constructively.

As a result, in Part I of the book we outline hallmarks of civil discourse and by exploring the components of **constructive** and **destructive dialogue**. In essence, these first two chapters are a combination of "things to practice and embrace" when engaging in dialogue, and "things to avoid." We outline cultural approaches to conflict management, explore the concepts of culture and power, and focus on ways to keep conversations going. We offer a brief reminder about the history of free speech and its centrality to democratic self-government; while warning about the dangers of censorship and cancel culture, both of which have been on the rise in our digital era, and offer prescriptions for how to navigate difficult subjects and learn the significance of keeping conversations going.

Part II explores the art and purpose of argumentation grounded in the tenets of **critical thinking**. While building more logically sound and rationally compelling arguments, it offers students strategies that are crucial for engaging in constructive dialogue. We also note that although objectivity is a laudable and aspirational goal, everyone has a unique set of biases and perspectives that shape behavior, values, and attitudes. These frameworks, which are shaped by our experiences and identity, which not only reflect the power-dynamics that shape the production of knowledge, but guide us when we analyze evidence and construct arguments. It is important to know when our filters need to be expanded or replaced, our lenses cleaned and defogged. To be effective independent and critical thinkers as well as communicators, we must consider the many lenses through which we all view the world.

Chapters 3 and 4 move from examining individual thinking habits to overall argumentative construction. They offer crucial insights and strategies for developing logical arguments devoid of emotion and fallacious reasoning. We further address how to deconstruct arguments people encounter in everyday life. What should one look for? What is effective listening? How does one both ascertain and ask the right questions? How do we interpret and understand statistics and whether or not they are misleading? We offer an analysis of what is referred to as conventional wisdom, the baseless and misleading information that frequently appears unchallenged in the so-called mainstream media. We note how one can address this kind of misinforma-tion and disinformation, i.e., propaganda, and the assumptions underlying our social fabric, all while working toward a more holistic type of argu-mentation and discourse that leads to a broader and more rational under-standing of the world around us. In order to have constructive dialogue, people must be adept at deconstructing and building arguments, which necessitates familiarity with the power-dynamics that shape knowledge. As a result, this section also looks at **critical theory** and explores the relationship between **identity** and **power** in order to understand political **ideologies** as well as how class, race, sexuality, ability, and age inform their perspectives. By applying a critical and intersectional lens to various historically con-tentious issues, we illustrate how many events can produce a litany of inter-pretations and perspectives, ones we need to grapple with, not ignore, if we are to be a truly self-governing and democratic society. We also warn of co-optation and how these very theories and concepts can be distorted and decontextualized, even weaponized against their own original proponents in a form of information warfare.

Part III focuses on the importance of critical media literacy education. In Chapter 5, we learn about investigating and evaluating mass media messages, how they are made, by and for whom, which is key to under-standing the modern world given how much we rely on media institu-tions to educate society about key issues. Here we move beyond argumentation to examine strategies for analyzing and evaluating evi-dence, especially in media-disseminated content. Whether we like it or not, marketing, public relations strategies, and ideologies all work to mold messaging. These chapters explore the ways media shape identity; project, ignore, or reflect representation; and serve as an extension of dominant power structures.

Chapter 6 goes on to address the importance of ethical journalism and the culture of news media. News outlets and journalists range from transparently legitimate to downright propagandists. As a result, this chapter shares ways of deconstructing news content that help determine fact from fiction while broadening news frames in an effort to transcend confirmation biases and motivated reasoning. We look at theories about the political economy of mass media for analyzing and evaluating many media sources. We introduce the Propaganda Model, which looks at the role of media owners and advertisers, as well as news makers and shapers, while exploring how these interests and subsequent ideologies influence media content. The concept of fake news is addressed, not as a new phenomenon, but as the latest iteration of propaganda, which has been with us a long time. We aim to take this opportunity, when so many in society seem so concerned about the veracity of the information they receive, to introduce critical media literacy components into people's daily news habits.

In Chapter 7, we specifically delve into the digital realm. Just as fish cannot see the water, internet users are seldom aware of or are unable to identify how social media platforms promote inaccurate information and influence attitudes and behaviors. News content is often used as sourcing for a particular argument or narrative. These narratives, and by extension our arguments, are often shaped by commercial interests, especially advertisements. Indeed, it is estimated that in the U.S. users encounter between 5,000 and 10,000 advertisements daily. It is crucial to understand what narratives these advertisements help proliferate in mainstream culture, especially on digital platforms, and develop strategies for analyzing advertisement content, especially that which is embedded in popular culture. It is also necessary for users to realize how they may be used by digital technology and their devices, all the while believing they are using them. Staying vigilant of how one understands and navigates this digital terrain is imperative for civic survival.

In Part IV, the concluding chapter offers a summary of the book that reiterates the ways in which readers can combine the previous three parts of the book to foster constructive dialogue in contentions times, offering more ways to keep difficult conversations going, and how individuals might ultimately agree to disagree (and comprehend what that may look like when disagreements are rooted in toxic prejudice, hatred, and bigotry). In other words, individuals do not have to tolerate intolerance or agree with it, but they do need to learn how to mitigate and deal with it in the real world.

In Chapter 8, we provide a checklist that aims to help us lead by example. As longtime consumer rights attorney and activist Ralph Nader reminds us, democracy is not a spectator sport. In order for individuals to be meaningfully engaged in civil society, we invite everyone to get *critical* by reviewing the main points of the previous chapters using the acronym C.R.I.T.I.C.A.L. as a mnemonic device:

1   C – Create constructive dialogue;
2   R – Reflect on communication practices;
3   I – Inquire: Be a critical thinker;

4   T – Test theory and spot ideology;
5   I – Investigate and evaluate mass media;
6   C – Critique content: "Fake news" and ethical journalism;
7   A – Assess, analyze, and evaluate digital media use and abuse;
8   L – Lead by example: Democracy is not a spectator sport.

A Critical Conclusion for a Constructive Future

No matter what ideology or identity one has, they will experience conflict and disagree with other people. Those with whom we disagree are not going away. There will always be liberals, conservatives, as well as people in between and beyond those parameters, along with a series of corresponding political parties. There will always be a diversity of racial, gender, sexuality, religious, class, and other identities. There will be rural and urban people. There will be educated and non-educated people. Maintaining a democracy is a full-time job for its citizens. Our job in a democracy is to maximize our factual knowledge and engage in dialogue for the purposes of accumulating social capital. Dialogue is essential in uniting people into mass movements that reassert the electorate's influence over the democratic process.[69] In fact, democracies have emerged from horrible histories after engaging in difficult, yet thoughtful and compassionate dialogue. For example, the Truth and Reconciliation Commission in South Africa was a crucial step in building social capital that moved the war-torn nation from the horrors of apartheid to a more functioning democracy.[70]

There is no progress without sacrifice, there is no way to pretend we are united when confronted with the evidence of the past several years, and there is no quick fix for the long-held conflicts the ruling class has worked to institutionalize in the name of neoliberal "reforms." Power elites sowing division and peddling lies are among the oldest tricks in the political handbook. Critical and independent thought are the antidote to these civic maladies, but we must learn to communicate clearly and effectively with those who hold disparate views and build upon our shared goals, which means we sometimes must agree to disagree, at least in fits and starts, as we honor the processes we present in the text that follows.

If one is disinterested in being an informed, productive citizen in a democratic society, that is a choice, one freedom ironically allows. Such detachment, disinterest, or inaction in these societies promotes a sort of cynicism, that becomes like a metastatic cancer of the body politic, eroding trust in institutions integral for promoting engagement in the public sphere. We hope that the material we lay out in the following pages works to bolster a new generation of fiercely independent and

critical thinkers as the antidote to such civic malaise. As the anarchist
Emma Goldman once said, "the most unpardonable sin in society is
independence of thought."[71] We hope to spawn a tsunami of such sin-
ners, and a torrent of open discourse around the issues that impact us
most, ever with the hopes of understanding, if not convincing each other,
on a path to an enlightened state where we can agree to disagree, and
keep the conversations going to learn more another day. We are all teachers, we are all students. We hope you enjoy this ongoing journey as
much as we do and that we may meet and engage with you on an ever
widening and enlightening path.

Notes

1 "America in 1968: An overview in 17 quotes – we take a quick look at the
   major events and pop culture highlights in a pivotal year in American history," *Saturday Evening Post*, January 18, 2018, https://www.saturdayeveningp
   ost.com/2018/01/america-1968-overview-17-quotes/.
2 Ibid.
3 Eric Foner, *Give Me Liberty: An American History*, 6th ed. (New York: W.W.
   Norton, 2020).
4 National Advisory Commission on Civil Disorders, "Report of the National
   Advisory Commission on Civil Disorders: Summary of Report" (United States
   Government Printing Office, 1968), https://www.hsdl.org/?abstract&did=
   35837.
5 Nolan Higdon and Mickey Huff, *United States of Distraction: Media Manipulation in Post-truth America (and what we can do about it)* (San Francisco, CA:
   City Lights Books, 2019); John Flesher, "6 men indicted in alleged plot to
   kidnap Michigan governor," *Associated Press*, December 17, 2020, https://ap
   news.com/article/gretchen-whitmer-michigan-indictments-coronavirus-pande
   mic-traverse-city-10f7e02c57004da9843f89650edd4510; Minyvonne Burke
   and Marianna Sotomayor, "James Alex Fields found guilty of killing Heather
   Heyer during violent Charlottesville white nationalist rally," *NBC*, December
   7, 2018, https://www.nbcnews.com/news/crime-courts/james-alex-fields-
   found-guilty-killing-heather-heyer-during-violent-n945186; Kenya Evelyn,
   "Capitol attack: The five people who died," *The Guardian*, January 8, 2021,
   https://www.theguardian.com/us-news/2021/jan/08/capitol-attack-police-offic
   er-five-deaths.
6 Linley Sanders, "Americans now see other Americans as the biggest threat to
   their way of life," *YouthGov*, January 20, 2021, https://today.yougov.com/top
   ics/politics/articles-reports/2021/01/20/americans-now-see-other-americans-bi
   ggest-threat.
7 Ibid.
8 Kevin Kruse and Julian Zelizer, *Fault Lines: A History of The United States
   Since 1974* (New York: W.W. Norton, 2020); Ross Douthat, *The Decadent
   Society America Before and After the Pandemic* (New York: Avid Reader Press,
   2021); Kurt Andersen, *Evil Geniuses: The Unmaking of America* (New York:
   Random House, 2020).
9 Ross Douthat, *The Decadent Society: America Before and After the Pandemic* (New
   York: Avid Reader Press, 2021).
10 Ibid.

11 Winston Churchill, Speech in House of Commons, November 11, 1947.

12 Larry Diamond and Leonardo Morlino, "The quality of democracy: An overview," *Journal of Democracy* 15, no. 4 (2004): 20–31.

13 Robert D. Putnam, "Tuning in, tuning out: The strange disappearance of social capital in America," *PS: Political Science & Politics* 28, no. 4 (1995): 664–684.

14 Ezra Klein, *Why We're Polarized* (New York: Simon & Schuster, 2020).

15 Amory Gethin, Clara Martínez-Toledano, and Thomas Piketty, "Brahmin Left versus Merchant Right: Changing Political Cleavages in 21 Western Democracies, 1948–2020," working paper, World Inequality Lab, May 2021.

16 Marilynn B. Brewer, "In-group bias in the minimal intergroup situation: A cognitive-motivational analysis," *Psychological Bulletin* 86, no. 2 (1979): 307; Geoffrey L. Cohen, "Party over policy: The dominating impact of group influence on political beliefs," *Journal of Personality and Social Psychology* 85, no. 5 (2003): 808; Donald P. Green, Bradley Palmquist, and Eric Schickler, *Partisan Hearts and Minds: Political Parties and the Social Identities of Voters* (New Haven, CT: Yale University Press, 2004), 28.

17 Michael Barber and Jeremy C. Pope, "Does party trump ideology? Disentangling party and ideology in America," *American Political Science Review* 113, no. 1 (2019): 38–54.

18 Henri Tajfel, "Experiments in intergroup discrimination," *Scientific American* 223 (1970): 96–102; Henri Tajfel and John C. Turner, "An integrative theory of intergroup conflict," in *The Social Psychology of Intergroup Relations,* eds William G. Austin and Stephen Worchel (Monterey, CA: Brooks-Cole, 1979), 33–47.

19 Shanto Iyengar and Sean J. Westwood, "Fear and loathing across party lines: New evidence on group polarization," *American Journal of Political Science* 59, no. 3 (2015): 690–707.

20 Gregory A. Huber and Neil Malhotra, "Political homophily in social relationships: Evidence from online dating behavior," *The Journal of Politics* 79, no. 1 (2017): 269–283.

21 Anna Brown, "Most democrats who are looking for a relationship would not consider dating a Trump voter," *Pew Research,* April 24, 2020, https://www.pewresearch.org/fact-tank/2020/04/24/most-democrats-who-are-looking-for-a-relationship-would-not-consider-dating-a-trump-voter/.

22 Shanto Iyengar and Sean J. Westwood, "Fear and loathing across party lines: New evidence on group polarization," *American Journal of Political Science* 59, no. 3 (2015): 693.

23 "Political polarization in the American public," *Pew Research,* June 12, 2014, https://www.pewresearch.org/politics/2014/06/12/political-polarizatio n-in-the-american-public/.

24 Drew Desilver, "Once again, nearly all Senate elections reflect states' presidential votes," *Pew Research,* January 8, 2021, https://www.pewresearch.org/fact-tank/2021/01/08/once-again-nearly-all-senate-elections-reflect-states-presi dential-votes/.

25 "Partisan antipathy: More intense, more personal majority of Republicans say Democrats are 'more unpatriotic' than other Americans," *Pew Research,* October 10, 2019, https://www.pewresearch.org/politics/2019/10/10/partisan-a ntipathy-more-intense-more-personal/?utm_source=link_newsv9&utm_campa ign=item_268982&utm_medium=copy.

26 Nolan Higdon and Mickey Huff, *United States of Distraction: Media Manipulation in Post-truth America (and what we can do about it)* (San Francisco, CA: City Lights Books, 2019).

27 Jenn Brandt and Callie Claire, *An Introduction to Popular Culture in the US, People, Politics, Power* (New York: Bloomsbury Press, 2018).

28 Nickie Louise, "These 6 corporations control 90% of the media outlets in America," *Tech Startups,* September 18, 2020, https://techstartups.com/2020/09/18/6-corporations-control-90-media-america-illusion-choice-objectivity-2020/; Forest Hunt, "The new podcast oligopoly Spotify and Liberty corner the market, while Amazon and Apple plot their ascent," *FAIR,* May 21, 2021, https://fair.org/home/the-new-podcast-oligopoly/; Chris Alcantara, Kevin Schaul, Gerrit De Vynck and Reed Albergotti, "How big tech got so big: Hundreds of acquisitions," *Washington Post,* April 21, 2021, https://www.washingtonpost.com/technology/interactive/2021/amazon-apple-facebook-google-acquisitions/.

29 Matt Taibbi, *Hate Inc: Why Today's Media Makes Us Despise One Another* (New York: OR Books, 2019).

30 Ed Pilkington, "Obama angers Midwest voters with guns and religion remark," *The Guardian,* April 14, 2008, https://www.theguardian.com/world/2008/apr/14/barackobama.uselections2008.

31 Mark Memmott, "Romney's wrong and right about the '47 percent'," *NPR,* September 18, 2012, https://www.npr.org/sections/thetwo-way/2012/09/18/161333783/romneys-wrong-and-right-about-the-47-percent-"takers".

32 Katie Reilly, "Read Hillary Clinton's 'Basket of Deplorables' remarks about Donald Trump supporters," *Time,* September 10, 2016, https://time.com/4486502/hillary-clinton-basket-of-deplorables-transcript/.

33 Nolan Higdon and Mickey Huff, *United States of Distraction: Media Manipulation in Post-truth America (and what we can do about it)* (San Francisco, CA: City Lights Books, 2019).

34 Dan Mangan, 'You're a damn liar, man!' – Joe Biden blasts Iowa voter, calls him 'fat' after man repeats Ukraine smear," *CNBC,* December 5, 2019, https://www.cnbc.com/2019/12/05/biden-calls-iowa-voter-damn-liar-and-fat-after-ukraine-accusation.html; Poppy Noor, "'A lying, dog-faced pony soldier': Just what was Joe Biden talking about? *The Guardian,* February 10, 2020, https://www.theguardian.com/us-news/2020/feb/10/joe-biden-lying-dog-faced-pony-soldier-new-hampshire.

35 Zaid Jilani, "Debunking Brian Stelter's call to deplatform Fox News," *YouTube,* https://www.youtube.com/watch?v=IbHTl_qwA9o&feature=youtu.be.

36 "Politics Hannity v. de Blasio: A 41-minute shouting match in 148 seconds," *Washington Post,* August 8, 2019, https://www.washingtonpost.com/video/politics/hannity-v-de-blasio-a-41-minute-shouting-match-in-148-seconds/2019/08/08/34fc277a-b4a2-461c-a46c-038a943d677c_video.html.

37 Allison Morrow, "CNBC's Rick Santelli starts shouting match on air over Covid-19 restrictions," *CNN Business,* December 4, 2020, https://www.cnn.com/2020/12/04/media/cnbc-santelli-sorkin-coronavirus/index.html.

38 Beatrice Verhoeven, "Watch Fox News' Leland Vittert get into shouting match with Trump campaign official over vote count," *Yahoo,* November 14, 2020, https://money.yahoo.com/watch-fox-news-leland-vittert-213440948.html.

39 Jerusalem Demsas, "In the final debate, Trump interrupted twice as much as Biden Trump 'only' interrupted 34 times this time," *Vox,* October 23, 2020, https://www.vox.com/2020/10/23/21529607/biden-trump-debate-won-interrupt-kristen-welker-presidential.

40 Maureen Groppe and John Fritze, "As Trump continues to interrupt during the debate, Biden says, 'Will you shut up, man?'" *USA Today*, September 29, 2020, https://www.usatoday.com/story/news/politics/elections/2020/09/29/biden-asks-trump-shut-up-president-keeps-interrupting-debate/3582754001/.

41 Bahman Fozouni, "A nation of Trolls: Is it even worthwhile to discuss with Trumpies anymore?," *Informed Comment*, July 13, 2020, https://www.juancole.com/2020/07/worthwhile-discuss-trumpies.html.

42 "All In transcripts / All In interview with Michael Moore," *All In w/ Chris Hayes*, December 13, 2019, www.msnbc.com/transcripts/all-in/2019-12-13.

43 Ashley McKinless, "Cornel West and Robert P. George on Christian love in the public square March 08, 2019," *American Magazine*, March 8, 2019, https://www.americamagazine.org/politics-society/2019/03/08/cornel-west-and-robert-p-george-christian-love-public-square.

44 Judith Hertog, "Prisoner of hope Cornel West's quest for justice," *The Sun Magazine*, September 2018, https://www.thesunmagazine.org/issues/513/prisoner-of-hope.

45 Marc Jansen, "International class solidarity or foreign interventions?: Internationalists and Latvian rifles in the Russian Revolution and the Civil War," *International Review of Social History* 31, no. 1 (1986): 68.

46 Greg Jaffe and Jenna Johnson, "In America, talk turns to something not spoken of for 150 years: Civil war," *Washington Post*, March 2, 2019, https://www.washingtonpost.com/politics/in-america-talk-turns-to-something-unspoken-for-150-years-civil-war/2019/02/28/b3733af8-3ae4-11e9-a2cd-307b06d0257b_story.html.

47 Ibid.

48 Eric Foner, *Give Me Liberty: An American History*, 6th ed. (New York: W.W. Norton, 2020).

49 Grace Kay, "A majority of Americans surveyed believe the US is in the midst of a 'cold' civil war," *Business Insider*, January 13, 2021, https://www.businessinsider.com/many-people-united-states-believe-cold-civil-war-survey-2021-1.

50 Ryan W. Miller, "Poll: Almost a third of US voters think a second civil war is coming soon," *USA Today*, June 27, 2018, https://www.usatoday.com/story/news/politics/onpolitics/2018/06/27/civil-war-likely-voters-say-rasmussen-poll/740731002/.

51 Reis Thebault, "Steve King posts meme warning that red states have '8 trillion Bullets' in the event of civil war," *Washington Post*, March 19, 2019, https://www.washingtonpost.com/politics/2019/03/18/steve-king-posts-meme-warning-that-red-states-have-trillion-bullets-event-civil-war/.

52 Steven Levitsky and Daniel Ziblatt, *How Democracies Die* (New York: Crown Publishing, 2018), 9.

53 Martin Gilens and Benjamin I. Page, "Testing theories of American politics: Elites, interest groups, and average citizens," *Perspectives on Politics* 12, no. 3 (2014): 564–581.

54 Ibid.

55 "Democracy Index 2018," *The Economist*, 2019, https://www.eiu.com/topic/democracy-index.

56 Ibid.

57 Sheldon Wolin, *Democracy Inc.: Managed Democracy and the Specter of Inverted Totalitarianism* (Princeton, NJ, Princeton University Press, 2008, 2017), xxi.

58 Yascha Mounk, "America is not a democracy," *The Atlantic*, March 2018, https://www.theatlantic.com/magazine/archive/2018/03/america-is-not-a-democracy/550931/.

59 Matthew Yglesias, "American democracy is doomed," *Vox,* October 8, 2015, https://www.vox.com/2015/3/2/8120063/american-democracy-doomed.

60 David Frum, *Trumpocracy: The Corruption of the American Republic* (New York: Harper Collins Publishers, 2018), ix.

61 Rick Shenkman, "The shocking paper predicting the end of democracy," *Politico,* September 8, 2019, https://www.politico.com/magazine/story/2019/09/08/shawn-rosenberg-democracy-228045.

62 Matthew Kroenig, *The Return of Great Power Rivalry: Democracy versus Autocracy from the Ancient World to the U.S. and China* (Oxford University Press, 2020).

63 Jill Patton, "An existential moment for democracy?" *Stanford Magazine,* December 2019, https://stanfordmag.org/contents/an-existential-moment-for-democracy.

64 Ruth Ben-Ghait, *Strongmen: Mussolini to the Present* (New York: W.W. Norton, 2020), 261.

65 David Kinsella and D.L. David, "Democracy and Conflict," in *The Sage Handbook of Conflict Resolution,* eds J. Bercovitch, V. Kremenyuk, and W. Zartman (London: Sage Publications, 2009), 475–491, doi: 10.4135/9780857024701.n25; William J. Dixon, "Democracy and the management of international conflict," *Journal of Conflict Resolution* 37, no. 1 (1993): 42–68.

66 Thích Nhất Hạnh, *The Art of Communicating* (London: Rider Books, 2013).

67 Richard Rorty, *Consequences of Pragmatism* (Minneapolis, MN: University of Minnesota Press, 1982), 197.

68 Robert D. Putnam, *Making Democracy Work* (Princeton, NJ: Princeton University Press, 1993), 167.

69 Bruce Levine, *Get Up, Stand Up: Uniting Populists, Energizing the Defeated, and Battling the Corporate Elite* (White River Junction, VT: Chelsea Green Publishing, 2011); Mark Engler and Paul Engler, *This is an Uprising: How Nonviolent Revolt is Shaping the Twenty-first Century* (New York: Nation Books, 2016).

70 Madeleine Fullard and Nicky Rousseau, "Truth telling, identities, and power in South Africa and Guatemala," Research Brief, International Center for Transitional Justice, New York (2009).

71 Emma Goldman, *Red Emma Speaks: An Emma Goldman Reader,* ed. Alix Kates Shulman, e-book edition (New York: Open Road Media, 1996, 2012).

Part I

Communication

As the late feminist scholar bell hooks once noted, "Honesty and openness is always the foundation of insightful dialogue."[1] hooks reminds us that, how people relate and share information with each other is as consequential as the validity of their messages. As a result, we begin our text by centering the importance of salubrious communication that accounts for the differing ways people interpret messages and the world around them. In Chapter 1, Create Constructive Dialogue, we explore processes of fostering constructive dialogue and effective conflict management as well as suggest ways to avoid destructive communication habits. Our hope is that readers will become more critical and compassionate listeners who keep conversations going, and feel comfortable agreeing and disagreeing with others.

In Chapter 2, Reflect on Communication Practices, we historicize the contemporaneous debates and practices that shape Americans' ability to engage in constructive dialogue. We delve into the history of free speech, free press, and free expression and argue that censorship and cancel culture are not productive ways to mitigate differences or build understanding between various groups in society. These first two chapters serve as a foundation for the rest of the text which further expands readers to build critical thinking and communicative skillsets. We hope that when taken together, these two chapters help readers. We hope you find these chapters as useful as they are informative.

DOI: 10.4324/9781003250906-2

Chapter 1

Create Constructive Dialogue

"I have worked a working-class job. I have waited tables in restaurants. I have ridden the subway. I have walked the streets in New York City. And this kind of language is not new." So explained U.S. Representative from New York, Alexandria Ocasio-Cortez (AOC), in a July 23, 2020 speech on the floor of the House of Representatives in the U.S. Capitol Building. She was responding to a series of incidences that occurred with fellow congressperson Rep. Ted Yoho of Florida. Reportedly, the day prior to her speech, as AOC was entering the U.S. Capitol Building, Yoho exclaimed that AOC was "out of [her] freaking mind!" In response, AOC accused Yoho of being "rude." As Yoho walked away, he muttered that AOC was a "f***ing b****!"[2]

In her measured response on the floor of the House of Representatives, AOC recounted that after hearing Yoho's comment,

> I honestly thought I was going to pack it up and go home. It's just another day, right? But then yesterday, Representative Yoho decided to come to the floor of the House of Representatives and make excuses for his behavior. And that I could not let go. I could not allow my nieces, I could not allow the little girls that I go home to, I could not allow victims of verbal abuse and, worse, to see that – to see that excuse and to see our Congress accept it as legitimate and accept it as an apology and to accept silence as a form of acceptance, I could not allow that to stand …. Mr. Yoho mentioned that he has a wife and two daughters. I am two years younger than Mr. Yoho's youngest daughter. I am someone's daughter too …. Now, what I am here to say is that this harm that Mr. Yoho levied, tried to levy against me, was not just an incident directed at me, but when you do that to any woman, what Mr. Yoho did was give permission to other men to do that to his daughters …. And so, what I believe is that having a daughter does not make a man decent. Having a wife does not make a decent man. Treating people with dignity and respect makes a decent man. And when a decent man messes up, as we all

DOI: 10.4324/9781003250906-3

are bound to do, he tries his best and does apologize. Not to save face, not to win a vote. He apologizes genuinely to repair and acknowledge the harm done, so that we can all move on.[3]

The events that transpired between Representatives Yoho and Ocasio-Cortez are an example of conflict. **Conflict** refers to

> some form of friction, disagreement, or discord arising between individuals or within a group when the beliefs or actions of one or more members of the group are either resisted by or unacceptable to one or more members of another group. Conflict pertains to the opposing ideas and actions of different entities, thus resulting in an antagonistic state.[4]

Democracies rightly assume that conflict is a fact of life. After all, citizens' diverging and competing preferences are always in conflict. Democratic institutions exist to shape processes for resolving conflicts civilly among competing political preferences.[5] Rather than seek to avoid or eradicate conflict, democratic systems focus on how to manage it constructively. Constructive conflict can seem cumbersome, but it is worth the effort. As a process, the arduous conflict management peregrination is not only efficacious for the participants involved, but the democracy as well. For those reasons, this chapter investigates and unpacks conflict management and dialogue.

Cultural Approaches to Conflict Management

As Fred Jantd explains in *Communication and Conflict*, much of our understanding of conflict is shrouded in myth.[6] For example, conflict is often viewed as abnormal when in fact, harmony is unusual and conflict is inescapable. Another myth is that conflicts are generally considered a breakdown in communication, when in fact it is communication that manages conflict. Furthermore, we mistakenly believe that conflict extinguishes relationships and stifles collaboration, but in actuality it is unresolved conflict that often destroys relationships and effective collaboration.

Communication scholars have long argued that human conflict is best addressed when people try to *manage* rather than *resolve* it. Herbert C. Kelman defines **conflict resolution** as the "process of shaping a mutually satisfactory and hence durable agreement between the two societies, reconciliation refers to the process whereby they learn to live together in the post-conflict environment."[7] In essence, conflict resolution, sometimes referred to as dispute resolution, is fixated on putting an end to conflict. Conversely, scholars argue that participants are better served by **conflict**

management, which according to Calvin Morrill, is "any social process by which people or groups handle grievances about each other's behaviors."[8]

Just as there are many myths about conflict, there are also myths about conflict management. There are two myths that Jandt highlights that are particularly instructive for how humans incorrectly perceive conflict management:[9]

- The best way to solve conflict is through compromise.
- Conflict is a global practice with global solutions that span across cultures.

Compromise is a way of managing conflict, but it is not the only way to resolve conflict. In fact, better approaches exist. To understand why this is the case, we must address the second myth. It is true that conflicts due indeed occur across all cultures. However, the ways in which they manifest and are resolved is culture specific. For example, in some cultures conflict is over when there is a final resolution.[10] In other cultures, conflict resolution is an ongoing process that continues as long as the relationship exists.[11]

Culture

Culture can be a decisive factor in conflict resolution. Western cultural approaches to conflict are shaped by individualism. **Individualism** is a dimension of culture that "refers to the rights and interdependence of individuals."[12] This concept helps shape dominant western cultural conflict management strategies, which include:

- **Avoiding** – a passive approach to conflict where one tries to ignore rather than confront the conflict. Due to lack of reciprocity, the avoidance of conflict is considered an approach that will likely weaken a relationship because when the conflict remains unresolved it is impossible for either, let alone both parties, to have their concerns satisfied.[13]
- **Accommodating** – a conflict style where one party attends to the needs of others rather than their own. It is considered an approach that will likely weaken a relationship due to its lack of reciprocity. Indeed, the accommodating style only allows one side to have their concerns met.[14]
- **Competing** – a conflict style where one party pursues their own goals and ignores the goals of the other party or parties. A competing approach, which many utilize in their childhood, will more than likely weaken a relationship.[15] Where accommodation allows for the

satisfaction of one party without considering the other, competition allows for the satisfaction of one party at the expense of the other.

- **Compromising** – a conflict style where participants seek to partially satisfy the concerns of both parties.[16] This can be a reasonable approach, but not when it comes to principles. Furthermore, since both parties are only partially satisfied in a compromise setting, that means that neither is fully satisfied.
- **Collaborating** – an approach to conflict occurs when both parties agree on an outcome that satisfies all party's concerns.[17] Communication scholars contend that a collaborative approach, although more complex, labor intensive, and disruptive – is ultimately the most effective.[18]

The influence of individualism is apparent in the first four approaches to conflict which seek to satisfy, at least partially, one party without much consideration for the satisfaction of others.

Non-western cultures are more collectivist and thus utilize different styles of conflict management. **Collectivism** is a dimension of culture that values groupthink, interdependence, and social cohesion.[19] For example, some non-western scholars view the use of avoidance as an illustration of waning commitment to one's self and others. Some Western Africa and Eastern Asia societies reveal a commitment to harmony in their conflict management. **Harmony** refers to "the maintenance of intricate relationships and complexities in a networked society."[20] Another example is China, where conflict management strategies are determined by a participant's efforts to save face. **Face** is a collectivist cultural concept denoting public image or reputation one has achieved regarding integrity and morality.[21] Beyond culture, conflict management approaches are also complicated by issues of power.

Power

Regardless of the culture or strategy employed, engaging in conflict is complicated by power dynamics. **Power**, in the broadest sense, refers to the authority or influence a person or group has over others.[22] Power informs conflict, and power imbalances can be a determinative factor in conflict outcomes. A power imbalance can be something as common as a manager and an employee, because the manager has the power to set and enforce the parameters of the conflict and its resolution, but the employee does not.

Recognizing power imbalances is essential for understanding **positionality**, which refers to the how differing social position and power shape identities and privilege in society. **Privilege** refers to the prestige, opportunity, and power that select identity groups have in society. For example, in the U.S. centuries of laws have been codified and enforced to ensure privilege for those with wealth and means, often whites, males, and heterosexuals. For starters, most people in the early so-called republic were not permitted to vote unless they owned land, and women and people of color could not participate at all in civic life. Further, federal courts once upheld a state's ability to racially segregate the population (Plessy v. Ferguson, 1896), reduce employment opportunities for females (Muller v. Oregon, 1908), and ban non-heterosexual relations (Bowers v. Hardwick, 1986). Communication scholars contend that laws such as these have engendered privileges that enable select individuals or groups to utilize power in a way that is not afforded to under-privileged ones.

Take the accommodation strategy, which only allows one side to have their concerns met.[23] When accommodation decides the outcome of a conflict, it can be a result of **coercive power,** which refers to "one stakeholder having the power to force (coerce) other stakeholders to take certain actions. Government and public sector agencies generally possess this type of power due to their role in policy development and resource allocations."[24] Those with this kind of power can use their positionality to provide or reduce resources in exchange for certain concessions. That is a privilege that some parties or nations have, while others do not. Deciding conflict based on which party has more power is a form of destructive conflict management.

Destructive Conflict and Communication

Destructive conflict refers to "dysfunctional conflicts in which the substantive issues become secondary to the parties getting even, retaliating, or hurting each other."[25] Conflict becomes destructive when one or more participants have little if any interest in repairing and maintaining the relationship. Instead, they are more interested in being perceived as right; convincing the other person; or "winning" the argument.[26] Disregarding the relationship for competing goals results in destructive behaviors such as:

- **Violence:** Threats or use of violence are illustrative of a dialogue that has broken down. If the goal was to change minds or find consensus, the participants have failed once violence is introduced. Furthermore, rather than foster creative dialogue, studies show that violence fosters more violence.[27]
- **Provocation:** This "refers to the action or occurrence that causes someone to do something or become angry."[28] Some media figures have been made for provocation, their role seems to be to create political enemies, including figures such as Anne Coulter, Richard Spencer, Ben Shapiro, and others like Michael Moore or Bill Maher.

Although it may help build a personal brand and draw attention to someone's content and viewpoint, provocation does not usually lead to constructive dialogue. Instead, it acts to boil down political differences to knee-jerk emotional reactions.

- **Condescension:** This occurs when one displays an attitude of superiority or disdain for the other person or party.[29] Rather than foster an inviting environment for dialogue it alienates participants, making them feel uncomfortable or incapable of engaging in equitable dialogue.
- **Patronizing:** This takes place when someone duplicitously communicates their desire to help or be kind to someone while simultaneously emphasizing that person or group's perceived or implied inferiority.
- **Name calling:** This refers to the act of using a term or label to describe someone without introducing an explanation of the evidence that warrants such a claim. This sentiment was summed up by conservative commentator Tomi Lahren, who described why name-calling did not impel her to question her alleged racism:

> I think a lot of Trump supporters feel as though we have been cast away and alienated .... we have been kind of pushed to the way side you're a racist, you're a bigot, you're intolerant, once we have been named called to that extend and we have had our character assassinated to such an extent, it is hard to repair that once you've called people such horrible names, once you've called people white nationalist, and racist just because they support his president. Naturally, we are going to be a little bit more defensive.[30]

Just because one party engages in destructive conflict does not mean that the other party has to as well. In order to bring the conflict to a more constructive space, participants should *avoid* language that escalates destructive communication such as:

- **"Calm down"** can be destructive because it is accusatory in that it assumes the listener's behavior is erratic. It also demeaning because it falsely empowers one to act as an authority on what is acceptable.
- **"Shut up"** is destructive because it demonstrates that the speaker is not interested in listening or dialogue, they just want to be heard.
- **"I know how you feel"** can be destructive because it may not be accurate. It is better to qualify with "I cannot imagine how you feel" or "I know my situation was different, or similar, but ...."
- **"You should not feel that way"** is destructive because it places a speaker in a corrective or admonishing mode, telling a listener what they should be feeling.

- "You need to ..." is destructive because the speaker is lecturing the listener on what they should do, or how they should do it.

- "We need to settle this now" is destructive because the speaker is demanding the listener's compliance by lecturing them on when something should or needs to be settled. Not all conflicts can be settled right away, and more complicated ones can take a long time.

- "You/they made me ..." blames another person or party rather than taking responsibility. One cannot control others' behaviors or feelings, nor should others control you. Thus, it is irrational to claim someone made you do something or believe something.

Constructive Conflict and Dialogue

Where destructive conflict seeks to eradicate or dismiss the possibility of growing or maintaining a relationship, **constructive conflict** refers to "conflicts that balance the interests of both parties to maximize opportunities for mutual gains. The process can result in increased productivity, greater cohesiveness within groups, and creative decisions."[31] When U.S. Representative AOC requested that Representative Yoho "apologizes genuinely to repair and acknowledge the harm done, so that we can all move on," she was making an appeal for a constructive conflict management approach known as restorative justice. A **restorative justice** approach to conflict "emphasizes repairing the harm done to people and relationships rather than mere retribution or punishment."[32] As a form of conflict management, restorative justice is not just aspirational, it is a well-documented approach to interpersonal and intergroup conflict management.[33] One of the most famous examples offered in terms of the success of restorative justice is post-apartheid South Africa,[34] where victims and witnesses to apartheid atrocities gave testimony and the accused were able to recount the acts of injustice and apologize for their participation.[35]

The nature of conflict is such that it violates principles and expectation of justice. **Justice** refers to "not only to enforcement of rights, and imposition of judgment or punishment, but also the restoration of what was lost."[36] The derogatory comment toward AOC was an act of injustice because it hindered a peaceful co-existence between the congresspersons. In response, AOC's speech called for a restorative justice approach to reconciliation. AOC believed that restorative justice could be achieved if Yoho would engage in dialogue and apologize for his behavior.

It is not just AOC; scholars have found that constructive conflict rests upon dialogue.[37] **Dialogue** is the process by which all parties are engaged in a series of messaging. Dialogue is the "transparent conversation that often creates unanticipated relational outcomes due to parties' profound respect for disparate voices."[38] As communications scholar Richard L. Johannesen once pointed out, dialogue requires listening, not to "command, coerce, manipulate, conquer, dazzle, or deceive,"[39] but for the purposes of engaging in "authenticity, inclusion, confirmation, presentness, spirit of mutual equality, and supportive climate."[40]

Communication scholars note that this is difficult because humans are often guarded in their approach to communication. For example, **uncertainty reduction theorists** explain that uncertainty makes people uncomfortable, which hinders the development of strong relationships.[41] In response, **social penetration theorists** argue that those seeking to engage in substantive dialogue must be patient and develop a reciprocal relationship that allows for the free flow of information.[42] Too often conflicts over ideas take a wrong turn to hostility and violence, but the exchange of differing perspectives should not be reduced to combat zones; rather, we should consider them construction zones, where we build understanding through sound argumentation. We would do well to remember the words of philosopher Friedrich Nietzsche in *Beyond Good and Evil*: "Whoever fights monsters should see to it that in the process he does not become a monster. And if you gaze long enough into an abyss, the abyss will gaze back into you."[43] This is why learning about and practicing constructive communication is such a vital skill.

Constructive Communication

Participants interested in constructive dialogue must work to cultivate **reciprocity**, which refers to the "exchanges of roughly equivalent values in which the actions of each party are contingent on the prior actions of the others in such a way that good is returned for good, and bad for bad."[44] The intersubjective nature of reciprocity allows for participants to sympathize and empathize with one another.[45] **Sympathy** is defined as "acknowledging another person's emotional hardships and providing comfort and assurance,"[46] while **empathy** is "an affective response more appropriate to someone else's situation than to one's own."[47] Empathy and sympathy allow for the constructive ways of handling conflict because they recognize the humanity in the other person, which is often missing in destructive conflicts, especially ones that manifest violently. Reciprocity emerges when participants trust in one another, and trust must be established over time.[48]

If participants seek constructive dialogue they must work collaboratively to develop trust. **Trust** refers to the expectations that participants have for the relationship.[49] Trust exists when participants must feel respected.[50] **Respect** is defined as "treating people from diverse backgrounds and cultures with courtesy, and vulnerable populations are singled out for additional protection."[51] It fosters trust between the participants.[52] Participants can display respect in their **tone**, which refers to the attitude displayed in communication. Although the words themselves may be respectful, if the tone if disrespectful, the dialogue will become destructive. This is because respect necessitates that participant's display decency. **Decency** refers to the display of attitude and values that emphasize respectability.[53] Participants can display decency and respect in a constructive manner by recognizing their stage of intellectual development, rather judging them for where they think they should be. This means avoiding **the curse of knowledge**, which is a cognitive bias where one assumes that other people should do or should know what *they* do or know. For example, in 2020, professor of organizational behavior and senior associate dean for academic affairs at Stanford University's Graduate School of Business, Brian S. Lowery, wrote in the *Washington Post*, "To my white friends, the time for talk has passed. Now is the time for work." The merits of his opinion are not in question, but the assumption that white people will take constructive actions toward addressing and remedying racial injustices assumes that white people are aware of and understand the realities of racial injustices.[54] A more constructive approach would be to meet people where they are on the topic, barring they are not violent or otherwise abusive (which is not tolerable behavior), by patiently listening and engaging, and then thoughtfully suggesting how parties might best move forward together.

In order to garner respect and trust, participants must display integrity, credibility, and humility. **Integrity** refers to the qualities of honesty, possessing strong moral principles, and moral uprightness. An old adage of integrity is "mean what you say and say what you mean." A more refined definition of integrity is "the consistency of an individual's words and actions that is observable by relevant stakeholders."[55] Integrity is important to constructive dialogue because it is required for fostering credibility. **Credibility** refers to "the intelligence, character, goodwill that audience members perceive in a message source."[56] Once a participant has credibility, other participants may disagree with them, but they trust that they are coming from a place of integrity and decency. Finally, participants cultivate trust by displaying humility. **Humility** refers to the "attribute of attaching low estimation to one's importance, using subtle ways of communicating this to others, presenting oneself in a ... modest way, and being hard working, caring, and down-to-earth."[57] Constructive dialogue requires **relational humility** which refers to "our being humble in personal relationships with others"[58] A long-standing practice of relational humility comes from the Jewish holiday of Yom Kippur which gives people an opportunity for atonement and repentance, where they can reflect on their treatment of others. For example, during Yom Kippur, Rabbi Dan Ain encourages people to go back and read their emails to see how they have communicated with others.[59] Another summation of the confluence of these practices from Buddhist monk and peace activist Thích Nhất Hạnh, in *The Art of Communicating*, reminds us to tell the truth, avoid exaggeration, be consistent, and use peaceful language.[60]

Listening

Reciprocity is not just a product of what participants say, but also how they listen. Too often, humans treat conversation as if it's "all about us." We are the ones shaping the narrative, staying on message, waiting to speak, and value is placed on what one projects not what one absorbs.[61] These non-reciprocal approaches to dialogue make destructive dialogue inevitable. Constructive dialogue rests upon listening while other participants communicate. American clinician Rachel Naomi Remen famously stated that

> the most basic and powerful way to connect to another person is to listen. Just listen. Perhaps the most important thing we ever give each other is our attention .... A loving silence often has far more power to heal and to connect than the most well-intentioned words.[62]

We often conflate listening with hearing, which prevents us from considering another person's point of view. However, as Stephen R. Covey notes, "most people do not listen with the intent to understand; they listen with the intent to reply."[63] Journalist Kate Murphy qualifies what listening entails in her 2019 book, *You're Not Listening, What You're Missing and Why It Matters*:

> Listening goes beyond just hearing what people say. It's also paying attention to how they say it, and what they do while they are saying it and in what context, and how what they say resonates within you. It's not about simply holding your peace while someone else holds forth. Quite the opposite. A lot of listening has to do with how you respond - the degree to which you elicit clear expression of another person's thoughts and, in the process, crystallize your own. Done well and with deliberation, listening can transform your understanding of the people in the world around you, which inevitably enriches and elevates your experience and existence. It is how you develop wisdom and form meaningful relationships.[64]

What Murphy describes is a form of responsiveness and attentiveness known as active listening. **Active listening** refers to "a process where the individual listens and, at the same time, attempts to discern, interpret and summarize what the speaker is saying."[65] When participants actively listen, they:

1   Hear the message
2   Decipher the meaning of the message
3   Recall what they heard
4   Think critically about the message
5   Provide feedback to the speaker[66]

More specifically, in *Intuition Pumps and Other Tools for Thinking*, philosopher Daniel Dennett points out four ways that participants can demonstrate to each other that they are practicing active listening:

1   Attempt to re-express the other person's position so clearly, vividly and fairly that they respond: "Thanks, I wish I'd thought of putting it that way."
2   List any points of agreement (especially if they are not matters of general or widespread agreement).
3   Mention anything you have learned from the other person.
4   Only then are you permitted to say so much as a word of rebuttal or criticism.[67]

When participants listen and consider, they are seeking to understand, not to pass judgment.

Constructive dialogue requires active listening, which also includes knowing how to use what is learned from active listening to help keep a conversating going. One must also be willing to do so, which may not always be easy when dealing with conflicts, especially those where power dynamics and hierarchies are in play. That noted, authors M. Neil Browne and Stuart M. Keeley, in their classic text *Asking the Right Questions: A Guide to Critical Thinking*, emphasize the significance of knowing how to keep dialogue happening, and to keep it constructive.[68] They lay out eight ways to keep a conversation going, thus paraphrased:

1   Try to clarify understanding of what the other person intends by asking "Did I hear you say?"
2   Ask the other person/party whether there is any evidence that would cause them to change their mind.
3   Suggest a time-out in which each party tries to find the best evidence they have to support their claims and beliefs.
4   Ask why anyone would find the evidence you have weak or faulty.
5   Try to come together on common ground after reviewing all the evidence. Is there a possibility that both parties have good points based on evidence?

6   Search for common values to serve as a basis for determining the roots of any disagreements.

7   Try to present a model of caring and calm curiosity when appropriate and possible; remember we are all learners not warriors.

8   Make sure body language suggests humility and models an environment open to reciprocal dialogue.[69]

Reciprocal dialogue suspends potential judgment and considers other participants' points of view with an open mind. Indeed, as Sean Bland notes, we too often assume the other person or side is "dumb" or "wrong" without considering that "it is possible we're not right about everything."[70] In fact, studies show that it is sometimes easier for observers to identify flaws in another person's thinking process than it is for them to recognize those same deficiencies in their thinking process.[71]

Active listening is further hampered by humans' destructive belief that they possess some innate intuition to "read" people. This practice has defined notions of racism, sexism, and other forms of discrimination because it assumes that people have an essence that defines them. An **essentialist** view interprets select categories of people – such as by gender, race, ethnicity, employment, or age – as having a set of attributes that are necessary to their identity and function.[72] In his bestselling book, *Talking To Strangers: What We Should Know About The People We Don't Know,* Malcolm Gladwell points out that choosing to "read" people rather than understand them has had catastrophic consequences. We have convinced ourselves that we have some intuition about humans that enables us to know them without listening. As Gladwell points out, our baseless assumption that we can read people by analyzing their words and intentions has facilitated horrendous outcomes. For example, people falsely "read" Amanda Knox to be a murderer; police officers' "read" of Sandra Bland led to her murder; and those who "read" Brock Turner and Jerry Sandusky to be harmless enabled numerous sex crimes to occur. In all of these cases, individuals were certain they had "read" the intentions or desires of the other person correctly.[73] Where reading a person in this way can be quick, because there is a pre-determined script, entering into constructive dialogue takes more time and patience, and is usually a purposeful activity.

Putting The Pieces Together: Cultivating Constructive Dialogue

Effective communicators work to produce an environment that is conducive to constructive dialogue. A set of agreements can be a useful tool for engendering constructive dialogue. Communicators benefit from taking the time to structure their dialogue around a set of agreements.

The following are a set of sample agreements based on the work of critical media literacy scholar Jeff Share and *Courageous Conversations About Race* by Glenn E. Singleton:[74]

- Stay engaged
  - Remain involved in the dialogue, Stay present, and embrace the conversation/dialogue.
- Experience discomfort
  - Openly and honestly deal with challenges, be authentic, push yourself, and recognize that discomfort can and often does engender growth.
- Make space/take space
  - Carefully balance making space for others while making sure you are heard
- Speak your truth
  - Share with humility, be honest, and take risks.
- Talk in first person
  - Use "I" statements only and avoid generalities
- Expect and accept non-closure
  - Do not expect a "quick fix." Instead, expect opportunities to learn and take meaningful action.
- Maintain confidentiality
  - Respect others by upholding privacy and discretion
- Listen with the intent to learn.
  - Be present and reciprocal.
- Suspend judgment

In addition to agreements, effective communicators use strategic questions. Community therapist and diversity trainer Lee Mun Wah encourages participants to:[75]

- Reflect back for clarity and understanding by asking questions such as "what I heard you say was...?" or "Tell me more about what you meant by...?"
- Reflect back to validate with question such as "what angered/hurt you about what happened?"

- Affirm for the purpose of making inclusive space by inquiring "how is this familiar?"
- Offer alternative positions by probing questions such as "have you considered...?"
- Set boundaries by requesting that certain statements or language be removed from the dialogue: "Can you please not say...again or around me?"
- Respond if feeling hurt or offended by asking "I am having a response to what you said, can I share it with you?"
- Make time and space for themselves by requesting time outs.
- Connect for realizable solutions or connections with the other participant(s) by asking "what do you need/want?"

Fostering constructive dialogue is a difficult task. It requires constant attention, energy, and measured acts.

Conclusion

"It has come to my attention that Representative Alexandria Ocasio-Cortez sent out a tweet a few hours ago in which she accused Senator Ted Cruz, in essence, of attempted murder," explained U.S. House of Representative from Texas Chip Roy in a January 29, 2021 letter to House Speaker Nancy Pelosi.

> As a member of this body who disagreed with 'objections' to the electors and who has expressed publicly my concerns about the events leading to January 6th, it is completely unacceptable behavior for a Member of Congress to make this kind of scurrilous charge against another member in the House or Senate for simply engaging in speech and debate regarding electors as they interpreted the Constitution. I ask you to call on her to immediately apologize and retract her comments.[76]

The letter followed a series of events the day previous, where market manipulation by companies such as the trading app Robin Hood led lawmakers such as AOC and U.S. Senator Ted Cruz to publicly state their interest in holding a hearing to investigate the claims. However, three weeks earlier, a group of individuals had stormed the U.S. capital to stop congress from recognizing Joe Biden as the President. In addition to white supremacist and internet conspiracy content, the individuals involved were found with paraphernalia designed to physically harm if not murder members of congress.[77] Cruz was one of the elected leaders who had publicly questioned the validity of Biden's victory, and thus, AOC and others accused him of being complicit in inciting the events at the Capitol.[78]

On January 28, 2021, when AOC expressed interest via Twitter to investigate the Robin Hood app, Ted Cruz publicly expressed his agreement.

However, soon thereafter AOC let it be known that she would work with members of Cruz's party, but not Cruz himself because he had still not apologized for the what she views as his complicity in the attempted murder of her and her colleagues.[79]

The Twitter spat is illustrative of destructive conflict. Neither party appears positioned to achieve their preferences, nor is there concern for the preferences of others. This is particularly problematic in a democracy, where representatives are supposed to collaborate for the betterment of the electorate. Such destructive forms of conflict – and it is one of many – are not a constructive force that strengthens American democracy, they are just the opposite. As AOC demonstrated in her speech about Rep. Yoho's comments, there are constructive approaches for managing conflict that produce better results than harassing language or empty apologies. However, as AOC's dialogue and interaction with Senator Cruz illustrate, the erudition of constructive processes is not a deterrent for destructive conflict. This is because just as conflict is not without encumbrance, humans are not without contradiction. These contradictions become

Ted Cruz ✅
@tedcruz

···

Fully agree.

🌟 **Alexandria Ocasio-Cortez** ✅ @AOC · Jan 28

This is unacceptable.

We now need to know more about @RobinhoodApp's decision to block retail investors from purchasing stock while hedge funds are freely able to trade the stock as they see fit.

As a member of the Financial Services Cmte, I'd support a hearing if necessary.
twitter.com/motherboard/st...

Show this thread

8:47 AM · Jan 28, 2021 · Twitter for iPhone

17K Retweets   **12.9K** Quote Tweets   **103.9K** Likes

Figure 1.1 **Tweet from U.S. Senator Ted Cruz's (R-TX) Twitter account on January 28, 2021.**

Alexandria Ocasio-Cortez ✔ @AOC · Jan 28   ···
I am happy to work with Republicans on this issue where there's common ground, but you almost had me murdered 3 weeks ago so you can sit this one out.

Happy to work w/ almost any other GOP that aren't trying to get me killed.

In the meantime if you want to help, you can resign.

> 🌑 **Ted Cruz** ✔ @tedcruz · Jan 28
> Fully agree. 🌫 twitter.com/AOC/status/135...

💬 48.4K   ⟲ 167.3K   ♡ 775.7K   ⬆️

Figure 1.2 Quoted retweet from U.S. House of Representative Alexandria Ocasio-Cortez's (D-NY) Twitter account on January 28, 2021.

difficult to temper in spaces that privilege destructive conflict. To better understand the ways in which the U.S. structuralizes destructive conflict, the next chapter focuses on the importance of not closing off channels of communication. We look at the relationship between free speech and democratic principles, how power shapes dialogue, and why censorship and cancel culture are the enemies of constructive, civic interactions.

Notes

1 bell hooks, *All about Love: New Visions* (New York: William Morrow and Company, 2000), 189.
2 Trace William Cowen, "Alexandria Ocasio-Cortez responds after reportedly being called a 'f*cking b*tch' by Republican Ted Yoho at Capitol," *Complex,* July 21, 2020, https://www.complex.com/life/2020/07/alexandria-ocasio-cortez-responds-called-bitch-by-republican-ted-yoho-at-capitol.
3 Ibid.
4 Oachesu Madalina, "Conflict management, a new challenge," *Procedia Economics and Finance* 39 (2016): 808.
5 David Kinsella and D.L. David, "Democracy and conflict," in *The Sage Handbook of Conflict Resolution*, eds J. Bercovitch, V. Kremenyuk, and W. Zartman (London: Sage Publications, 2009), 475–491. doi: 10.4135/9780857024701.n25.
6 Fred E. Jandt, *Conflict Communication* (Thousand Oaks, CA: Sage Publications, 2017), 2–3.
7 Herbert C. Kelman, "Conflict resolution and reconciliation: A social-psychological perspective on ending violent conflict between identity groups," *Landscapes of Violence* 1, no. 1 (2010): 1.
8 Calvin Morrill, "Conflict management, honor, and organizational change," *American Journal of Sociology* 97, no. 3 (1991): 586.
9 Fred E. Jandt, *Conflict Communication* (Thousand Oaks, CA: Sage Publications, 2017), 2–3.

10 Ibid., 2–3.
11 Ibid.
12 Ibid., 239.
13 Ibid., 38.
14 Ibid., 39.
15 Ibid., 41.
16 Ibid., 42.
17 Ibid., 43.
18 Ibid., 2–3.
19 Ibid., 237.
20 Ibid., 45.
21 Ibid., 239.
22 Shane Thye, "Power, theories of," in *The Blackwell Encyclopedia of Sociology*, ed. George Ritz (Malden, MA: Blackwell Publishing, 2007), 1.
23 Fred E. Jandt, *Conflict Communication* (Thousand Oaks, CA: Sage Publications, 2017), 237.
24 Hiroaki Saito and Lisa Ruhanen, "Power in tourism stakeholder collaborations: Power types and power holders," *Journal of Hospitality and Tourism Management* 31 (2017): 192.
25 Ibid., 238.
26 Kenneth J. Gergen, Sheila McNamee, and Frank J. Barrett, "Toward transformative dialogue," *International Journal of Public Administration* 24, no. 7–8 (2001): 679–707.
27 Charles Stangor, "The Violence around us: How the social situation influences aggression," in *Principles of Social Psychology – 1st International Edition,* ed. Dr. Charles Stangor (BC Campus, 2014), https://opentextbc.ca/socialpsychology/chapter/the-violence-around-us-how-the-social-situation-influences-aggression/.
28 Nader Sohrabi Safa, Carsten Maple, Steve Furnell, Muhammad Ajmal Azad, Charith Perera, Mohammad Dabbagh, and Mehdi Sookhak, "Deterrence and prevention-based model to mitigate information security insider threats in organisations," *Future Generation Computer Systems* 97 (2019), 7.
29 Gloria Wong, Annie O. Derthick, E.J.R. David, Anne Saw, and Sumie Okazaki, "The what, the why, and the how: A review of racial microaggressions research in psychology," *Race and Social Problems* 6, no. 2 (2014): 181–200; Thomas Huckin, "Critical discourse analysis and the discourse of condescension," *Discourse Studies in Composition* 155 (2002): 176.
30 "Ana Kasparian vs Tomi Lahren at Politicon 2019," *YouTube*, Oct 28, 2019, https://youtu.be/geNzraekJ-s.
31 Ibid., 238.
32 Ramy Bulan, "Dispute resolution: Restorative justice under native customary justice in Malaysia," in *Indigenous Peoples' Access to Justice, Including Truth and Reconciliation Processes*, eds Wilton Littlechild and Elsa Stamatopoulou, pp. 319–343 (New York: Institute for the Study of Human Rights, Columbia University), 320.
33 Tina Opie and Laura Morgan Roberts, "Do black lives really matter in the workplace? Restorative justice as a means to reclaim humanity," *Equality, Diversity and Inclusion: An International Journal* 36 (2017): 707–719; Declan Roche, "Dimensions of restorative justice," *Journal of Social Issues* 62, no. 2 (2006): 217–238.
34 Tinneke Van Camp, "Understanding victim participation in restorative practices: Looking for justice for oneself as well as for others," *European Journal of Criminology* 14, no. 6 (2017): 679–696; Lode Walgrave, "Domestic terrorism: A challenge for restorative justice," *Restorative Justice* 3, no. 2 (2015): 282–

290; Theo Gavrielides, "Clergy child sexual abuse and the restorative justice dialogue," *Journal of Church and State* 55, no. 4 (2013): 617–639.

35   Madeleine Fullard and Nicky Rousseau, "Truth telling, identities, and power in South Africa and Guatemala," Research Brief, International Center for Transitional Justice, New York, NY (2009).

36   Ramy Bulan, "Dispute resolution: Restorative justice under native customary justice in Malaysia," in *Indigenous Peoples' Access to Justice, Including Truth and Reconciliation Processes*, eds Wilton Littlechild and Elsa Stamatopoulou, pp. 319–343 (New York: Institute for the Study of Human Rights, Columbia University), 320.

37   Cathy Driscoll, "Fostering constructive conflict management in a multistakeholder context: The case of the forest round table on sustainable development," *International Journal of Conflict Management* 7, no. 2 (1996), 156–172. https://doi.org/10.1108/eb022780.

38   Em Griffin, Andrew Ledbetter, and Glenn Sparks, *A First Look at Communication Theory* (New York: McGraw-Hill, 2019), 472.

39   Richard L. Johannesen, "The emerging concept of communication as dialogue," *Quarterly Journal of Speech,* 58 (1971): 373–382.

40   Fred E. Jandt, *Conflict Communication* (Thousand Oaks, CA: Sage Publications, 2017), 17.

41   Charles R. Berger and Richard J. Calabrese, "Some explorations in initial interaction and beyond: Toward a developmental theory of interpersonal communication," *Human Communication Research* 1, no. 2 (1974): 99–112; Richard L West and Lynn H. Turner, *Introducing Communication Theory: Analysis and Application* (New York: McGraw-Hill).

42   Irwin Altman and Dalmas A. Taylor, *Social Penetration: The Development of Interpersonal Relationships* (New York: Holt, Rinehart & Winston, 1973).

43   Friedrich Nietzsche, *Beyond Good and Evil*, Aphorism 146.

44   Robert O. Keohane, "Reciprocity in international relations," *International Organization* 40, no. 1 (Winter, 1986): 8.

45   Jean Decety and Meghan Meyer, "From emotion resonance to empathic understanding: A social developmental neuroscience account," *Development and Psychopathology* 20, no. 4 (2008): 1053–1080.

46   Martin L. Hoffman, "The contribution of empathy to justice and moral judgment," in *Empathy and its Development*, eds Nancy Eisenberg and Janet Strayer (Cambridge, MA: Cambridge University Press, 1987), 47–80.

47   Ibid.

48   Robert O. Keohane, "Reciprocity in international relations," *International Organization* 40, no. 1 (Winter, 1986): 8.

49   Pamela Shockley-Zalabak, Kathleen Ellis, and Gaynelle Winograd, "Organizational trust: What it means, why it matters," *Organization Development Journal* 18, no. 4 (2000): 35.

50   Michalinos Zembylas, "The "crisis of pity" and the radicalization of solidarity: Toward critical pedagogies of compassion," *Educational Studies* 49, no. 6 (2013): 504–521.

51   Donna M. Mertens, "Philosophy in mixed methods teaching: The transformative paradigm as illustration," *International Journal of Multiple Research Approaches* 4, no. 1 (2010): 11.

52   Michalinos Zembylas, "The "crisis of pity" and the radicalization of solidarity," *Educational Studies* 49, no. 6 (2013): 504–521.

53   Omayya M. Al-Hassan, Theodora De Baz, Fathi Ihmeideh, and Ibrahim Jumiaan, "Collectivism and individualism: Jordanian mothers' child-rearing values," *International Journal of Early Years Education* (2020): 1–12.

54 Brian S. Lowery, "Opinion: To my white friends, the time for talk has passed. Now is the time for work," *Washington Post*, June 12, 2020, https://www.wa shingtonpost.com/opinions/2020/06/12/my-white-friends-time-talk-has-passe d-now-is-time-work/.

55 Michael E. Palanski and Francis J. Yammarino, "Integrity and leadership: A multi-level conceptual framework," *The Leadership Quarterly* 20, no. 3 (2009): 409.

56 Em Griffin, Andrew Ledbetter, and Glenn Sparks, *A First Look at Communication Theory* (New York: McGraw-Hill, 2019), 467.

57 Ali Dastmalchian, Mansour Javidan, and Kamran Alam, "Effective leadership and culture in Iran: An empirical study," *Applied Psychology* 50, no. 4 (2001): 544.

58 Edward C. Watkins, Joshua N. Hook, David K. Mosher, and Jennifer L. Callahan, "Humility in clinical supervision: Fundamental, foundational, and transformational," *The Clinical Supervisor* 38, no. 1 (2019), 61.

59 "Jewish/Black Relations; Dialogue in Contentious Times with Rabbi Dan Ain," Along the Line Ep. 96, *YouTtube*, July 3, 2020, https://www.youtube. com/watch?v=rNdl0bO59v0.

60 Thích Nhⵯt Hⵯnh, *The Art of Communicating* (London: Rider Books, 2013); Nicole Fenton, *Swell Content*, November 2, 2013, https://swellcontent.com/ 2013/11/the-art-of-communicating/.

61 Kate Murphy, *You're Not Listening, What You're Missing and Why It Matters* (New York: Celadon Books, 2019).

62 Rachel Naomi Remen, "Listening: A powerful tool for healing," *Science of Mind* 70, no. 7 (1997): 14–19.

63 Stephen R. Covey, *The 7 Habits of Highly Effective People: Powerful Lessons in Personal Change* (New York: Simon and Schuster, 1989, 2013), 252.

64 Kate Murphy, *You're Not Listening, What You're Missing and Why It Matters* (New York: Celadon Books, 2019), 4.

65 Jonathon Timothy Newton, "Matching perception with reality: How patients develop perceptions of treatment," *Primary Dental Journal* 4, no. 1 (2015): 51.

66 Fred E. Jandt, *Conflict Communication* (Thousand Oaks, CA: Sage Publications, 2017), 15–16.

67 Daniel Dennett, *Intuition Pumps and Other Tools for Thinking* (New York: W.W. Norton, 2013), 33–34.

68 M. Neil Browne and Stuart M. Keeley, *Asking the Right Questions: A Guide to Critical Thinking*, 12th ed. (New York: Pearson, 2018).

69 Ibid., 12–13.

70 Sean Blanda, "The 'other side' is not dumb: Is it possible we're not right about everything?" January 7, 2016, https://humanparts.medium.com/the-o ther-side-is-not-dumb-2670c1294063.

71 Daniel Kahneman, *Thinking Fast and Slow* (New York: Farrar, Strauss Giroux, 2011), 4.

72 Richard Delgado and Jean Stefancic, *Critical Race Theory: An Introduction* (New York: New York University Press, 2001); Kimberlé Williams Crenshaw, "Twenty years of critical race theory: Looking back to move forward," *Conn. L. Rev.* 43 (2010): 1253; Sumi Cho, Kimberlé Williams Crenshaw, and Leslie McCall, "Toward a field of intersectionality studies: Theory, applications, and praxis," *Signs: Journal of Women in Culture and Society* 38, no. 4 (2013): 785–810.

73 Malcolm Gladwell, *Talking to Strangers: What We Should Know About the People We Don't Know* (New York: Little, Brown and Company, 2019).

74 Glenn E. Singleton, *Courageous conversations about race*, (Thousand Oaks, CA: Corwin Press, 2005 2021); Email correspondence with Jeff Share; Staff, "Agreements for Courageous Conversations and Active Learning, The Denver Foundation, 2021, www.nonprofitinclusiveness.org/agreements-courageous-conversations-and-active-learning.

75 Lee Mun Wah, "Mindful Facilitation Training for the Workplace," 2018, http s://bhdp.sccgov.org/sites/g/files/exjcpb716/files/lp-mindfully-resolving-conflict s-for-diversity-issues-handout-04-02-18.pdf.

76 Biba Adams, "GOP lawmaker demands AOC apologize to Cruz for tweets," *Yahoo*, January 29, 2021, https://news.yahoo.com/gop-lawmaker-demands-a oc-apologize-165903575.html.

77 Jamil Smith, "White entitlement, on parade: The Trump mob's siege on the Capitol was white supremacy in full, a violent assertion that only they are fit to select a president," *Rolling Stone*, January 7, 2021, https://www.roll ingstone.com/politics/political-commentary/trump-mob-capitol-attack-jamil-1110820/.

78 See Senator Ted Cruz on Twitter, https://twitter.com/tedcruz/status/ 1354833603943931905; Dareh Gregorian, Julie Tsirkin and Frank Thorp, "Senate Democrats file ethics complaint against Republicans Hawley, Cruz over roles in Capitol riot," *NBC News*, January 21, 2021, https://www. nbcnews.com/politics/congress/senate-dems-file-ethics-complaint-against-gop -sens-hawley-cruz-n1255228.

79 Representative Alexandria Ocasio-Cortez on Twitter, https://twitter.com/ AOC/status/1354848253729234944.

Chapter 2

Reflect on Communication Practices and Censorship

> Our cultural institutions are facing a moment of trial. Powerful protests for racial and social justice are leading to overdue demands for police reform, along with wider calls for greater equality and inclusion across our society, not least in higher education, journalism, philanthropy, and the arts. But this needed reckoning has also intensified a new set of moral attitudes and political commitments that tend to weaken our norms of open debate and toleration of differences in favor of ideological conformity. As we applaud the first development, we also raise our voices against the second. The forces of illiberalism are gaining strength throughout the world and have a powerful ally in Donald Trump, who represents a real threat to democracy. But resistance must not be allowed to harden into its own brand of dogma or coercion.[1]

So read the letter published in *Harper's Magazine* in fall of 2020, signed by over 150 authors, intellectuals, and others professing their commitment to free speech and democratic discourse.

The signatories included writers such as Canadian poet Margaret Atwood, British-Indian novelist and essayist Salman Rushdie, and Harry Potter creator J.K. Rowling; intellectuals such as the political theorist Noam Chomsky, cognitive psychologist Steven Pinker, and political scientist Francis Fukuyama; journalists such as Vox co-founder Matthew Yglesias, author Malcolm Gladwell, and CNN's Fareed Zakaria; liberals such as feminist writer and activist Gloria Steinem and Liberal Party of Canada Michael Ignatieff; along with conservatives like former Republican speech writer David Frum and *New York Times* writer David Brooks.

The bi-partisan and ideologically diverse signatories were concerned over what they viewed as the normalization of censorship. **Censorship** refers to "the prohibition on publication of information in various products (e.g., newspaper articles, cultural channels, and official publications) that challenge the themes of the dominant conflict-supportive narratives."[2] The signatories claimed that the use of censorship in response to perceived transgressions had resulted in a series of anti-democratic trends:

DOI: 10.4324/9781003250906-4

Editors are fired for running controversial pieces; books are withdrawn for alleged inauthenticity; journalists are barred from writing on certain topics; professors are investigated for quoting works of literature in class; a researcher is fired for circulating a peer-reviewed academic study; and the heads of organizations are ousted for what are sometimes just clumsy mistakes.

The letter made clear that they were not interested in protecting an individual, but the idea of protecting individuals' right to free speech and expression:

Whatever the arguments around each particular incident, the result has been to steadily narrow the boundaries of what can be said without the threat of reprisal. We are already paying the price in greater risk aversion among writers, artists, and journalists who fear for their livelihoods if they depart from the consensus, or even lack sufficient zeal in agreement.[3]

The letter also addressed that many of the signatories were people of privilege who were concerned that the normalization of censorship would ultimately hurt the under-privileged:

This stifling atmosphere will ultimately harm the most vital causes of our time. The restriction of debate, whether by a repressive government or an intolerant society, invariably hurts those who lack power and makes everyone less capable of democratic participation. The way to defeat bad ideas is by exposure, argument, and persuasion, not by trying to silence or wish them away. We refuse any false choice between justice and freedom, which cannot exist without each other.[4]

The subtext of their letter expressed fear that intolerance and repression were leading citizens to engage in self-censorship. **Self-censorship** refers to decisions by individuals or organizations to curtail their own expressions out of fear of negative consequences.[5] Scholars have found that rather than create more space for truth to percolate, censorship campaigns create a chilling effect – when fears of persecution, legitimate or otherwise, result in acts of self-censorship – among the electorate that fosters an anti-democratic climate that produces repressive regimes.[6] Once the public is aware that censorship is being employed, it often results in a chilling effect that stifles freedom of speech and expression for unintended targets.[7]

Despite their best efforts, the letter seemed to engender the very destructive conflict it sought to minimize. First a destructive and inaccurate hyper-partisan frame was applied to the letter. The conservative *Washington Times* ignored the conservative signatories to focus on how

"Liberals J.K. Rowling, Noam Chomsky sign letter denouncing 'ideological conformity,' cancel culture."[8] To further the partisan divide, the conservative *New York Post* and *Fox News* fixated on stories of liberals who opposed the letter and some of its signatories.[9] For example, Vox's Emily VanDerWerff lambasted her company's founder Matthew Yglesias for being a signatory because "the letter, signed as it is by several prominent anti-trans voices and containing as many dog whistles towards anti-trans positions ...." VanDerWerff went on to claim, without explanation, that knowing Yglesias signed the letter "makes me feel less safe at Vox," and her job "slightly more difficult." Similarly, Professor Jennifer Finney Boylan, an American author, transgender activist and reality television personality, recanted her signature not because she changed her mind about the content, but because she rejected previous attitudes and behaviors of some of the signatories including Rowling.[10] Ironically, the guilt by association premise from which Boylan operated did more to demonstrate rather than ameliorate the concerns of the original letter.

What these critiques did not address was whether censorship is, or could be, successful in stifling targeted content. As policy, censorship not only limits access to some information, but has been shown to popularize the ideas it seeks to erase. Scholars refer to this as the **Streisand Effect**, which is "defined as the inadvertent popularity of any material as a result of its suppression."[11] This occurred in 2020 when big-tech platforms decided to remove a story about then presidential candidate Joe Biden's son Hunter from *The New York Post*, one of the oldest newspapers in the country, which was in turn correlated to increased popularity of the article.[12] The efforts to censor the story attracted new audiences to the very content that big-tech platforms aimed to conceal. These actions by censors have the exact opposite effect of their stated purpose.

Nonetheless, others made a more nuanced critique of the *Harper's* letter. Arionne Nettles, a lecturer, organized 150 people from academia and media to sign the "A More Specific Letter on Justice and Open Debate."[13] It criticized the *Harper's* letter for being written by and for people of privilege who already have a platform, while ignoring those who have been traditionally marginalized or cancelled. What was most revealing about the competing letters was that just like the *Harper's* letter, Nettles' letter had people refuse to sign and some chose anonymity out of fear of "professional retaliation."[14] The organizer of the *Harper's* letter, Thomas Chatterton Williams, pointed out that the fact people were afraid to sign either letter proves the point of the letter itself– that the current climate is punitive for those who speak freely and think outside of the box.[15] The fact that people were afraid to sign the *Harper's* letter gives the signatories' fears about the normalization of censorship some merit.

However, the signatories of the *Harper's* letter, like all humans, are full of their own contradictions and hypocrisies. Jillian C. York, Director for

International Freedom of Expression at the Electronic Frontier Foundation, pointed out that some of the signatories to the original letter had in fact acted to cancel or censor others in the past and many remained silent on censorship matters when it was inconvenient for them to speak up. For example, while at Columbia University, one of the signatories, Bari Weiss, formerly of the *New York Times*, toiled to get a professor fired for inviting speakers to campus that Weiss opposed.[16]

In essence, no one seems immune from the tendency to censor or cancel, contingent upon relative circumstances. If anything, these developments suggest we need to have more conversations around these issues, not fewer. Indeed, noted scholar and civil rights activist Cornel West warned in 2018 about Americans' seeming unwillingness to engage in dialogue by noting

> nowadays it is rare to see a right-wing person and a left-wing person who love and respect each other and engage in dialogue. We live in a society where it's all about the will to power, the will to dominate, the will to conquer.[17]

Here, we operate from the assumption that Americans are not unwilling to engage in dialogue, but simply lack the spaces and tools to do so.

This chapter looks at some of the behaviors and attitudes that prevent constructive dialogue. Despite the use of seemingly new language such as "cancel culture" and "deplatforming," it is our contention that these concepts reflect long-term anti-dialogical, even anti-intellectual practices that act in opposition to the free and open debate allowances that define a functioning democracy. That is not to say that all efforts to censor derive from ill will, as some efforts to quell debate may be very well-intended, at least at the time and by the party calling for censorship. Nonetheless, we point out in this section that these censorious approaches not only fail to achieve many of their stated goals, they often backfire.[18] For example, in the mid 1980s, Parents Music Resource Center (PMRC), a high-profile campaign launched by Washington, D.C. insiders Tipper Gore and Susan Baker, wives of Senator Al Gore and Secretary of State James Baker respectively, forced labeling of record albums they viewed as "obscene" with a "parental advisory" notice.[19] Ironically, these efforts boosted sales of many recordings that brandished the warning label, thus backfiring as artists often wore the advisory sticker/label as a badge of honor. Despite these modest victories, threats to freedom of speech – and as a consequence liberty and constructive discourse – persist, though this is a struggle a long time in the making.[20]

The First Amendment, Free Speech, and Democracy

In the U.S., the conception of freedom of speech and censorship is framed by the First Amendment to the U.S. Constitution. The five freedoms protected by the First Amendment to the Constitution's Bill of Rights (religion, speech, expression, assembly, and the press), are requisite for any republican form of government. Such principles long predate the founding of the U.S., harkening back to ancient Greece. As media scholar Andy Lee Roth of Project Censored reminds us, pulling from the work of 20th century philosopher Michel Foucault, the Athenians had what they called *parrhesia*, which literally translated to "saying everything." *Parrhesia*, as a form of truth-telling, was seen as "a moral activity that was a central characteristic of Athenian democracy.[21] The belief that liberty rests upon unfettered free speech is such a defining feature in the U.S. that it was shared by the privileged and unprivileged alike, such as slave owner President Thomas Jefferson, and those battling this most horrific form of exploitation like former slave Frederick Douglass.[22]

In his First Inaugural Address, President Jefferson spoke in favor of unfettered free speech, stating that "error of opinion may be tolerated where reason is left free to combat it."[23] Moving through early history in the U.S., free speech protections moved beyond the elite political classes and played a key role in advancing pro-democracy movements for civil rights, voting rights, women's rights, and abolitionism. In 1860, former slave and radical abolitionist Frederick Douglass stated:

> Liberty is meaningless where the right to utter one's thoughts and opinions has ceased to exist. That, of all rights, is the dread of tyrants. It is the right which they first of all strike down. They know its power .... Slavery cannot tolerate free speech.[24]

This message can easily be extended to other hierarchical arrangements of power in purportedly free societies, as illustrated by the open and free expression of suffragists leading to the formal inclusion of women into the civic sphere by 1919 in the U.S. when they won the right to vote and participate in federal elections.

Despite its perceived centrality to democracy, limitations on the First Amendment have been debated throughout U.S. history. From the founding of the country with the Alien and Sedition Acts of 1798 to the Espionage and Sedition Acts of 1917 and 1918, and up to the present day in the so-called War on Terror, certain forms of speech and expression have been suppressed and deemed punishable by the government. One prominent example occurred during World War I; thousands of people were imprisoned and deported for protesting the war, including socialist Eugene Debs, who was arrested, tried, and sentenced to ten years in prison under the Sedition Act for delivering an anti-war speech in Canton, Ohio. Debs had urged working people to not join the war efforts which would contribute to bank profits and mass violence against other working people, thus obstructing the draft (which was considered illegal as it interfered with the government's war efforts).[25] He ran for president from prison on the Socialist Party ticket garnering almost a million votes, and sentence was subsequently commuted in 1921 by President Warren G. Harding.[26]

While upholding speech restrictions during and just after World War I, there have also been numerous attempts to expand and protect freedom of speech, most famously by Supreme Court Justice Louis Brandeis, who wrote in the 1927 *Whitney v. California* decision that

> no danger flowing from speech can be deemed clear and present, unless the incidence of the evil apprehended is so imminent that it may befall before there is opportunity for full discussion. If there be time to expose through discussion the falsehood and fallacies, to avert the evil by the processes of education, the remedy to be applied is more speech, not enforced silence.[27]

In 1929, in his historic opinion for *United States v. Schwimmer*, Supreme Court Justice Oliver Wendell Holmes, Jr., wrote:

> If there is any principle of the U.S. Constitution that more imperatively calls for attachment than any other, it is the principle of free thought — not free thought for those who agree with us but freedom for the thought we hate.[28]

Although it was a dissenting opinion at the time, Holmes' remarks served as the basis for future generations to free political thought by strengthening freedom of expression and speech, and by extension the press, as bulwarks of democratic societies. Not long after, in *Near vs. Minnesota*, 1931, the same court further protected freedom of speech and the press by ruling that prior restraint on publications was unconstitutional.[29] Justice Charles Evans Hughes noted in that ruling that, "It is no longer open to doubt that the liberty of the press, and of speech, is within the liberty safeguarded by the due process clause of the Fourteenth Amendment from invasion by state action."[30]

After the atrocities of the Second World War (1939–1945), with the rise of the Nazis in Germany and assaults on personal freedoms that were hallmarks of fascism, the U.S. like much of the world sought to ensconce democratic freedoms. In 1948, the United Nations General Assembly adopted The Universal Declaration of Human Rights. In it, Article 19 addressed free speech and expression declaring, "Everyone has the right to freedom of opinion and expression; this right includes freedom to hold opinions without interference and to seek, receive and impart information and ideas through any media and regardless of frontiers."[31] In the 1960s, students like Mario Savio and their First Amendment allies formed The Free Speech Movement (FSM) centered around the University of California–Berkeley, which helped lead to many reforms and protections involving student rights and paved the way for more robust public protests around civil and human rights for which the decade of the 1960s is largely known. The civil rights and anti-war marches in particular are squarely rooted in the spirit and practice of the First Amendment.

In the 1970s, historic whistleblower Daniel Ellsberg leaked the Pentagon Papers to the press about government misdeeds during the Vietnam War, leading to a Supreme Court showdown with President Richard Nixon in the *New York Times Co. v. United States*.[32] The *Times* won that case, which was a huge victory for press freedom. Ellsberg has been a staunch supporter of the public's right to know ever since and later wrote of the significance of the free flow of information and the need for citizens to demonstrate what he called "civil courage," or what is known as whistleblowing, or fearless speech, which is a contemporary example of *parrhesia* the ancient Greeks might have recognized.[33] By providing information that shapes citizens' knowledge of powerful institutions and actors, whistleblowers play an important role in a democracy. So important were whistleblowers, that by the 1980s, the U.S. Congress passed the Whistleblower Protection Act which protected whistleblowers employed by the government that reported crimes or abuses in government.[34] But, as history often shows, the pendulum of support for one policy, in this case whistleblower protections of politics later swings back against that very same policy.

In the 21st century, the 2001 War on Terror saw Presidents George W. Bush and Barack Obama with new powers granted by controversial legislation – such as the U.S.A. P.A.T.R.I.O.T. Act (Uniting and Strengthening America by Providing the Appropriate Tools Required to Intercept and Obstruct Terrorism Act), which seriously encroached on First, Fourth, Fifth, Sixth, and Eighth Amendment Rights in particular, targeting whistleblowers, activists, and racial and ethnic minorities' freedoms.[35] It also drew serious criticism from the right and left, from prominent Republicans like Bob Barr and Arlen Specter to more progressive coalitions like the Bill of Rights Defense Committee, now Defending Rights and Dissent.[36] The early 21st century saw several states pass laws to silence activists such as the so-called ag-gag bills – which make it a crime to discuss the cruelty witnessed in factory farming.[37] Similarly, over half of U.S. states have passed specific laws which aim to disrupt and criminalize those engaged in the efforts to boycott, divest, and sanction Israel (called the BDS movement) for its treatment of the

Palestinians.[38] Although a similar movement against apartheid South Africa was celebrated for its success in furthering social justice, some states now consider the BDS movement to be a hate crime – meaning that is it is a prejudice-motivated crime.[39] The legal tide may be turning, however, as in May 2021, a federal district court ruled in favor of the First Amendment rights of journalist Abby Martin in her case against Georgia's anti-BDS law.[40]

Closer to the present, the moral panic over so-called fake news has engendered calls for censorship. **Fake news**, in its most basic sense, can be any false or misleading information presented as legitimate journalism. The post-2016 fears that fake news was responsible for undesired electoral outcomes and violence saw open dialogue in the U.S. about censoring content. After the January 2021 conflict over the outcome of the 2020 U. S. Presidential Election resulted in thousands of people storming the U.S. Capitol in a clash that ultimately saw five people die, MSNBC's Anand Giridharadas blamed Fox News Channel and tweeted, "It's time for this question to be front and center: Should Fox News be allowed to exist?"[41] Zaid Jilani of *The Intercept* countered that a productive response

> isn't to say that people just shouldn't be allowed to watch it [Fox News Channel]. At that point, I'm stepping out of the boundaries of liberal democratic discourse. I'm telling other people I should dictate to them what they can believe rather than having any kind of conversation with them, and I think that's the fatal error really what he's arguing.[42]

In addition, even more recent debates have focused on the utility of the First Amendment in regards to hate speech. **Hate speech** is defined as speech that expresses a "profound disrespect, hatred, and vilification for the members of minority groups."[43] In a 2019 opinion piece for the *Washington Post*, Richard Stengel, the former managing editor of *Time* magazine and as of 2021 the head of the U.S. Agency for Global Media, argued for more stringent hate speech laws in the U.S. He explained that "the First Amendment ... should not protect hateful speech that can cause violence by one group against another."[44] Some scholars have noted that hate speech is incorrectly classified as expressive speech, and should be defended like any other form of speech that is protected by the First Amendment.[45] However, some contend that this narrow interpretation protects those speaking at the expense of the targets. At the heart of this argument is the belief that inclusiveness is a public good from which all benefit, and hate speech undermines inclusivity by emaciating individual dignity.[46] Those who oppose the criminalization of hate speech argue that people must learn to tolerate the thoughts that they hate. However, advocates for criminalization of content note that this view does not consider the targets: "can their lives be led, can their children be brought up, can their hopes be maintained and their worst fears dispelled, and a social environment polluted by these materials?"[47] The current debates about freedom of speech and censorship are further complicated by the advent of the internet and dysfunctions of social media platforms, but that does not mean these discussions are not worth having, quite the contrary, they may be the most important matters we consider as a society.

Algorithmic Censorship

Contemporaneous arguments about censorship center on whether removal of content online by big-tech companies can be considered censorship, or if that is something that only governments can do. In the last few years, concerns over fake news and hate speech has resulted in public pressure on technology companies such as Facebook, Twitter, Apple, Alphabet (Google/YouTube), and Spotify to moderate content on their platforms.[48] Supporters of this movement argue that they are private companies buckling under public pressure to serve the interests of their users. Indeed, the First Amendment to the U.S. Constitution protects citizens from government censorship, but not corporate censorship. However, some argue that tech-censorship simply amounts to **censorship by proxy**, which refers to the censorship of information performed by a third party, but at the behest of government.[49] This practice pre-dates the internet.[50] More widely covered cases occurred during the Cold War, where elites in the film industry and university system blacklisted employees in the entertainment industry and university system respectively, often at the suggestion or behest of the government.[51]

However, since America's War on Terror, technology companies have further transformed into government proxies when it comes to censoring content.[52] The major tech-companies have contracts to assist in surveillance for the federal government, which includes a litany of individuals who have gone from working for the federal government to big-tech, and vice versa, and they are dependent upon government loans and subsidies.[53] In fact, the Defense Advanced Research Projects Agency (DARPA), a U.S. laboratory that works with the Pentagon, the Central Intelligence Agency (CIA), the National Security Agency (NSA), and other agencies, was born during the Cold War after the U.S.S.R. launched Sputnik in 1957. Since then, it has been a technological source of innovation behind everything from the internet and drones to self-driving cars and mass surveillance tools (like Global Positioning Systems, or GPS), all originally designed for military purposes with public money, and purportedly, for public good.[54]

These companies' unparalleled control over communication makes them a valuable proxy for government agencies struggling with political and legal obstacles to censorship.[55] It is telling that after the events of January 6, 2021 many argued that fake news on social media had precipitated the storming of the U.S. Capitol building. What was revealing was that the former First Lady Michelle Obama and U.S. Congressperson AOC reached out to big-tech, rather than legislators, to solve the problem by removing apps and people.[56] What is rarely talked about is how their commitment to free speech is tenuous at best, considering that companies such as Google, Microsoft, Apple, Facebook, Twitter, and Wikipedia[57] regularly work with regimes like China to censor content and regularly censor pages of journalists and activists in so-called free world.

Big-tech companies' awesome power to censor is rooted in their ability to surveil users. Surveillance enables effective censorship, as data from the former can feed the party pushing the latter, sometimes without context and with harmful, silencing effect on a target. Prominent figures like NSA whistleblower Edward Snowden exposed wanton and lawless surveillance of millions of innocent people that the U.S. government and NSA were lying about to cover up. He tried to leak this information to the press in the U.S., but only the U.K.-based paper *The Guardian* and journalist Glenn Greenwald took interest enough to report on the revelations in 2013. Snowden is still living in Russia in exile as the State Department revoked his passport as an effort to stop him when he was trying to meet with Greenwald and documentarian Laura Poitras in Hong Kong. Snowden warned that these dangers went beyond government entities to include big-tech companies, especially around social media, noting that "Facebook's data policies are exploitative and resemble the work of a surveillance company."[58] He said these companies were "just as untrustworthy as the NSA."[59] On Twitter he remarked:

> Businesses that make money by collecting and selling detailed records of private lives were once plainly described as 'surveillance companies.' Their rebranding as 'social media' is the most successful deception since the Department of War became the Department of Defense."[60]

Snowden reminds us that

> Facebook's internal purpose, whether they state it publicly or not, is to compile perfect records of private lives to the maximum extent of their capability, and then exploit that for their own corporate enrichment. And damn the consequences ... This is actually precisely the same as what the NSA does. Google ... has a very similar model.[61]

Now that these companies are used so ubiquitously for communications by much of the world, an extraordinary amount of power has amassed in the hands of a few corporate CEOs who can decide what is or is not acceptable speech, what is or is not public or private. Critics contend that the power of the internet coupled with the public's intolerance for select speech and content has created a "cancel culture."

Cancel Culture

Cancel culture is a nebulous phrase that refers to the practice of withdrawing support for – the canceling of – individuals and institutions due to expressed attitudes or behaviors outside of the **Overton Window,** which refers to the range of political ideas tolerated in public discourse. Also known as online shaming, **cancel culture** involves drawing attention to perceived *faux pas* or wrongheadedness as a pretext for getting someone removed from popular culture, their place of employment, or other related institutions.[62]

The term "cancel culture" emerged from a 1981 song by the Chic titled "Your Love Is Canceled," which compared the end of a romantic relationship to the cancellation of TV shows.[63] The song inspired screenwriter Barry Michael Cooper to script a woman being "canceled" in the 1991 film New Jack City.[64] By 2014, the Me Too Movement - a social movement aimed at comabtting sex crimes by publicizing allegations of sexual abuse and sexual harassment - had begun using the phrase "call-out culture" to communicate their desire to draw public attention to sex crimes.[65] Soon transgressors were publicly shamed, ostracized, and professionally and legally punished for accusations of non-sex crimes such as offensive language behaviors and attitudes.[66] People began to describe what was already being termed "call-out culture" and "cancellation" as a singular phenomenon known as "cancel culture." Although it had been used prior, there was large increase in the use of cancel culture on the internet starting in 2019.[67]

Scholars argue that people's desire to punish, humiliate, shame, and cancel people is not solely rooted in morality or notions of justice, but in pleasure. Indeed, studies show that people get a hit of dopamine – a chemical messenger in the brain that provides people with feelings of pleasure - when someone is held accountable for a transgression.[68] This is summed up in the word *Schadenfreude,* which combines the words malicious and damage with joy, to describe the pleasure people feel when they see other people's misfortune. Scholars argue that pleasure from a powerful person's misfortune, such as a celebrity or politician, is particularly satisfying because the pleasure from seeing a person they envy experience misfortunate alleviates feelings of inferiority.[69]

So-called cancel culture's emphasis on public shame and humiliation for transgressors is not an historical aberration.[70] For example, at one time, those accused of committing offenses in China were locked in a cage outside of the entrance gates to the city; offenders had their heads shaved, bodies stoned, and houses labeled with public notices in the Ancient Mediterranean; and the word ostracization emerged from the Ancient Greeks, who voted to banish citizens with shards of pottery known as "ostraka."[71] Similarly, around the 12th century, England began to tar and feather people, lock women's mouths shut for disapproved of behavior or speech with an iron mask known as the scold's helm or dame's bridle; force people to wear a giant wooden barrel known as the drunkards cloak for excessive public intoxication; a cuck-stule which humiliated women accused of sexual offenses, an early form of slut shaming, by hanging them in a sitting position and parading them around the town; and the ducking stool which seated offenders in a chair from which they could not escape and they were dunked under water.[72] In the 13th century the pillory was developed. It locked accused individuals head and arms into a piece of wood where they were mocked as they paraded to the gathering sight to be insulted, pelted with items, and in some cases murdered.[73]

By the late 20th century, public shaming over speech transgressions focused on issues of political correctness. Legendary sociologist and cultural theorist Stuart Hall explains:

> According to one version, political correctness actually began as an in-joke on the left: radical students on American campuses acting out an ironic replay of the Bad Old Days BS (Before the Sixties) when every revolutionary groupuscule had a party line about everything. They would address some glaring examples of sexist or racist behaviour by their fellow students in imitation of the tone of voice of the Red Guards or Cultural Revolution Commissar: "Not very 'politically correct,' Comrade!"[74]

However, by the late 20th century, conservative commentators such as Dinesh D'Souza had used "political correctness" to denote a belief that liberals were creating rules and policies around acceptable speech that amounted to censorship and thought control.[75] Some leftists agreed such as education expert and historian Diane Ravitch, who warned that the political correctness in schools was robbing students of their education. Ravitch cited textbook manufacturers' intention of eliminating sexist and racist language and imagery as stupefying because it removes necessary resources to historically contextualize and resist such ideologies.[76] Furthermore, it leaves students ignorant of prescient issues that are important, albeit controversial.[77]

Cancel culture is viewed as the next chapter in the long saga of public shaming as censorship.[78] Cancel culture critics argue that college campuses are normalizing cancel culture as a response to a range of transgressions. Groups such as The Foundation for Individual Rights in Education and affiliated scholars argue that today's college students have been conditioned to accept what they call "great untruths," including concepts of fragility, emotional reasoning, and "us versus them" binary mindsets that lead to a culture of fear, insecurity, entitlement, and ultimately to reactionary cancellation, or "calling out" of different people or ideas that are perceived to be existential threats, even if they are not.[79] They cite the college campuses faculty and campus speakers who were cancelled for past transgressions.[80] For example, Bret Weinstein, a white faculty member at Evergreen College in Olympia, WA, entered his campus on their "Day of Absence," which sought to limit the population to marginalized students for the purpose of creating a safe space to discuss campus issues.[81] On college campuses, **safe spaces** "refers to the need to feel emotionally comfortable to facilitate oral participation and maximize learning."[82] Weinstein would eventually feel compelled to leave his faculty position citing the criticisms he received for dismissing the "Day of Absence."

Comedians have also derided higher education for leaving students unable to recognize the value in humor.[83] Their concern is that **humor** is dichotomous when it comes to communication: It can be both destructive and constructive. It can be a destructive force if participants do not share the same humor. Worse, it can be a tool that masks hate. For example, racist jokes, sexist memes, and derisive posts have been defended as "humor," but that does not change the pernicious tropes and perspectives they spread. On the other hand, humor can also bring people to together to share the involuntary response of laughter. It can de-escalate tensions and perceived divisions, especially when those with privilege use self-depreciation. Finally, some of the most provocative thoughts and ideas that bind people have derived from standup comedians over the years. This may especially be the case if humor "punches up" at the powerful, not down, toward those whom are oppressed in society.

Although educational institutions have bore the brunt of frustration over cancel culture, it emerges in many other spaces. For example, former San Francisco 49ers quarterback Colin Kaepernick is believed to have lost his position in the National Football League because he knelt during the National Anthem.[84] In 2017, social media users' ire over Kathy Griffin posting a picture of herself holding a bloody severed head of President Trump, prompted employers to rescind job offers to the comedian.[85] In 2018, Roseanne Barr was accused of being a racist and removed from her television show for tweeting that African American Valerie Jarrett was the offspring of the "Muslim Brotherhood & Planet of the Apes."[86] During the protests for racial justice that followed George Floyd's murder, social media users lambasted David Shor for tweeting an academic study about the political consequences of violent and peaceful protests because they perceived it as an effort to conflate the protests for racial justice with violence.[87] He was fired shortly after from Civics

Analytics, although they claim it was not due to the tweet. During those same protests, Lee Fang of *The Intercept* tweeted out an interview he performed with a mixed-race man who identifies as black, and who said he was worried that black Americans were only concerned with black lives when they were taken by white people, but not when they are taken by black or brown people.[88] Fang did not fabricate the interview and provided the video, yet he was so heavily criticized on social media that his co-worker Akela Lacy accused him of "continuing to push racist narratives." Fang made a formal apology on social media.[89] It is not just celebrities who are targeted for cancellation, but average people as well. For example, Emmanuel Cafferty was fired from his job for a public utility company after photo emerged of him flashing the OK finger gesture, which is associated with white supremacist groups, while in his company's vehicle. Cafferty, who is Latinx, claims he was exercising his fingers. He lost his job after social media users amplified the picture and besmirched his character.[90]

Rather than deconstruct "cancel culture" and assess its democratic utility, it has largely been debated along partisan lines. Michigan State University's Keith Hampton argues that "shame and blacklisting do not change opinions," instead they are "likely to increase the polarization" of American society.[91] Indeed, even "cancel culture" as a concept has become polarized. Conservatives have increasingly argued that they are the victims of "cancel culture," but liberals argue that it is conservatives who engage in hate speech and fake news are simply being held accountable.[92] They argue that the real victims of such cancellation are the underprivileged.[93] They point out the systemic ways in which the underprivileged have been canceled from traditional discourses for centuries.[94] In the U.S., there is a long history of African Americans being shamed and violently censored with lynchings.[95] The same is true for women who have been silenced and marginalized through acts of slut shaming and domestic violence.[96] Similarly, members of the LGBTQIA community with violent forms of bullying such as gay-bashing.[97] These are just some of the ways the underprivileged are censored or canceled. According to many liberals, if conservatives were actually concerned with cancel culture they would not only take umbrage with the attacks on conservatives, but also with the systemic ways in which the underprivileged are censored or canceled.

Meanwhile, conservatives claim that cancel culture's stronghold over debates in education and media is a "revolution" or attempt at forced acculturation that is "spinning out of control."[98] Professor of law at the University of Miami School of Law, Mary Anne Franks, dismisses such arguments, claiming that "the assertion that conservative ideas are being violently suppressed on college campuses is as untrue today as it was in the 1970s."[99] Other liberals agree with conservatives such as former president Barack

Obama, who in 2019 warned leftists about how they had conflated "cancel culture" with activism.[100] Some liberals contend that while conservatives claim to favor free speech, they relish in the censorship of liberals.[101] Indeed, in the 21st century, conservative groups have distributed lists of "the Most Dangerous Professors" who they encourage students to target on college campuses, and shamed physicians for performing abortions who were subsequently murdered.[102] This partisan lens to censor serves to strengthen rather than hinder so-called cancel culture.

Historically, censorship for anyone, including one's ideological opponent, works to weaken democracy for all because it enables anyone to be censored. Chris Hedges reminded liberals of this, noting that historically "cancel culture was pioneered by the red baiting of the capitalist elites and their shock troops in agencies such as the Federal Bureau of Investigation (FBI) to break, often through violence, radical movements and labor unions. Tens of thousands of people, in the name of anti-communism, were cancelled out of the culture. He notes that "this cancel culture is embraced by corporate media platforms."[103] This lesson was made painfully clear to the *World Socialist Web Site* Labor Editor Jerry White, who appeared on *The Jimmy Dore Podcast* in 2021 to discuss big-tech's decision to ban Donald Trump and his supporters messaging from their platforms:

WHITE: Our opposition to [President Joe] Biden is from the left.
DORE: Yes.
WHITE: We're not joining in you know with the extreme right. We did not jump on the bandwagon and say it's the horror of horrors that Trump's twitter account was taken away.

White's contention was that it was not in his interest or the interest of working people to fight for Trump's access to Twitter. Dore countered, arguing that the power ceded to big-tech was dangerous. A day later, Facebook banned accounts associated with White's *World Socialist Web Site*. It was a quick lesson on how cheerleading or even by-standing censorship matters can be short-sighted. Indeed, many self-defined liberals and even some progressives have supported censorship online (especially when happening to conservatives), but big-tech is using this power to marginalize and demonetize progressive websites such as *Common Dreams, Truthout, MintPress News*, and *The Intercept* among others; censor academic conferences that challenge big-tech such as the Critical Media Literacy Conference of the Americas; and manipulate electoral outcomes such as Prop 22 in California.

Conclusion: Calling-In

Far from achieving restorative justice, calling people out simply sets boundaries, and raises awareness about the ways in which an individual's words or actions were harmful. It is effective in preventing further harm because it interrupts an transgressor's momentum. However, it does not resolve the conflict. As a result, Smith College Professor Loretta J. Ross argues that people should call others in for dialogue rather than calling them out.[104] Calling-in is a collaborative approach to conflict where the transgressor is invited to participate in constructive dialogue. It provides participants with an opportunity to make meaning, explore issues and actions more deeply, and develop understanding across difference. Once called in, a transgressor is better positioned to learn because they are in a situation that values reflection over reaction. As a result, they are able to entertain or imagine competing perspectives, possibilities, and outcomes.[105]

Calling-in is hampered in societies where dissent and contrary opinions are stifled. This is a principle that civil libertarians, both from right *and* left, have long understood. For example, iconic liberal figures like Ralph Nader even argued, in *Unstoppable: The Emerging Left-Right Alliance to Dismantle the Corporate State*,[106] that people need to work together across the aisles to make common cause on issues as significant as those relating to our collective Bill of Rights protections, which extend beyond government to the corporate world, given how much the two have become intertwined. Censorship is not just a problem for who or what is being censored, it's a potential threat to anyone who may be the censor's next target.

It is crucial to call-in one's ideological opponent. In a nation of 330 million people, conservatives and liberals will always exist. We must seek to mollify rather than eradicate philosophical divisions. The questions are not how or when to censor, erase, or cancel one side or the other. Rather, the questions before us in a democracy should involve how to openly engage in civic dialogue civilly and uphold First Amendment principles. The purpose is not to win, or even agree, it is simply to seek out collaborative efforts and understanding that strengthen democratic discourse and the lived experience of all involved – while maybe persuading each other along the way. We are aware that we sometimes enter into dialogue with a differing set of knowledge and evidence. This complicates matters and makes constructive dialogue difficult to achieve, but that doesn't mean it is not ultimately worth the effort. As a result, the next chapters of this book examine critical thinking, analysis of evidence, and sound argumentation. The purpose is to better position the reader to engage in robust, yet constructive, democratic dialogue.

Notes

1   "A letter on justice and open debate," *Harper's Magazine,* July 7, 2020, http s://harpers.org/a-letter-on-justice-and-open-debate/.

2   Boaz Hameiri, Daniel Bar-Tal, and Eran Halperin, "Self-censorship as a socio-psychological barrier to peacemaking," in *Self-Censorship in Contexts of Conflict*, eds Daniel Bar-Tal, Rafi Nets-Zehgut, and Keren Sharvit, pp. 61–78 (Cham, Switzerland: Springer, 2017), 65.

3   Ibid.

4   Ibid.

5   Judith Townend, "Freedom of expression and the chilling effect," in *The Routledge Companion to Media and Human Rights*, eds Howard Tumber and Slivio Waisbord (Abingdon, UK: Routledge, 2017), 73–82; Margot E. Kaminski and Shane Witnov, "The conforming effect: First Amendment implications of surveillance, beyond chilling speech," *U. Rich. L. Rev.* 49 (2014): 465.

6   Antoon De Baets, "Taxonomy of concepts related to the censorship of history," in *Government Secrecy*, ed. S. Maret (Research in Social Problems and Public Policy, Vol. 19), (Bingley, UK: Emerald Group Publishing Limited), 53–65; Jennifer Earl and Katrina Kimport, *Digitally Enabled Social Change: Activism in the Internet Age* (MIT Press, 2011).

7   Judith Townend, "Freedom of expression and the chilling effect," in *The Routledge Companion to Media and Human Rights*, eds Howard Tumber and Slivio Waisbord (Abingdon, UK: Routledge, 2017), 73–82; Margot E. Kaminski and Shane Witnov, "The conforming effect: First Amendment implications of surveillance, beyond chilling speech," *U. Rich. L. Rev.* 49 (2014): 465.

8   Jessica Chasmar, "Liberals J.K. Rowling, Noam Chomsky sign letter denouncing 'ideological conformity,' cancel culture," *The Washington Times*, July 8, 2020, https://m.washingtontimes.com/news/2020/jul/8/jk-rowling-noam-chomsky-sign-letter-denouncing-ide/.

9   Kelly Jane Torrance, "The left goes nuts over liberals who dare to defend free speech," *New York Post*, July 8, 2020, https://nypost.com/2020/07/08/the-left-goes-nuts-over-liberals-who-dare-to-defend-free-speech/; Joseph A. Wulfsohn, "Conservatives defend Vox journalist after he's shamed by colleague for signing letter combatting 'cancel culture': The open letter penned by 150 prominent liberals has caused quite the stir on social media," *Fox News*, July 7, 2020, https://www.foxnews.com/media/conservatives-defend-vox-journalist-signs-cancel-culture-letter.

10   Emma Nolan, "Trans Author Jennifer Finney Boylan recants 'cancel culture' letter signed by J.K. Rowling," *Newsweek*, July 8, 2020, https://www.newsweek.com/author-jennifer-finney-boylan-recants-cancel-cultureletter-jk-rowling-1516235.

11   Zubair Nabi, "Resistence censorship is futile," *First Monday* 19, no. 11 (2014).

12   Abby Ohlheiser, "Twitter's ban almost doubled attention for Biden story: The social media company's attempt to stop misinformation from spreading brought the Streisand Effect into action," *MIT Technology Review*, October 16, 2020, https://www.technologyreview.com/2020/10/16/1010644/twitter-ban-hunter-biden-emails-backfires/.

13   Jennifer Schuessler, "An open letter on free expression draws a counter-blast," *The New York Times*, July 10, 2020, https://www.nytimes.com/2020/07/10/arts/open-letter-debate.html.

14   Ibid.

15   Reed Dunlea and Daniel Halperin, "Useful idiots: Thomas Chatterton Williams on the open letter on cancel culture plus, hosts Matt Taibbi and

Katie Halper discuss Bari Weiss leaving 'The New York Times'," *Rolling Stone,* July 19, 2020, https://www.rollingstone.com/politics/politics-news/useful-idiots-taibbi-thomas-chatterton-williams-cancel-culture-bari-weiss-n yt-1030497/.

16 Jillian C. York, "The people who signed the Harper's letter seem blinded to what censorship is in the real world," *The Conversationalist,* July 9, 2020, http://conversationalist.org/2020/07/09/the-people-who-signed-the-harpers-letter-seem-blinded-to-what-censorship-is-in-the-real-world/.

17 Judith Hertog, "Prisoner of hope Cornel West's quest for justice," *The Sun Magazine,* September 2018, https://www.thesunmagazine.org/issues/513/p risoner-of-hope.

18 See the Network of Concerned Historians at http://www.concernedhistoria ns.org; see also Antoon De Baets, "Censorship backfires: A taxonomy of concepts related to censorship," in *Censored 2013: Dispatches from the Media Revolution,* eds Mickey Huff and Andy Lee Roth with Project Censored (New York: Seven Stories Press, 2012), 223–234.

19 Kory Grow, "PMRC's Filthy 15: Where are they now?" *Rolling Stone,* September 17, 2015, https://www.rollingstone.com/music/music-lists/pmrcs-fil thy-15-where-are-they-now-60601/.

20 Ibid.

21 Mickey Huff and Andy Lee Roth, eds, *Censored 2014: Fearless Speech in Fateful Times* (New York: Seven Stories Press, 2013), 25. For more on the concept of *parrhesia,* see Michel Foucault, *Fearless Speech,* ed., Joseph Pearson (Los Angeles: Semiotext(e), 2001).

22 President Thomas Jefferson, First Inaugural Address, March 4, 1801, accessed from the University of Virginia, Miller Center, https://millercen ter.org/the-presidency/presidential-speeches/march-4-1801-first-inaugural-a ddress; Frederick Douglass, "Plea for free speech in Boston," December 9, 1860, accessed at Law & Liberty, https://lawliberty.org/frederick-douglass-p lea-for-freedom-of-speech-in-boston/.

23 President Thomas Jefferson, First Inaugural Address, March 4, 1801, accessed at the University of Virginia, Miller Center, https://millercenter.org/the-presi dency/presidential-speeches/march-4-1801-first-inaugural-address.

24 Frederick Douglass, "Plea for free speech in Boston," December 9, 1860, accessed at Law & Liberty, https://lawliberty.org/frederick-douglass-plea -for-freedom-of-speech-in-boston/.

25 Howard Zinn, *A People's History of the United States* (New York: Perennial Classics, 2003 [1980]), 367–368.

26 Frederick C. Gamst, "Labor hero Eugene V. Debs: 'A dedication to unpopu-larity'," *Journal of Transportation Law, Logistics, and Policy* 74, no. 2 (2007): 241.

27 Whitney v. California, 274 U.S. 357, U.S. Supreme Court (1927). Search-able online at the Bill of Rights Institute, https://billofrightsinstitute.org.

28 United States v. Schwimmer, 279 U.S. 644, U.S. Supreme Court (1929). Searchable online at the Bill of Rights Institute, https://billofrightsinstitute.org.

29 Near v. Minnesota, 283 U.S. 697, U.S. Supreme Court (1931). Searchable online at the Bill of Rights Institute, https://billofrightsinstitute.org.

30 Ibid.

31 United Nations General Assembly, "Universal Declaration of Human Rights," Article 19, December 10, 1948, https://www.un.org/en/about-us/universal-declaration-of-human-rights.

32 *New York Times Co. v. United States,* 403 U.S. 713 (1971), also known as The Pentagon Papers Case.

33 Daniel Ellsberg, "On civil courage and its punishments," in *Censored 2014: Fearless Speech in Fateful Times*, eds Mickey Huff and Andy Lee Roth with Project Censored (New York: Seven Stories Press, 2013), 208–213.

34 The Whistleblower Protection Act of 1989, 5 U.S.C. 2302(b)(8)-(9), Pub. L.

35 Nancy Chang, *Silencing Political Dissent: How Post-September 11 Anti-Terrorism Measures Threaten Our Civil Liberties* (New York: Seven Stories Press, 2002); Spencer Ackerman and Ed Pilkington, "Obama's war on whistleblowers leaves administration insiders unscathed," *The Guardian,* March 16, 2015, https://www.theguardian.com/us-news/2015/mar/16/whistleblowers-double-standard-obama-david-petraeus-chelsea-manning; Jason Ralph, *America's War on Terror: The State of the 9/11 Exception from Bush to Obama,* (Oxford: Oxford University Press, 2013).

36 ACLU, "Conservative Voices Against the USA PATRIOT Act," https://www.aclu.org/other/conservative-voices-against-usa-patriot-act; Defending Rights and Dissent, https://rightsanddissent.org.

37 Kelsey Piper, "'Ag-gag laws' hide the cruelty of factory farms from the public," *Vox,* January 11, 2019, https://www.vox.com/future-perfect/2019/1/11/18176551/ag-gag-laws-factory-farms-explained.

38 Aila Slisco, "Companies boycotting Israel can't do business with these U.S. States," *Newsweek,* May 19, 2021, https://www.newsweek.com/companies-boycotting-israel-cant-do-business-these-us-states-1593099.

39 Karine Lamarche. "The backlash against Israeli human rights NGOs: Grounds, players, and implications," *International Journal of Politics, Culture, and Society* 32, no. 3 (2019): 301–322.

40 Jordan Howell, "In challenge to Georgia's anti-BDS law, federal district court sides with journalist disinvited from Georgia Southern University," *The FIRE,* May 27, 2021, https://www.thefire.org/in-challenge-to-georgias-anti-bds-law-federal-district-court-sides-with-journalist-disinvited-from-georgia-southern-university/.

41 Armin Rosen, "Journalists mobilize against free speech: A new generation of media crusaders clamor for government control over what you see, hear, and read—and for banning their competition," *Tablet,* January 24, 2021, https://www.tabletmag.com/sections/news/articles/jounalists-against-free-speech; Jordan Freiman, "4 dead after Trump supporters storm U.S. Capitol," *CBS News,* January 7, 2021, https://www.cbsnews.com/news/trump-supporters-us-capitol-4-dead/.

42 Zaid Jilani, "Debunking Brian Stelter's call to deplatform Fox News," *YouTube,* https://www.youtube.com/watch?v=IbHTl_qwA9o&feature=youtu.be.

43 Jeremy Waldron, *The Harm in Hate Speech* (Cambridge, MA: Harvard University Press, 2012), 27.

44 Richard Stengel, Why America needs a hate speech law," *Washington Post,* October 29, 2019, https://www.washingtonpost.com/opinions/2019/10/29/why-america-needs-hate-speech-law/.

45 Jeremy Waldron, *The Harm in Hate Speech* (Cambridge, MA: Harvard University Press, 2012).

46 Ibid.

47 Ibid., 33.

48 Aja Romano, "Apple banned Alex Jones's Infowars. Then the dominoes started to fall," *Vox,* August 6, 2018, https://www.vox.com/policy-and-politics/2018/8/6/17655516/infowars-ban-apple-youtube-facebook-spotify; Joseph Cox and Jason Koebler, "Facebook bans white nationalism and white separatism," *Vice,* March 27, 2019, https://www.vice.com/en_us/article/nexpbx/facebook-bans-white-nationalism-and-white-separatism; The Times Editorial Board, "Facebook has the right to ban

extreme voices, but it needs to tread lightly," *Los Angeles Times,* May 7, 2019, http s://www.latimes.com/opinion/editorials/la-ed-facebook-ban-20190507-story.html.

49 Seth F. Kreimer, "Censorship by proxy: The First Amendment, internet intermediaries, and the problem of the weakest link." *U. Pa. L. Rev.* 155 (2006): 11.

50 Meredith D. Clark, "DRAG THEM: A brief etymology of so-called 'cancel culture'," *Communication and the Public* 5, no. 3–4 (2020): 88–92.

51 Ibid.

52 Ibid.; Matthew Potolsky, *The National Security Sublime: On the Aesthetics of Government Secrecy* (New York: Routledge, 2019).

53 Nolan Higdon, *The Anatomy of Fake News: A Critical News Literacy Education* (Oakland, CA: University of California Press, 2020).

54 See more about DARPA online at https://www.darpa.mil/about-us/about-da rpa; "From DARPA to Google: How the military kickstarted AV," *Arrow,* February 27, 2020, https://www.arrow.com/en/research-and-events/articles/ from-darpa-to-google-how-the-military-kickstarted-av-development.

55 Kreimer

56 Darrell Etherington, "Michelle Obama calls on Silicon Valley to permanently ban Trump and prevent platform abuse by future leaders," *Tech Crunch,* January 7, 2021, https://techcrunch.com/2021/01/07/michelle-o bama-calls-on-silicon-valley-to-permanently-ban-trump-and-prevent-platfor m-abuse-by-future-leaders/; see Twitter online at https://twitter.com/aoc/sta tus/1347679332014161920?lang=en.

57 Mary Meisenzahl, "These 6 tech companies have made the controversial decision to try to operate in China, where the government can demand social media posts be removed or search results be censored," *Business Insider,* October 10, 2019, https://www.businessinsider.com/tech-companies-censoring-content-for-china-apple-microsoft-2019-10.

58 Jason Murdock, "Snowden: Facebook is a 'surveillance company' that exploits user data," *Newsweek,* March 19, 2018, https://www.newsweek.com/ edward-snowden-facebook-surveillance-company-851428.

59 Shirin Ghaffary, "Edward Snowden says Facebook is just as untrustworthy as the NSA," *Vox: Recode,* October 31, 2019, https://www.vox.com/recode/ 2019/10/31/20940532/edward-snowden-facebook-nsa-whistleblower.

60 Edward Snowden, @Snowden, Twitter, March 17, 2018, https://twitter. com/snowden/status/975147858096742405?lang=en.

61 Ghaffary, "Edward Snowden says Facebook is just as untrustworthy as the NSA," *Vox: Recode,* https://www.vox.com/recode/2019/10/31/20940532/ edward-snowden-facebook-nsa-whistleblower.

62 Kristine Gallardo, "Taming the internet pitchfork mob: Online public shaming, the viral media age, and the communications decency act," *Vand. J. Ent. & Tech. L.* 19 (2016): 721; Ganaele Langlois and Andrea Slane, "Economies of reputation: The case of revenge porn," *Communication and Critical/Cultural Studies* 14, no. 2 (2017): 120–138.

63 Clyde McGrady, "The strange journey of 'cancel,' from a Black-culture punchline to a White-grievance watchword," *Washington Post,* April 2, 2021, www. washingtonpost.com/lifestyle/cancel-culture-background-black-culture-white-gr ievance/2021/04/01/2e42e4fe-8b24-11eb-aff6-4f720ca2d479_story.html.

64 Ibid.

65 Kaitlynn Mendes, Jessica Ringrose, and Jessalynn Keller. "# MeToo and the promise and pitfalls of challenging rape culture through digital feminist activism." *European Journal of Women's Studies* 25, no. 2 (2018): 236-246.

66   Ryan Schocket, "13 Celebs Who Were Actually Canceled In 2020 Featuring Ellen, J.K. Rowling, and more," January 3, 2021, BuzzFeed, https://www.buzzfeed.com/ryanschocket2/celebs-cancelled-in-2020.

67   "Google Trends: Cancel Culture," Google, https://trends.google.com/trends/explore?date=today%205-y&geo=US&q="cancel%20culture".

68   Tiffany Watt Smith, *Schadenfreude: The joy of another's misfortune*, (United Kingdon: Little Brown and Company, 2018);

69   Ibid.

70   Smith; Kristy Hess and Lisa Waller. "The digital pillory: media shaming of 'ordinary'people for minor crimes." *Continuum* 28, no. 1 (2014): 101-111.

71   Timothy Brook, Jérôme Bourgon, and Gregory Blue. *Death by a thousand cuts*, (Cambridge, Massachusetts: Harvard University Press, 2008); Sara Forsdyke, "Street theatre and popular justice in Ancient Greece: shaming, stoning and starving offenders inside and outside the courts." *Past and Present* 201, no. 1 (2008): 3-50; A. R. Hands, "Ostraka and the Law of Ostracism—Some Possibilities and Assumptions." *The Journal of Hellenic Studies* 79 (1959): 69-79.

72   Alice Morse Earle, *Curious Punishments of Bygone Days*, (Chicago, Illinois: Herbet S. Stone and Company, 1896); Jörg Wettlaufer, "The shame game." *RSA Journal* 161, no. 5564 (2015): 36-39.

73   Jörg Wettlaufer, "The shame game." *RSA Journal* 161, no. 5564 (2015): 36-39.

74   Stuart Hall, "Some 'politically incorrect' pathways through PC," in *The War of the Words: The Political Correctness Debate*, ed. Sarah Dunant (London: Virago, 1994), 164–183.

75   Dinesh D'Souza, *Illiberal Education: The Politics of Race and Sex on Campus* (New York: Free Press, 1991).

76   Diane Ravitch, *The Language Police: How Pressure Groups Restrict What Students Learn* (New York: Vintage, 2003, 2004).

77   Ibid.

78   Daniel Kovalik, *Cancel This Book: The Progressive Case Against Cancel Culture* (New York: Hot Books, 2021).

79   Greg Lukianoff and Jonathan Haidt, *The Coddling of the American Mind: How Good Intentions and Bad Ideas Are Setting Up a Generation for Failure* (New York: Penguin, 2018), 4–5.

80   Jason Wilson, "How to troll the left: Understanding the rightwing outrage machine," *The Guardian,* March 18, 2018, https://www.theguardian.com/us-news/2018/mar/18/how-the-right-trolls-the-left-college-campus-outrage.

81   Scott Jaschik, "Who defines what is racist? Students demand firing of Evergreen State professor," *Inside Higher Ed,* May 30, 2017, https://www.insidehighered.com/news/2017/05/30/escalating-debate-race-evergreen-state-students-demand-firing-professor.

82   Nora W. Lang, "Teachers' translanguaging practices and "safe spaces" for adolescent newcomers: Toward alternative visions." *Bilingual Research Journal* 42, no. 1 (2019): 73-89.

83   Mark Y. Herring, "Roosting chickens?" *Against the Grain* 27, no. 6 (2016); Cori Healy, "Reexamining political correctness through feminist rhetoric in the stand up of George Carlin," *Comedy Studies* 7, no. 2 (2016): 137–142.

84   Ta-Nehisi Coates, "The cancellation of Colin Kaepernick: "Cancel culture" has always existed – for the powerful, at least. Now, social media has democratized it," *New York Times,* November 22, 2019, https://www.nytimes.com/2019/11/22/opinion/colin-kaepernick-nfl.html.

85   Carly Mallenbaum, "Social media reacts, Kathy Griffin apologizes for 'decapitated' Trump photos," *USA Today*, May 31, 2017, https://www.usa today.com/story/life/people/2017/05/30/kathy-griffin-donald-trump-photo-shoot/102327772/.

86   Ellis Clopton, "'Roseanne' canceled after star's racist tweets," *Variety*, May 2018, https://variety.com/video/roseanne-canceled-racist-tweets/.

87   Rachel E. Greenspan, "How 'cancel culture' quickly became one of the buzziest and most controversial ideas on the internet," *Insider*, August 6, 2020, 5, https://www.insider.com/cancel-culture-meaning-history-origin-phrase-used-negatively-2020-7.

88   Jonathan Chait, "The still-vital case for liberalism in a radical age," *New York Magazine*, June 11, 2020, https://nymag.com/intelligencer/2020/06/case-for-liberalism-tom-cotton-new-york-times-james-bennet.html.

89   Ibid.

90   Priya Sridhar, "BLACK LIVES MATTER SDG&E Worker Fired Over Alleged Racist Gesture Says He Was Cracking Knuckles," *NBC*, June 15, 2020, https://www.nbcsandiego.com/news/local/sdge-worker-fired-over-alleged-racist-gesture-says-he-was-cracking-knuckles/2347414/.

91   Agence France Presse, "The 'cancel culture', a new weapon of the anonymous and a factor of polarization," *Agence France Presse*, July 22, 2020, http s://www.journaldemontreal.com/2020/07/22/la-cancel-culture-nouvelle-arme-des-anonymes-et-facteur-de-polarisation.

92   Margaret Sullivan, "So you're being held accountable? That's not 'cancel culture'," *Washington Post*, January 31, 2021, https://www.washingtonpost. com/lifestyle/media/cancel-culture-criticism-accountability/2021/01/29/8d2 4d2d4-6180-11eb-9061-07abcc1f9229_story.html; Jacob Jarvis, "Republicans blame 'cancel culture' for backlash after U.S. Capitol riot," *Newsweek*, January 13, 2021, https://www.newsweek.com/republicans-blame-cancel-culture-capitol-backlash-1561121.

93   Sarah Hagi, "Cancel culture is not real—at least not in the way people think," *Time*, November 21, 2019, https://time.com/5735403/cancel-culture-is-not-real/.

94   Meredith D. Clark, "DRAG THEM: A brief etymology of so-called 'cancel culture'," *Communication and the Public* 5, no. 3–4 (2020): 88–92.

95   David, W. Blight, *Race and Reunion: The Civil War in American Memory*, (Cambridge, MA: Harvard University Press, 2001, 2009).

96   Kate Manne, *Down Girl: The Logic of Misogyny*, (New York, New York: Oxford University Press, 2018, 2019).

97   Van Der Meer, Theo. "Gay bashing–a rite of passage?." *Culture, Health & Sexuality* 5, no. 2 (2003): 153-165.

98   John Leo, "Free inquiry? Not on campus," *City Journal*, Winter (2007), https:// www.city-journal.org/html/free-inquiry-not-campus-12989.html.   William McGowan, *Coloring the News: How Political Correctness Has Corrupted American Journalism* (San Francisco, California Encounter Books, 2003); Fox News Flash, "Howard Kurtz warns cancel culture is 'clearly spinning out of control,' reaching the 'point of absurdity'," *Fox News*, June 12, 2020, https://www.fox news.com/media/howard-kurtz-cancel-culture-out-of-control; Kevin D. Williamson, "Social justice warriors are waging a 'Cancel Cultural Revolution'," *New York Post*, June 13, 2020, https://nypost.com/2020/06/13/social-justice-warriors-are-waging-a-cancel-cultural-revolution/; Martin Jay, "Dialectic of counter-enlightenment: The Frankfurt School as scapegoat of the lunatic fringe," *Salmagundi* 168/169 (2010): 30.

99   Mary Anne Franks, "The miseducation of free speech," *Virginia Law Review Online* 105 (2019): 218.

100   Emily S. Rueb and Derrick Bryson Taylor, "Obama on call-out culture: 'That's not activism,'" *New York Times,* October 31, 2019, https://www.nytimes.com/2019/10/31/us/politics/obama-woke-cancel-culture.html.

101   "2019 Politicon panel gets HEATED," *YouTube,* October 26, 2019, https://youtu.be/NDC8Xhc18hM.

102   David M. Perry, "The right-wing plot to take over student governments," *Pacific Standard,* April 20, 2018, https://psmag.com/education/the-right-wing-plot-to-take-over-student-governments; Gabriel Winant, "O'Reilly's campaign against murdered doctor," June 11, 2009, Salon https://web.archive.org/web/20090611145732/http://www.salon.com/news/feature/2009/05/31/tiller/.

103   Chris Hedges, "Cancel culture, where liberalism goes to die," *Scheerpost,* February 15, 2021, https://scheerpost.com/2021/02/15/hedges-cancel-culture-where-liberalism-goes-to-die/.

104   Jessica Bennett, "What if Instead of Calling People Out, We Called Them In? Prof. Loretta J. Ross is combating cancel culture with a popular class at Smith College," *New York Times,* February 24, 2021 https://www.nytimes.com/2020/11/19/style/loretta-ross-smith-college-cancel-culture.html.

105   For more on Calling-out versus callin-in see "Interrupting Bias: Calling Out vs. Calling In," Advanced Racial Equity Tools," www.racialequityvtnea.org/wp-content/uploads/2018/09/Interrupting-Bias_-Calling-Out-vs.-Calling-In-REVISED-Aug-2018-1.pdf.

106   Ralph Nader, *Unstoppable: The Emerging Left-Right Alliance to Dismantle the Corporate State* (New York: Nation Books, 2014).

Part II

Critical Thinking

The American linguist, political activist, and dissident Noam Chomsky explains that he

> encourage[s] people to think for themselves, to question standard assumptions ... Don't take assumptions for granted. Begin by taking a skeptical attitude toward anything that is conventional wisdom. Make it justify itself. It usually can't. Be willing to ask questions about what is taken for granted. Try to think things through for yourself.[1]

Chomsky's statement reveals that in addition to being constructive in their dialogue, individuals must be critical in their analysis of arguments and others.

Among other guarantees, the First Amendment to the U.S. Constitution protects citizens' right to a free press and speech. This allows citizens to share and access information that can be debated in a civil fashion. Although we often hear that there are at least two sides to everything, that does not mean that all sides have a compelling argument. Free speech guarantees the right to speak; it is not an indication of the sophistication of an argument presented. Civil discourse is best served by a populace of critical thinkers: People who are guided by the evidence and reason rather than other competing interests or appeals to emotion.

Critical thinking is among the best tools citizens have at their disposal to make sense of an increasingly complex and contentious world. Given that humans are an emotionally driven and reactive species, it is essential to not only know and understand tenets of the critical thought process, but actually practice and employ them on a regular basis. With our 21st century technologically ubiquitous communication and media-saturated culture, citizens need these skills, perhaps more than any other time in history, to make sense of the world; contribute to the growth of knowledge and understanding; and be situated to make intelligent, well-informed decisions about key elements of their lives as individuals and as a society.

DOI: 10.4324/9781003250906-5

Part II of this text begins with Chapter 3, Inquire: Be a Critical Thinker, which introduces critical thinking basics and provides tools that can help readers think more logically and rationally, and communicate more effectively with others. Chapter 4, Test Theory and Spot Ideology, looks at critical theory and outlines how it can be useful for making sense of the world. These tools not only support thought processes, but they are keys to open and expand possibilities for others, to help bridge gaps between people and groups in society, and assist us in understanding the perspectives of others including those with differing views. Part II teaches readers how to agree to disagree and reduce tensions and troubles associated with so many conflicts.

Chapter 3

Inquire: Be a Critical Thinker

We begin by recounting the following false but widely circulated claims recently posted across the World Wide Web: 1) "Hitler also defunded the police and installed his own enforcers." 2) "National Public Radio wants people to burn books written by white people." 3) "A tweet from the Obama Foundation featuring a picture of George Floyd went out on May 17, more than a week before his death, suggesting the nonprofit was aware of Floyd well before he died." 4) "When Minneapolis residents call 911 they are now told there are 'no officers available' due to the defunding of the police department after protests in the city against police brutality."[2]

These statements represent only a tiny fraction of the false claims that spread throughout the internet during the 2020 demonstrations for social and racial justice. This outpouring of anti-racist activism followed the release of video showing a Minneapolis, Minnesota police officer murdering an unarmed African American man, George Floyd, as he used his last breaths to call for his mother. Across the nation, the protests further sparked violent clashes with reactionary demonstrations from white supremacists and pro-police groups.[3]

Whether they were anti-racists, police, or white supremacists, the overwhelming majority of people had never met George Floyd or visited his community. Their decision to participate or not participate in these demonstrations, and what side they aligned themselves with, was based on the information they gleaned from media, especially social media. Just as the video of Floyd's murder motivated thousands of citizens to ignore the risks posed by the COVID-19 pandemic and protest for racial justice, the false statements and claims noted at the start of this chapter led many racist and bigoted reactionaries to take aggressive action that they too felt was warranted. The conflicting interpretations of these events illustrate how dependent people are on the information they receive.

Furthermore, it illuminates the danger of false content flowing through media systems, which can compel otherwise upstanding people to feel justified in taking horrendous actions. After all, if someone believes the statements at the start of this chapter are true, which they are not, and

DOI: 10.4324/9781003250906-6

acts upon them, one would not see oneself as fighting against racial justice. Instead, one would see themselves as taking part in righteous action against Hitlerism, a war on white people, the eradication of public safety posed by those wanting to defund police, and a conspiracy connected to former President Barack Obama.

Some scholars have argued that the waning agreement about facts and arguments constitutes an epistemological crisis, referred to as a **post-truth** era in the U.S. The *Oxford Dictionary* even proclaimed "post-truth" as word of the year after the 2016 presidential election. They defined it as "relating to or denoting circumstances in which objective facts are less influential in shaping public opinion than appeals to emotion and personal belief."[4] The history of the specific term goes back to the early 1990s after the Iran-Contra scandal and first Iraq War, where Serbian-American playwright Steve Tesich wrote about the Iran-Contra scandal and the Persian Gulf War for *The Nation* magazine. He bemoaned that "we, as a free people, have freely decided that we want to live in some post-truth world." Since then, prominent satirists like Stephen Colbert on his Comedy Central late-night program riffed on this concept, calling it "truthiness" (which Merriam-Webster cited as its word of the year in 2006). Colbert claimed:

> Truthiness is 'What I say is right, and [nothing] anyone else says could possibly be true.' It's not only that I feel it to be true, but that I feel it to be true. There's not only an emotional quality, but there's a selfish quality.[5]

By 2009, media scholars and critics Peter Phillips and Mickey Huff of Project Censored declared a "truth emergency" in the U.S. based on the increase of censorship and propaganda in a post-9/11 world. A truth emergency reflects the cumulative failures of the fourth estate to act as a truly free press in the public interest. It further implies that we are awash in a sea of information in the digital era, yet we have a paucity of understanding.[6]

By the 2016 presidential election, the truth emergency escalated and Colbert's satire became reality as the post-truth concept rose to the fore, accompanying terms like "fake news" and "alternative facts" as they became mainstays of American politics in the campaign and presidency of Donald Trump.[7] The societal impacts of these epithets have led scholars and journalists to apply various correctives, from fact-checking services to outright labeling and censorship. The former of these is based on critical thinking and analysis, and marks a more intellectually honest path. The latter contributes to so-called cancel culture and breeds suspicion and anti-intellectualism. The entire post-truth construct has led to an epistemic crisis. Harvard scholars Yochai Benkler, Robert Faris, and Hal Roberts, in their 2018 book *Network Propaganda*, stated that it is this "epistemic crisis in media and politics that threatens the integrity of democratic processes, erodes trust in public institutions, and exacerbates social divisions."[8] Such a situation requires empirical correctives from educational, journalistic, and other civic institutions.

In fact, at the root of solutions one will find that critical thinking is the antidote to this post-truth construct. While the term *critical* has several meanings such as to find fault, judge, or criticize, when we use it we are referring "to an intellectual skill of analysis—critical thinking— as well as to a body of scholarship—Critical Theory."[9] We argue that a combination of critical thinking and theory is necessary for developing a democratic society grounded in truth. This chapter looks at the first dimension of critical thinking, the acquisition of knowledge, while the next chapter analyzes the second dimension of critical thinking, the context in which knowledge is produced, validated, and circulated.[10]

Knowledge and Critical Thinking

The first dimension of critical thinking is the acquisition of knowledge. **Knowledge** refers to the facts, information, and skills acquired through experience or education that provide a person or persons with the theoretical or practical understanding of a subject. A **fact** is verifiable. A fact is beyond argument. For example, in the U.S., the federal holiday of Christmas is recognized on December 25th annually. That is a fact. It is different than an **opinion**, which is an attempt to draw an honest judgment based upon the facts. For example, if a person found evidence confirming that the state of the economy was preventing the majority of people from purchasing Christmas gifts, they could form an opinion that the government should cancel Christmas. Fact and opinion both differ from a **belief**, which is a conviction based on something other than evidence such as faith, morals, or values. They cannot be disproven because they do not rest upon evidence. For example, some may believe that if we treated everyone like we do on Christmas all the time, there would be no more conflict in the world.

This leads to a discussion of the concept of what it means for something to be **true**. To be true implies being in accordance with demonstrable, discernible reality. According to the Merriam-Webster dictionary, **truth** as a noun is that which is true, i.e., that which is so, the body of real things, events, and facts. Harry G. Frankfurt, professor emeritus of philosophy at Princeton University and author of the books *On Truth* and *On Bullshit*, notes that "We all know what it means to tell the truth about various things with which we are authoritatively familiar ... we understand with equal clarity, moreover, what it means to give false accounts of such things." He goes on to argue about the truth, "that the evidence for a certain proposition is conclusive, and that there can be no further reasonable question of whether the proposition is true."[11]

To know something is true, based on the collation of factual evidence, is different than believing it is true. To believe is to trust or have confidence that something is true based on faith rather than facts. This is not the same as "knowing" something is true. **Epistemology** is the discipline that studies how humans come to "know" anything at all. Epistemological research considers knowledge a resource with a strong connection to the knower. Knowledge always belongs to someone, whether it is an individual or groups of individuals. Groups can synthesize their knowledge for the benefit of society and its members. In fact, this is a democratic ideal.[12] For example, public health officials are tasked with synthesizing scientific knowledge to implement policy that is beneficial to the citizenry. The aforementioned "epistemic crisis" implies that citizens are becoming less capable of discerning truth from fiction, and suggests that they cannot be sure we know anything with great certainty, or that they live in a "post-truth" era – in short, we have a crisis in confidence about knowledge, and what is real. This chapter and section in the book are designed to address and alleviate this condition.

Philosophers have several views on epistemology. **Rationalists** contend that reason rather than experience is the bedrock of certainty in knowledge.[13] **Empiricists** reject the idea that knowledge is innate to humans. Instead, they view it as deriving from sense-making experiences. They consider any science that is hypothetical in nature as distracting from the pursuit of truths.[14] Rather than rely on abstraction, empiricism relies on an observational approach and excludes any activity of a hypothetical nature. **Realists** argue that the aim of science is to develop both an understanding and truth. As a result, they not only pursue truths, but also seek to develop informed speculation about the nature of the real world.[15] **Skepticism** is the philosophical branch dedicated to fostering self-consciousness about what people know through inquiry and reflection.

Understanding skepticism depends upon recognition of the crucial difference between impression, what a person see without judging, and a judgment, the acceptance or rejection of an impression. Proper judgments result in knowledge where acceptance of impressions as fact result in mistakes. Skeptics try to resist all judgments, which is not easy, by raising a lot of "what ifs." In the process, they shift the burden of proof to those making the claims, including themselves.[16]Although skepticism is useful in mitigating the mistakes concerning knowledge, it can also create a barrier to constructive dialogue. As Jennifer Nagel explains:

> given that the skeptic has promised to raise doubts about everything you say, there is not much hope for finding common ground with him on the basis of which you will convince him that he is mistaken. Those who choose to start with only premises the skeptic accepts will have trouble digging themselves out of the pit. Those who choose

instead to start from a common sense worldview have the easier task of building some defense mechanisms against the charms of skepticism, while accepting our common sense assumption that there is a good deal we know.[17]

Skepticism is constructive when it is remonstrative, and employed effectively, and thus referred to as a "healthy" type of skepticism. However, determining how much skepticism is warranted is case-by-case specific. If one is radically skeptical of everything, it could lead to a state of **nihilism** which rejects the existence of an independently existing reality and the possibility of knowledge, objective truth, and certainty.[18]

Other philosophers, known as postmodernists, have rejected the concept of finite knowledge for competing realities. This is known as the **relativist theory** of knowledge, which understands truth as relative to the subject, i.e., some things are true for one person and other things are true for another. Although it is an intriguing concept, at its heart is a self-refuting claim because if everything is subjective then no one ever makes a mistake. In other words, if things are always the way they appear, then appearances can never be misleading because that would enable the possibility of an incorrect or inaccurate interpretation.[19]

Building Knowledge Through Confidence

Regardless of one's view on epistemology, the process of critical thinking engenders confidence in knowledge. **Critical thinking**, as a process, refers to "general strategies which might be used in a variety of problem situations to gather and evaluate data, generate hypotheses, assess evidence and arrive at conclusions."[20] The process results in critical thinkers making persuasive arguments. An **argument** refers to a conclusion based on a series of inferences which are supported by evidence. Conceptually, a cogent argument is like a building. None of the components is independent, they all support and are supported by other components of the argument. If they are deemed to be well supported then the argument is logical. **Logic** refers to the process and assessment of reasoning in accordance with strict principles of validity.[21] A missing floor or weak foundation results in a feeble building. Similarly, baseless claims and weak evidence result in a feeble argument, what would be called illogical. If there is widespread confidence that the argument is logical then it is knowledge.

Claims

Knowledge is predicated on widespread confidence in a claim. A **claim** asserts the truth of something, but is typically disputed or in doubt. For example, suppose someone makes the claim that *every time* they are on YouTube, they see videos of politicians lying. This may not be true – they only have to go on YouTube one time without seeing a politician for it to be disproved. To avoid false claims such as these while still making a similar point, critical thinkers use qualifiers. A **qualifier** is a word or phrase that modifies how certain, absolute, or generalizable a statement is. Rather than *"every time* I am on YouTube see videos of politicians lying," they would replace *every time* with the qualifier *sometimes: "sometimes* when I am on YouTube, I see videos of politicians lying." Strong claims offer qualifiers and exceptions. A qualifier limits the claims and an exception denotes the instances where the claim does not apply.

Example of a qualified claim:
There is a history of corruption in politics.
Example of an unqualified claim:
All politicians are corrupt.
Common qualifiers: A minority, a small number, commonly, few, for a long time, frequently, hardly any, infrequently, many, not many, often, rarely, repeatedly, seldom, sometimes, sporadically, usually.
Example of an exception would take a claim such as
Sometimes, politicians are corrupt
and add:
Seldom do politicians pay any consequences for it.

Qualifiers only serve to strengthen a claim if they are accurate. Some of the most common qualifiers include possible, probable, and plausible. Although closely related, they each have differing definitions that are crucial for determining the validity of a claim.

- **Probability** quantifies chance in the absence of certainty. Probability is "linked to the future: Any genuine probability statement refers to something that will happen."[22] A probability attempts to quantify future events.
- **Possibility** refers to what can exist or happen. In this way, the possible is "conceivable, doable, realizable, acceptable, believable, permitted, eventual, likely, etc."[23]
- **Plausibility** is "the most problematic qualifier of the three, because it refers to a rather hybrid notion, hovering between probability, likeliness, credibility and being reasonable."[24] Rather than refer to knowledge, as possibility and probability do, plausibility depends upon judgment and conviction. It is less about being logically sound and more about convincing the audience that something can happen.

Unlike plausibility, probability is based on knowledge. Four of the main probabilities are the classic, frequentist, conditional, and subjective probabilities. Classic probability looks at well-defined phenomena that have symmetry and equal likelihood, for example, dice and coin flips. Frequentist probability looks at how likely a particular result will be. For instance, if one wants to know if a consumer prefers a certain strain of marijuana, experiments are conducted on people to see how often the outcome occurs. Conditional probabilities determine the likelihood of an event occurring given that another one has occurred. Suppose that there is a one percent chance that a person will vomit in a day, but the person is sick today, the event of their illness increases the probability of their vomiting. Subjective probability derives from an opinion, for example, if someone says there is a 50 percent chance they will vote on Election Day.[25]

Certain approaches do not work for other phenomena. To illustrate, conditional probabilities must have some influence on each other or correlation is being measured rather than causation. For example, if someone wins a one-on-one basketball game at 6 P.M. two nights in a row, their probability of winning at 6 P.M. tomorrow, or losing at 6 A.M. for that matter, is not impacted.

Probability's limits are explained through variables. Variables refer to the inconsistent or pattern-less events of phenomena that occur. They complicate analysis and limit the potential of some probability measurements because they cannot be accounted for. For example, Nassim Taleb's black swan theory posits that financial investors put themselves at risk because they do not account for the randomness of economically catastrophic events such as the 2008 financial collapse until after the event has occurred.[26] The 2008 financial collapse, and the response of the financial sector and government, saw 40 percent of the U.S. wealth disappear and consolidation and collapse of the banking and housing industry in the U.S. among others.[27] The black swan theory posits that if one looked at home prices from 2000 to 2007, which were increasing annually, a frequentist probability would assume that home values would increase by the end of 2009.[28] However, home prices collapsed in 2008. The same prediction being made at the end of 2008 would expect home prices to decline.

Evidence

In order to determine the veracity of the claim and its qualifiers, critical thinkers evaluate the available evidence. Without evidence the claim cannot be evaluated, which means there is no argument to be made and no dialogue to be had. For example, if someone claims on a Yelp Review that the service at a local restaurant is terrible, but does not offer evidence to prove it, how can a person determine if the restaurant has terrible service? Who's to say the customer is not the problem or maybe it is one employee rather than the entire restaurant? Without evidence, the claim cannot be verified.

Scholars generally examine two forms of evidence: Primary and secondary sources. A **primary source** is from a point of origin, such as an eyewitness account, interviews, diaries, birth certificates, or original historic documents. A **secondary source** derives from somewhere other than the original, such as textbooks, biographies, editorials, journal articles, or literary criticisms. Another, a **tertiary source**, is a third hand source, one that collates and summarizes primary and secondary sources, often for didactic purposes, like a database, encyclopedia, or library catalog.[29]

Take a look at the following five sources and determine if they are primary, secondary, or tertiary sources:

1   Video of George Floyd's murder;
2   The Pentagon Papers (government documents leaked by Daniel Ellsberg);
3   *Confidence Men: Wall Street, Washington, and the Education of a President* by Ron Suskind (a biography of President Barack Obama);[30]
4   The *Encyclopedia of Censorship*;[31]
5   Greta Thunberg's pre-prepared remarks on the global climate crisis.

If you said that the 1, 2, and 5 were primary, 3 was secondary, and 4 was tertiary, then you would be correct. The primary sources are historical documents or materials (including other media), they are points of origin for what has been said about them later. The Suskind book compiles and interprets primary sources as well as works by other historians, journalists, and academics, but is not primary itself. The reference book, an encyclopedia, is a general overview citing major primary and secondary sources around a specific topic.

Regarding some of the most common types of evidence:

- **Academic evidence** includes journals, books, and essays produced and reviewed by intellectuals and topical experts. Academic evidence offers a testable hypothesis that is replicable and peer reviewed.
- **Analogical evidence** compares things that are similar to draw comparisons.
- **Anecdotal evidence** depicts a singular event as representative of a larger story, event, or institution. For example, a story about co-worker who made a sexist joke in the lunchroom would be introduced as an anecdote to conclude that the entire workplace has a sexist culture.

- **Character evidence** centers on an individuals' character at a specific point in time to determine if they behaved in a certain way at a different point in time. For example, if a person is known for dismissing other students' viewpoints in the classroom, it is assumed that it is in their character to dismiss the viewpoint of a family member at home.
- **Circumstantial evidence**, sometimes known as indirect evidence, is used to infer something grounded in a series of facts that are distinct from the fact that the argument is attempting to prove.
- **Demonstrative evidence** is evidence that directly illustrates and proves a fact.
- **Digital evidence** derives from digital sources such as email, social media, search engines, and websites. Ways for analyzing this evidence are explored further in Chapter 7.
- **Direct evidence** or **primary evidence** is the best available substantiation of the existence of something because by existing it acts as the proof: No inference is needed.
- **Documentary evidence** is media, most often written, proof of something.
- **Exculpatory evidence** is evidence that can exonerate an individual or group.
- **Forensic evidence**, also known as scientific evidence, includes such evidence as DNA or fingerprints.
- **Hearsay evidence** comes from witnesses who were not present at the event in which they are commenting upon.
- **Physical evidence** refers to tangible objects.
- **Prima facie evidence**, also known as presumptive evidence, is considered sufficient in proving something until it is disproved.
- **Statistical evidence** is numbers, such as statistical analysis, for example, surveys and polls.
- **Testimonial evidence** is spoken or written evidence provided under oath.

Remember, just because there is evidence does not mean it is sufficient to prove a given thesis or claim.

Inferences

There is agreement between the claim and the evidence when a reasoned inference is made. An **inference** is a reasoning step that generates a conclusion based on given information that is assumed to be factual in nature. **Reasoning** refers to "a set of processes and abilities that act as a feasible tool in problem solving and enable us to go beyond the information given."[32] Informally, humans consistently use reasoning to engage in a serious decision such as which car to buy, which policy they support, or the person they should hire at their workplace. Critical thinkers apply reasoning to evidence and draw interferences. There are three main types of inference:

- **Deductive inference:** Reasoning from premises to logically necessary conclusions. In deductive reasoning all available premises, which are assertions or propositions, are rationally analyzed to draw a conclusion. Deductive inferences are as true as the premises considered. In other words, deductive inferences are as true as the premise.
- **Inductive inference:** Broad generalizations drawn from particular observations or empirical data. The data derives from the documentation of patterns of behavior through experimentation. Inductive reasoning relies on probability to draw an inference based on patterns. Inductive reasoning relies on probability to draw an inference based on observed patterns.
- **Abductive inference:** An incomplete set of observations from which one chooses the likeliest to draw a conclusion. If a person wakes up and the weather app on their phone claims it will rain in their area most of the day, but their friend sends them a text saying that they heard it was going to be high temperatures and dry today, they would need to choose the likeliest of the two in order to decide how to dress for the day. The process by which they decide which is the more likely is an abductive inference.

Here we have a table demonstrating the different ways in which people make inferences about social media users.

Just because someone goes through the inference process does not mean that their claim is valid. The **validity** of an inference refers to "the estimated degree of certainty about the truth of the inference and a main

Table 3.1 Abduction, deduction, and induction applied to TikTok users

Abduction	Deduction	Induction
All of my followers on TikTok are at least 18 years old	All of my followers on TikTok are at least 18 years old	These social media users must be on TikTok
These social media users are at least 18 years old	These social media users must be on TikTok	These social media users are at least 18 years old
These social media users must be on TikTok	These social media users are at least 18 years old	All of my followers on TikTok are at least 18 years old

validity will be based on empirical methods and the resulting data, as well as on the knowledge space."[33] When the inference is invalid, it engenders fallacious thinking.

Fallacies

When there is a lack of agreement between the evidence and the claim, this is known as a fallacy. **Fallacies** are faulty or inaccurate claims made based on the evidence or lack thereof. For example, if a friend tells another friend that they need to get the new smart phone by Saturday, because everyone is getting the phone, this a bandwagon fallacy (see below). The fact that everyone or many people are doing something is insufficient evidence to prove a *need*. Fallacies can be mistakes in reasoning, or employed deliberately as a form of propaganda to cajole or trick an audience. Common informal logical fallacies include:[34]

- **Ad hominem**: Attacking a person or source rather than addressing the argument being made.
- **Appeal to authority**: Believing claims because an alleged expert is cited in argument.
- **Appeal to emotion**: Exploiting emotional entanglements to build support for an argument.
- **Appeal to ignorance**: Preying on one's lack of knowledge regarding a particular topic.
- **Bandwagon/ad populum**: Believing something is true because a majority of people agree.
- **Begging the question/circular reasoning**: Restating premise as conclusion without evidence.
- **Cum hoc, post hoc, ergo propter hoc**: Correlation does not imply causation.
- **False analogy**: Comparing unlike things as though they were more related than they are.
- **False dilemma**: Either/or, forcing an option between two choices when there are multiple alternatives.
- **Halo effect**: Assigning positive attributes to a source based on one issue or situation.
- **Hasty generalization**: Jumping to a conclusion after a limited or weak observation.
- **Red herring**: Changing the topic of an argument for strategic purposes.
- **Slippery slope**: Claiming that, because one negative thing may occur, others will automatically follow.
- **Straw person**: Distorting someone's argument or viewpoint so it is easier to tear apart.

- **Sweeping generalization:** Casting inclusive categorization for complicated or diverse things.
- **Wishful thinking:** When we want to believe something is true, we convince ourselves it is, regardless of what the evidence suggests.

Building Knowledge Through Truth

Although confidence is crucial for developing knowledge, it is not sufficient on its own. People can be persuaded by illogical arguments. For example, rather than rely on the language itself to sway audiences, **sophistry** persuades audiences by introducing an argument that seems plausible even though it is fallacious or misleading. Traditionally, there are three persuasion techniques that appeal to audiences: Logos, pathos, and ethos. **Logos** relies on logic and appeals to reason. **Pathos** involves appealing the audiences' needs, emotions, values, and beliefs. For example, a politician is seeking to garner support for harsher traffic penalties from an audience who has experienced the death of a family member recently; a discussion about how a single car crash impacted a family may be more persuasive than introducing the number of driving fatalities per year. **Ethos** relies on the character of the person making the argument to persuade audiences. For example, some people tend to believe experts simply because they are experts. So, they may accept a doctor's recommendations for a particular type of medicine simply because they come from a doctor, not because they know anything about the medicine or its capabilities.[35]

Yuval Noah Harari points out in *Sapiens: A Brief History of Humankind* that the very same thing that enables humans to identify truth and develop knowledge is what makes them more susceptible and dependent upon falsehoods.[36] Gossip theory argues that humans evolved in a way that their survival depends upon social connection which humans fortify through gossip.[37] **Gossip** refers to "unverified news about the personal affairs of others, which is shared informally between individuals."[38] Gossip helped humans create social binds and relationships. Studies show that animal relations collapse or prove inefficient when they involve more than 150 beings because the binds are too weak.[39] Humans may have avoided this pitfall by using fiction to create massive societies and institutions.

In fact, Kurt Andersen argues in *Fantasyland* that fictitious thinking has been a mainstay of the U.S. for centuries.[40] For example, two-thirds of Americans believe that angels and demons are active in the world. At least half are absolutely certain. A third of Americans believe that our earliest ancestors were humans just like humans today, and that the government has through collusion with the pharmaceutical industry hidden evidence of natural cancer cures. A quarter of Americans believe that vaccines cause autism and that Donald Trump won the popular vote in 2016 and actually won reelection in 2020. A quarter of voters believed that Barack Obama was an antichrist. A quarter of Americans also believe in witches.[41]

Harari explains that the adoption of fiction is what separates humans from animals is not that they communicate through sound, but that they have complex messages and can talk about things that do not exist such as "legends, myths, gods, and religion."[42] Harari points out that it would be impossible to convince a monkey to give up something valuable, such as a banana, with the promise of a lifetime supply of more valuables in the afterlife, but humans believe it.[43] However, fiction is consequentially central to human society because it can justify societal organization and cooperation, and change to adapt to the environment such as 1789 France which shed the myth of divine right of kings. In order to hinder the genetic complication of fiction from obfuscating human thinking, critical thinkers strive for objectivity. They go where the facts lead them. They are reminded of the words of wisdom and warning from Indian poet Rabindranath Tagore nearly 100 years ago when he wrote, "The truth comes as conqueror only because we have lost the art of receiving it as guest."[44] These words can be hard to follow, however, due to humans' susceptibility to mental roadblocks known as cognitive biases.

Objectivity and Cognitive Biases

In order to ensure that they are not swayed by self-serving fictions and interests, critical thinkers strive for objectivity. **Objectivity** denotes impartial and balanced thinking about the evidence. Objectivity refers to incidents where individuals allow the evidence rather than their preferences to guide the decision-making process. For example, a voter may want a politician from their party to be found innocent of the crime. However, an objective analysis of the evidence leaves them no choice but to conclude that the politician is guilty. It is contrary to **subjective thinking**, which is based upon the feelings and preferences of the thinker.

Objective thinkers try to mitigate the influence of their bias on their conclusion. A **cognitive bias** refers to the prejudice or inclination of the thinker, oft unbeknownst to them. Since the 1970s, psychologists' research around this subject has increased significantly. Biases become problematic when they lead to the thinker deviating from a rationale thought process and/or the truth. Biases can work to undermine the process of **cognitive dissonance**, which occurs when one encounters information that counters their preordained beliefs or ideas about a certain matter or topic. For example, a person may consider themselves to be someone who cares about the environment, but at the same time they constantly use a smart phone which contributes to the erosion of the environment. This experience is often unpleasant, causing stress or confusion as a result of being subjected to new facts or perspectives. Some biases work to alleviate such mental discomfort, called dissonance reduction, but this does not likely lead to the best possible or reasoned conclusions. In fact, it motivates people to do the opposite.[45] Other scholars argue that it is impossible to completely remove bias so we should at least be familiar with what they are and how they impact our thinking. Some of the most common cognitive biases include the following:

- **Unconscious or implicit bias** asserts that bias can express itself without a conscious realization from the thinker. Unconscious bias "refers to ways that humans unknowingly draw upon assumptions about individuals and groups to make decisions about them."[46] Essentially, it is when we have a bias that we are not aware of. Professor of Psychology and MacArthur genius grant recipient Jennifer L. Eberhardt, author of *Biased: Uncovering the Hidden Prejudice That Shapes What We See Think and Do* says implicit bias "is a kind of distorting lens that's a product of both the architecture of our brain and the disparities in our society."[47] She particularly focuses on the role implicit bias plays in different manifestations of racism, noting:

  "We all have ideas about race, even the most open-minded among us. Those ideas have the power to bias our perception, our attention, our memory and our actions – all despite our conscious awareness or deliberate intentions. Our ideas about race are shaped by the stereotypes to which we are exposed on a daily basis ... Confronting implicit bias requires we look in the mirror."[48]

- **Confirmation bias** creates a cognitive preference for information that coincides with our preexisting beliefs while ignoring counter-evidence. This is one of the most pervasive forms of bias, closely linked to other specific effects of biases that we'll mention, including motivated reasoning and inferred justification. It is like when something happens and we can't make sense of it because we don't want to accept what the facts suggest, rather, we seek evidence to support what we already believe, or want to conclude. (See additional examples below.)

- **Self-serving bias** is a practice in which individuals attribute positive outcomes to their own behavior and negative outcomes to others, for example, when a student fails a test they blame the teacher, but if they pass they credit themselves. Or, if a candidate wins an election, it's due to their superior policy positions and popularity, and if they lose, it's because the process was unfair or rigged, as outgoing President Trump claimed after losing the 2020 election.

- **Curse of knowledge bias** is displayed when an individual assumes that everyone should know what *they* know. This is flawed logic because it ignores the period of time in which the individual did not have this knowledge. This curse can be summarized pithily by observing someone say how obvious something now is that they themselves just learned yesterday.

- **Hindsight bias** occurs when individuals claim that an outcome was obvious because they know what happened. For example, an individual in 2020 may have claimed it was obvious that Trump would be "electored" in 2016, even though they believed at the time he would not be. This is also referred to as "armchair quarterbacking," especially when applied to the outcomes of sporting events. Of course, most are familiar with the phrase "hindsight is 20/20," referring to the recent obviousness of an outcome for something in the past that just occurred, but wasn't necessarily so obvious or predictable prior.

- **Optimism/pessimism bias** occurs when individuals' predictions about a negative or positive outcome reflect the positive or negative feelings they have at that particular moment. It is a form of emotional bias, but one that can be very powerful and influential over how someone arrives at a particular position. Barack Obama's mantra of "hope and change" reflected the positive bias of anticipating better times ahead if he is elected, or the inverse when Ronald Reagan quipped in 1980, "Are you better off now than you were four years ago?" thus implying if we continued with the presidency of Jimmy Carter, America would be doomed.

- **Declinism bias** refers to the contention that the past was better than the present. For example, those that claim the internet is taking down society (that we are all "going to hell in a handbasket"). However, Socrates said the same thing about the written word ages ago. This is also manifest by other popular phrases pining for a so-called "golden age," when one sees the past with "rose colored glasses" or is susceptible to appeals to nostalgia. This bias can manifest is interesting ways. For example, the Trump campaign's slogan, "Make America Great Again" appealed to such a mythic, vague time, as did speeches by presidents John F. Kennedy, Ronald Reagan, and Barack Obama, all of whom invoked this notion under the guise of returning to better days, like the founding of the colonies and Puritan John Winthrop's declaration "that we shall be as a city upon a hill — the eyes of all people are upon us."

- **In-group bias** occurs when an individual displays a tendency to say favorable things about a person from their group based solely on the fact they are from the same group. Political partisans do this routinely and it can easily lead to holding double standards, one for those in the party, another for those in another party. Understanding how this bias works is an important component of achieving fairness in judgment, like how "our side" does not commit atrocities or conduct torture, that's what the "other side" does. The late comic and critic George Carlin once reminded us, "Let's not have a double standard here, one standard will do just fine."

As social scientists have long noted, biases are influential on individuals' decision-making processes. First, biases inform our perception of reality. Biases influence our behavioral and attitudinal responses such as how friendly or receptive we are to others. For example, how little or much we comfort individuals can be shaped by bias about the person or what they are experiencing. Lastly, biases guide our attention. For example, our biases inform which aspects of a person or event we focus on or ignore. Bias acts as a hindrance to logically sound argumentation. Indeed, some of the effects of bias, with relevant examples, include:

- **The Forer effect** (a.k.a. **the Barnum effect**) refers to the practice of personalizing vague information to one's self without consideration of the fact that it could be applied to anyone and could have many different interpretations than the one applied to the individual. For example, individuals read horoscopes and conclude that the vague information is a reflection of what is occurring in their unique lives.
- **The Dunning–Kruger effect** sees people with more knowledge about a topic acting with caution to display they know less than they do, while those with less knowledge treat the topic as simplistic, acting as if they have more knowledge than they actually do. The Trump presidency was filled with such Dunning–Kruger moments, like when he claimed with great authority he knew better than noted doctors and public health experts serving his administration regarding COVID-19 treatments that included things as absurd as injecting bleach or subjecting the virus to sunlight.
- **Motivated reasoning/inferred justification** are more specific types, or effects of the confirmation bias. **Motivated reasoning** is defined as an individual's tendency to consider and evaluate evidence in a way that only allows for their preferred conclusion.[49] The smokers' conclusion is a form of motivated reasoning. According to the Centers for Disease Control and Prevention (CDC) as of 2020, "Cigarette smoking is the leading preventable cause of death in the United States."[50] A year earlier, the CDC found that 14 percent of U.S. adults smoke cigarettes.[51] The reasons why individuals do or do not smoke cigarettes is complex. However, a 2007 study found that nearly half of smokers in France convinced themselves that only the people who smoke more than themselves were at risk of contracting cancer.[52] Not only does this ignore the current evidence, it fabricates arbitrary numbers to conclude that they are not at risk of cancer.

Motivated reasoning and irrational thinking have infected our democratic system. Quite similarly, **inferred justification** implies that we as humans assume there must be a reason or reasons that a particular event has taken place. The process of ascribing explanation to said event based on value assumptions and confirmation bias rather than actual factually supported information is inferred justification. Sociologist Steven Hoffman highlighted this in a major study looking at post-9/11 America, the war in Iraq, and supposed weapons of mass destruction (WMDs). The study, titled "There Must Be a Reason: Osama, Saddam, and Inferred Justification," looked at how Americans rationalized the invasion of Iraq; even though WMDs were not found, they concluded that there must be a reason we were there. The researchers concluded that "People were basically making up justifications for the fact that we were at war," and the study showed motivated reasoning and inferred justification posed a "serious challenge to democratic theory and practice that results when citizens with incorrect information cannot form appropriate preferences or evaluate the preferences of others."[53]

- **Pseudoscience** usually occurs as a result of confirmation bias. It relies on non-replicable results that utilize opinions, beliefs, or practices that are introduced as facts, but are discordant with the scientific method. For example, after **cherry picking**, which refers to the practice of selecting only the information that bolsters your argument, and misunderstanding historical evidence about the Mayan calendar, pseudoscience led many to believe that the world was going to end in 2012. It did not.[54] Noted astrophysicist and author Carl Sagan warned that increased interest and reliance on pseudoscience is a major symptom of a society in cognitive decline, one rapt by the illusions of knowledge. In his 1995 book, *The Demon Haunted World*, he noted,

"I have a foreboding of an America in my children's or grandchildren's time ... when the people have lost the ability to set their own agendas or knowledgeably question those in authority; when, clutching our crystals and nervously consulting our horoscopes, our critical faculties in decline, unable to distinguish between what feels good and what's true, we slide, almost without noticing, back into superstition and darkness."[55]

Lies, Damned Lies, and Statistics

A common misconception is that numbers do not lie. Statistical analysis depends upon putting a numerical value on anything or anyone to make inferences. This requires a sample, which is collection of data such as a group of people. Studies seek to attain a large enough sample size that it is generalizable for the larger population. For example, if only one child is used in a study, their experience would not be generalizable for the nearly 75 million children in the U.S. However, if 7.5 million children were a part of the study that would increase the confidence that their findings are generalizable to the larger population. When the sampling process systematically removes or mitigates members of the larger population from the study this is known as a **sampling bias**. Some forms of sampling bias include the following:

- **Participation bias or non-response bias** occurs when individuals who do respond or participate have a set of characteristics different from those who do not respond to the request to participate.
- **Selection bias** refers to the selection of data without achieving randomization. The result is a sample that is not representative of the target population.

Sampling bias is just one example of how the objectivity of numbers is suspect.

In addition to sampling bias, the numbers can be reported in a way that demonstrates bias. This is known as reporting bias which refers to the selective revealing and suppression of data to portray a preferred result or finding. Although it is not uncommon to report partial data for a litany of legitimate reasons, sometimes this can indicative of a reporting bias. In *Weaponized Lies: How to Think Critically in the Post-Truth Era,* Daniel Levitin explains the process of how reporting bias occurs and how people can spot it. Humans often use "average" interchangeably with common, normal, or expected. However, Levitin encourages people to consider what is meant by average. Averages are another often manipulated form of statistical analysis. There are three types of averages: Mean, median, and mode. Depending on which one is chosen can greatly shape the outcomes.[56] For example, let's say we wanted to present the average amount of years people are sentenced to in prison. Let's use the following data sample:

- Prisoner 1 – 1 year;
- Prisoner 2 – 1 year;
- Prisoner 3 – 1 year;
- Prisoner 4 – 1 year;
- Prisoner 5 – 1 year;
- Prisoner 6 – 5 years;
- Prisoner 7 – 20 years;
- Prisoner 8 – 20 years;
- Prisoner 9 – 25 years;
- Prisoner 10 – 25 years.

The mean average would require adding all of the numbers together (the sum of which is 100) and dividing it by the number of prisoners (the sum of which is 10). The mean average of prison sentences would be 10 years. The mode average is calculated by determining which number appears the most in the sentences. The mode average of prison sentences would be 1 year. The median average is decided by selecting the middle number. In this case the middle is between prisoners 5 and 6. That number is calculated by adding prisoner 5's (1 year) sentence to prisoner 6's (5 year) sentence and dividing by 2. The median average for this data set would be 3 years. Depending on how one wanted to frame their argument they could introduce the average as 1 year, 3 years, or 10 years.

Finally, sometimes evidence is compiled into visual depictions of numbers such as pie charts or bar graphs that reveal their creator's bias. These are often used to make large data sets more digestible to audiences. Some basic questions to consider when evaluating visual depictions of evidence:

- Are the sizes of the bars or slices proportionally correct?
- If it has percentages, do they add up to 100?
- Are they properly numbered?

Sometimes the reporting bias and visual bias can make the numbers difficult to discern.[57] For example, a 2019 *MSNBC* graphic depicting the Democratic presidential candidates with the most support among black South Carolinian voters completely removed Bernie Sanders, who had the second-most support, from the list of five candidates:[58]

Figure 3.1 6/17/19, MSNBC.

In other cases, news media will cherry-pick evidence to make the claims in their headlines and graphics that are discounted by the very evidence they provide. For example, in October 2019, a *CNN* headline ignored that Sanders was polling in second place in Iowa to emphasize how close to first place Buttigieg and Biden were polling, despite coming in third and fourth place respectively. See figure 3.2.

A November 2019 *New York Times* headline simply ignored that Sanders was the only Democrat out-polling Trump in order to mention how close Biden and Warren were to Trump in the polls. See figure 3.3.

The major networks were also involved in erasing the Sanders campaign. In December 2019, even though Sanders was polling among the top three candidates in a *WBUR* New Hampshire primary poll, a *CBS* graphic removed Sanders for Warren. See figure 3.4.

In April 2019, *MSNBC* distorted a poll that found that Sanders had more support among non-white voters than Biden, by creating a graphic that added more percentage points to Biden's support among non-white voters. See figure 3.5.

Similarly, in May 2019, Chuck Todd of *MSNBC* displayed an incorrect graphic that claimed Sanders had dropped five points in the Quinnipiac poll of Democratic candidates from the previous month:

In reality, the senator had increased five points. Thus, Todd's graphic represented a 10-point swing in the opposite direction for Sanders. See figures 3.7 and 3.8.

In July 2019, *MSNBC* showed the correct polling numbers, but *reordered* the candidates to have Sanders, who was polling in second place, appear in fourth place. See figure 3.9.

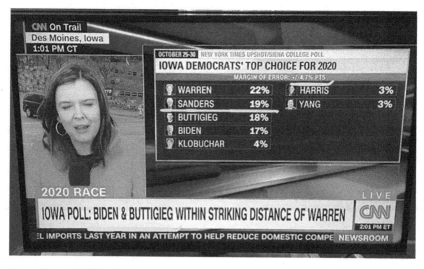

Figure 3.2 11/5/19, CNN.

One Year From Election, Trump Trails Biden but Leads Warren in Battlegrounds

Signs that the president's advantage in the Electoral College has persisted or even increased since 2016.

By Nate Cohn

Published Nov. 4, 2019   Updated Nov. 27, 2019   f y ✉ ➔ 🔖 3027

Despite low national approval ratings and the specter of impeachment, President Trump remains highly competitive in the battleground states likeliest to decide his re-election, according to a set of new surveys from The New York Times Upshot and Siena College.

How Trump fares among **registered voters**

	Biden	Sanders	Warren
Trump VS.			
Michigan	Even	Sanders +2	Trump +6
Pennsylvania	Biden +3	Sanders +1	Even
Wisconsin	Biden +3	Sanders +2	Even
Florida	Biden +2	Trump +1	Trump +4
Arizona	Biden +5	Trump +1	Warren +2
North Carolina	Trump +2	Trump +3	Trump +3

Based on a New York Times/Siena College poll of 3,766 registered voters from Oct. 13 to Oct. 26.

Figure 3.3 11/27/19, *The New York Times.*

Figure 3.4 12/14/19, CBS.

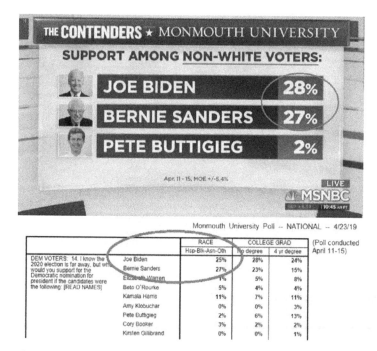

Figure 3.5 4/29/19, MSNBC. (Originally published by Fairness And Accuracy In
Reporting.)

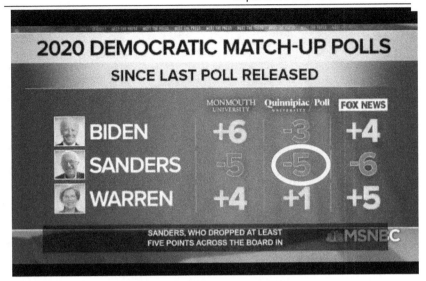

Figure 3.6 5/24/19, MSNBC. (Originally published by Fairness And Accuracy In Reporting.)

April 30, 2019

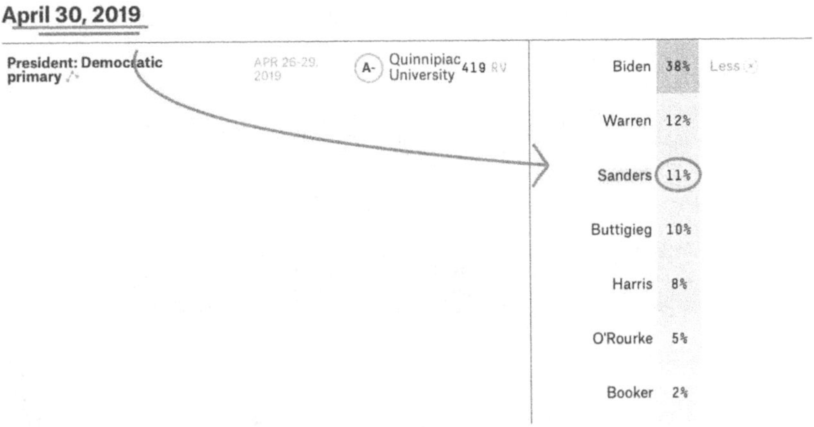

Figure 3.7 5/24/19, MSNBC. (Originally published by Fairness And Accuracy In Reporting.)

Added May 21, 2019

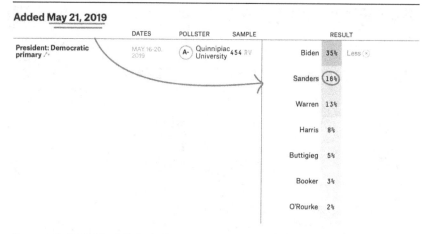

	DATES	POLLSTER	SAMPLE	RESULT		
President: Democratic primary	MAY 16-20. 2019	Quinnipiac University	454 RV	Biden	35%	Less
				Sanders	16%	
				Warren	13%	
				Harris	8%	
				Buttigieg	5%	
				Booker	3%	
				O'Rourke	2%	

Figure 3.8 5/24/19, *MSNBC.* (Originally published by Fairness And Accuracy In Reporting.)

2020 MATCHUPS:
AMONG REGISTERED VOTERS

	DEM	TRUMP
JOE BIDEN	53%	43%
KAMALA HARRIS	48%	46%
ELIZABETH WARREN	48%	48%
BERNIE SANDERS	49%	48%
PETE BUTTIGIEG	47%	47%

ABC NEWS/WASHINGTON POST POLL, JUNE 28 - JULY 1

Figure 3.9 7/7/19, *MSNBC.* (Originally published by Fairness And Accuracy In Reporting.)

That same month in another graphic, *MSNBC* pulled the same chicanery, dropping Sanders to third place despite his poll numbers being the second-highest among the candidates. See figure 3.10.

MSNBC was hardly the only 24-hour network to engage in graphic deception. In August 2019, *CNN* displayed all potential match-ups with a candidate against Trump in ascending order except Sanders, who was placed third despite polling in second. See figure 3.11.

Similarly, in December 2019, *CNN* ignored Sanders's poll numbers among California Latino voters by falsely noting that Warren and Biden led among the Golden State's fastest-growing demographic. See figure 3.12.

Figure 3.10 7/15/19, MSNBC. (Originally published by Fairness And Accuracy In Reporting.)

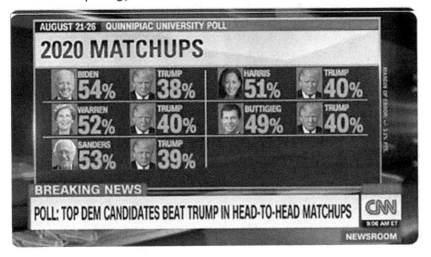

Figure 3.11 8/28/19, CNN.

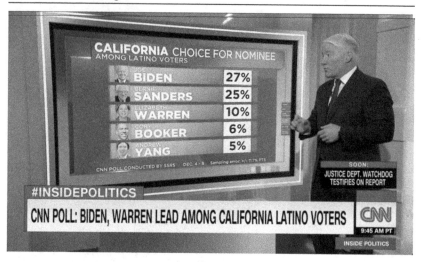

Figure 3.12   12/11/19, CNN.

Honing Critical Thinking Skills with Reading and Writing

Critical thinking is not just a process, but a skill. As with any skill, one's critical thinking abilities can drastically diminish without sustained use. That is why critical thinkers constantly read and write. Writing helps foster cognition and metacognition, which are essential for critical thinking. Professor of English Howard Tinberg describes the difference between the two as "knowing what we know, and knowing that we know."[59] Cognition, which refers to "the acquisition and application of knowledge trough complex mental processes," is developed when writers demonstrate an understanding of a question, the ability to meet the needs of an audience, their capability to fulfill a genre requirement, and that they can accurately and purposefully deploy concepts, knowledge sets, and terms to reveal expertise.[60] Writers can display **metacognition**, which refers to an awareness and understanding of one's own thought process, when they discern the structure of a draft, identify erroneous patterns in their writing, and distinguish what is necessary and unnecessary content.[61] Writing is an activity, and by examining their own writing process, readers are better positioned to think about and understand how writers' editorial decisions reflect their motivation, goals, ideology, and biases.[62]

In addition to writing, reading is essential for development of critical thinking skills. Readers mistakenly view the reading process as one of attaining knowledge from the author. However, reading is conducive to critical thinking when it is understood as a process of reflection, research, and writing.[63] Reading allows the author to control the conversation, but when audiences stop reading and reflect, write, and research, the reader takes over the process and begins to respond to the author.[64] Rather than just look for the writer's main argument, audiences should consider the larger context of the conversation that the reader is engaging with. This is achieved by asking: What arguments are the reader responding to? What other evidence or arguments exist in relation to this topic?[65] This demonstrates that one is not passively accepting the author's argument, but instead engaging in a process of critical thinking to understand, evaluate, analyze, and interrogate the text.

Clarity and Conclusion

The protesters and reactionaries who took to the streets following the murder of George Floyd were often operating from a different set of evidence that ranged from valid to unfounded. Their inability to engage in constructive dialogue not only illustrates the need for conflict management, but also an acceptability and accessibility of critical thinking skills. Although any of those individuals could rightly disagree on what to infer from the facts, a critically thinking society does not disagree on what are demonstrable facts. As Mark Twain once quipped, "get your facts first, then you can distort them as much as you please."[66] In that same vein, the late Senator from New York Daniel Patrick Moynihan, famously remarked, "Everyone is entitled to his own opinion, but not his own facts."[67] Recognizing and constructing rational arguments depends upon understanding the definition and importance of critical thinking and knowledge, and reflecting upon one's biases and listening capabilities. The next chapter explores how power-dynamics complicate these efforts.

Notes

1 Chris Hedges, "Noam Chomsky has 'never seen anything like this'," *Common Dreams,* April 19, 2010, https://www.commondreams.org/views/2010/04/19/noam-chomsky-has-never-seen-anything.

2 Arijeta Lajka, Ali Swenson, Amanda Seitz, and Beatrice Dupuy, "Politics not real news: Debunking false stories about Black Lives Matter, George Floyd, Antifa," *ABC13,* June 13, 2020, https://abc13.com/antifa-protest-black-lives-matter-lincoln-memorial/6246465/.

3 "Violence erupts as outrage over George Floyd's death spills into a new week," *NPR,* June 1, 2020, https://www.npr.org/2020/06/01/866472832/violence-escalates-as-protests-over-george-floyd-death-continue.

4 "Word of the Year 2016," *Oxford Dictionary,* https://languages.oup.com/word-of-the-year/2016/.

5 "'Truthiness': Can something 'seem,' without being, true?" *Merriam-Webster,* https://www.merriam-webster.com/words-at-play/truthiness-meaning-word-origin.

6 Mickey Huff and Peter Phillips, "Inside the military-industrial-media complex: Impacts on movement for social justice," *Truthout*, December 28, 2009, https://truthout.org/articles/inside-the-militaryindustrialmedia-complex-impacts-on-movement-for-social-justice/.

7 For more on these terms and concepts, see Mickey Huff and Andy Lee Roth, eds, *Censored 2018: Press Freedoms in a Post-Truth World* (New York: Seven Stories Press, 2017), 17–30.

8 Yochai Benkler, Robert Faris, and Hal Roberts, *Network Propaganda: Manipulation, Disinformation, and Radicalization in American Politics* (Oxford: Oxford University Press, 2018), https://oxford.universitypressscholarship.com/view/10.1093/oso/9780190923624.001.0001/oso-9780190923624-chapter-1.

9 Ozlem Sensoy and Robin DiAngelo, *Is Everyone Really Equal?: An Introduction to Key Concepts in Social Justice Education* (New York: Teachers College Press, 2017), 23.

10 Sensoy and DiAngelo, *Is Everyone Really Equal?*

11 Harry G. Frankfurt, *On Truth* (New York: Alfred A. Knopf, 2006), 11–12. See also Harry G. Frankfurt, *On Bullshit* (Princeton, NJ: Princeton University Press, 2005).

12 Ibid.

13 Stanford University, "Rationalism vs. empiricism," Stanford University, September 2, 2021, https://plato.stanford.edu/entries/rationalism-empiricism/; Jennifer Nagel, *Knowledge, A Very Short Introduction* (Oxford: Oxford University Press, 2014), 28–29.

14 Craig Dilworth, "Empiricism vs. realism revisited," in *The Metaphysics of Science*, pp. 183–192 (Dordrecht: Springer, 1996); Stanford University, "Rationalism vs. empiricism;" Nagel, *Knowledge, A Very Short Introduction.*

15 Dilworth, "Empiricism vs. realism revisited"; Nagel, *Knowledge, A Very Short Introduction.*

16 Ibid.

17 Nagel, *Knowledge, A Very Short Introduction,* 28–29.

18 Tracy Llanera, "Rorty and Nihilism," in *A Companion to Rorty*, ed. Alan Malachowski (Hoboken, NJ: John Wiley & Sons, 2020), 482–489.

19 Nagel, *Knowledge, A Very Short Introduction.*

20 Geoff Norman, "Critical thinking and critical appraisal," in *International Handbook of Research in Medical Education*, eds Geoff R. Norman, Cees P.M. van der Vleuten, David I. Newble, Diana H.J.M. Dolmans, Karen V. Mann, Arthur Rothman, and Lynn Curry, pp. 277–298 (Boston, MA: Kluwer Academic Publishers, 2002), 278.

21 Felix Kaufmann, "Truth and logic," *Philosophy and Phenomenological Research* 1, no. 1 (1940): 59–69.

22 Ruud Van der Helm, "Towards a clarification of probability, possibility and plausibility: How semantics could help futures practice to improve," *Foresight* 8, no. 3 (2006): 20.

23 Van der Helm, "Towards a clarification of probability, possibility and plausibility," 13.

24 Ibid.

25 Daniel Levitin, *Weaponized Lies: How to Think Critically in The Post Truth Era* (New York: Dutton, 2016).

26 Nassim Nicholas Taleb, *Incerto 4-Book Bundle: Fooled by Randomness, The Black Swan, The Bed of Procrustes, Antifragile* (New York: Random House, 2016).

27 Ylan Mui, "Americans saw wealth plummet 40 percent from 2007 to 2010, the Federal Reserve says," *Washington Post*, June 11, 2012, https://www.washingtonpost.com/business/economy/fed-americans-wealth-dropped-40-percen

t/2012/06/11/gJQAlIsCVV_story.html; Matt Taibbi, *Griftopia: A Story of Bankers, Politicians, and the Most Audacious Power Grab in American History* (New York: Random House Digital, Inc., 2011).

28 Federal Reserve Bank of St. Louis, "Median sales price of houses sold for the United States," Federal Reserve Bank of St. Louis, August 13, 2020, https://fred.stlouisfed.org/series/MSPUS.

29 For more on primary, secondary, and tertiary sources, see the University of California History Department's "Research and Writing Guide" compiled by Professor Mark Brilliant at https://history.berkeley.edu/undergraduate/academic-resources/research-writing-guide.

30 Ron Suskind, *Confidence Men: Wall Street, Washington, and the Education of a President* (New York: Harper-Collins, 2011).

31 Jonathon Green and Nicholas J. Karolides, *Encyclopedia of Censorship* (New York: Facts on File Library of World History, 2014).

32 Marios Pittalis and Constantinos Christou, "Types of reasoning in 3D geometry thinking and their relation with spatial ability," *Educational Studies in Mathematics* 75, no. 2 (2010): 196.

33 Thorleif Lund, "A metamodel of central inferences in empirical research," *Scandinavian Journal of Educational Research* 49, no. 4 (2005): 385–398.

34 For more on formal and informal logical fallacies, see *The Fallacy Files,* Taxonomy of Logical Fallacies, https://www.fallacyfiles.org/taxonnew.htm; see also Jacob E. Van Vleet, *Informal Logical Fallacies: A Brief Guide*, revised edition (Lanham, MD: Hamilton Books, 2021).

35 OWL, "Using rhetorical strategies for persuasion," Purdue University, 2020, https://owl.purdue.edu/owl/general_writing/academic_writing/establishing_arguments/rhetorical_strategies.html.

36 Yuval Noah Harari, *Sapiens: A Brief History of Humankind* (New York: Random House, 2014).

37 Ibid.

38 Jordan A. Litman and Mark V. Pezzo, "Individual differences in attitudes towards gossip," *Personality and Individual Differences* 38, no. 4 (2005): 963.

39 Harari, *Sapiens: A Brief History of Humankind.*

40 Kurt Andersen, *Fantasyland: How America Went Haywire. A 500-Year History* (New York: Random House, 2017).

41 Ibid.

42 Harari, *Sapiens: A Brief History of Humankind*, 24.

43 Harari, *Sapiens: A Brief History of Humankind.*

44 Rabindranath Tagore, *The Fourfold Way of India*, 1924.

45 Lee McIntyre, *Post-Truth* (Cambridge, MA: The MIT Press, 2018), 43–45.

46 Brenda J. Allen and Kavita Garg, "Diversity matters in academic radiology: Acknowledging and addressing unconscious bias," *Journal of the American College of Radiology* 13, no. 12 (2016): 1426.

47 Jennifer L. Eberhardt, *Biased: Uncovering the Hidden Prejudice That Shapes What We See Think and Do* (New York: Viking, 2018), 6.

48 Ibid. 6–7.

49 Ziva Kunda, "The case for motivated reasoning," *Psychological Bulletin* 108, no. 3 (1990): 480.

50 CDC, "Health effects of cigarette smoking," Centers for Disease Control and Prevention, April 28, 2020, https://www.cdc.gov/tobacco/data_statistics/fact_sheets/health_effects/effects_cig_smoking/index.htm.

51 CDC, "Current cigarette smoking among adults in the United States," Centers for Disease Control and Prevention, November 18, 2019, https://www.

cdc.gov/tobacco/data_statistics/fact_sheets/adult_data/cig_smoking/index.htm
#:~:text=In%202018%2C%20nearly%2014%20of,with%20a%20smoking-r
elated%20disease.

52 Patrick Peretti-Watel, Jean Constance, Philippe Guilbert, Arnaud Gautier, François Beck, and Jean-Paul Moatti, "Smoking too few cigarettes to be at risk? Smokers' perceptions of risk and risk denial, a French survey," *Tobacco Control* 16, no. 5 (2007): 351–356.

53 Ibid.

54 Suzan Clarke, "2012: End-of-the-world countdown based on Mayan calendar starts today," *ABC News,* December 21, 2011, https://abcnews.go.com/blogs/headlines/2011/12/2012-end-of-the-world-countdown-based-on-mayan-calendar-starts-today.

55 Carl Sagan, *The Demon Haunted World: Science as a Candle in the Dark* (New York: Random House, 1995), 12.

56 Daniel Levitin, *Weaponized Lies: How to Think Critically in the Post-Truth Era* (New York: Dutton, 2016).

57 Nolan Higdon and Mickey Huff, "The Bernie blackout is real, and these screenshots prove it," *Truthout*, January 30, 2020, https://truthout.org/articles/the-bernie-blackout-is-real-and-these-screenshots-prove-it/.

58 Maya King, "Why black voters are backing two old white guys: A divide among African Americans between Joe Biden and Bernie Sanders has major implications for the race heading into the fall," *Politico,* September 2, 2019, https://www.politico.com/story/2019/09/02/black-voters-sanders-biden-2020-1479234.

59 Howard Tinberg, "Metacognition is not cognition," in *Naming What We Know: Threshold Concepts of Writing Studies*, eds Linda Adler-Kassner and Elizabeth Wardle (Boulder, CO: University of Colorado Press, 2015), 75.

60 Ibid., 76.

61 Ibid., 76.

62 Linda Adler-Kassner and Elizabeth Wardle, "Metaconcept: Writing is an activity and a subject of study," in *Naming What We Know: Threshold Concepts of Writing Studies*, eds Linda Adler-Kassner and Elizabeth Wardle (Boulder, CO: University of Colorado Press, 2015).

63 Richard E. Miller and Ann Jurecic, *Habits of the Creative Mind: A Guide to Reading, Writing, and Thinking* (New York: Bedford/St. Martins, 2015, 2019).

64 David Bartholomae and Tony Petrosky, *Ways of Reading: An Anthology for Writers* (New York: Bedford/St. Martins, 1987, 2003).

65 Cathy Birkenstein and Gerald Graff, *They Say/I Say: The Moves That Matter in Academic Writing* (New York: Gildan Media, 2014).

66 "An Interview with Mark Twain," in Rudyard Kipling, *From Sea to Sea: Letters of Travel (Part II)* (New York: Charles Scribner's Sons, 1899), 285.

67 Daniel Patrick Moynihan, "More than social security was at stake," *Washington Post*, January 18, 1983, A17, col. 5, Washington, D.C.

Chapter 4

Test Theory and Spot Ideology

"[I will] never agree with anybody disrespecting the flag of the United States of America" explained New Orleans' Saints quarterback Drew Brees during a 2020 interview.[1] His comment was in response to questions about former NFL quarterback Colin Kaepernick's 2016 decision to protest police brutality by kneeling during the National Anthem. Brees' reflection on Kaepernick's activism occurred in 2020, when the murder of George Floyd sparked prolonged public protests against racial injustice. Brees' comments, which were viewed as insensitive, spawned public criticism including from his teammates. New Orleans Saints' wide receiver Malcolm Jenkins explained in social media that "even though we're teammates, I can't let this slide … [kneeling during the national anthem has] nothing to do with the disrespect of [the United States flag] and our soldiers."[2]

After days of criticism from other sports figures and his fellow teammates, Brees told the press that

> I love and respect my teammates, and I stand right there with them in regard to fighting for racial equality and justice .... I also stand with my grandfathers, who risked their lives for this country, and countless other military men and women who do it on a daily basis.[3]

In response, the Los Angeles' Laker LeBron James tweeted:

> WOW MAN!! Is it still surprising at this point. Sure isn't! You literally still don't understand why Kap was kneeling on one knee?? Has absolutely nothing to do with the disrespect of and our soldiers (men and women) who keep our land free. My father-in-law was one of those men who fought as well for this country. I asked him question about it and thank him all the time for his commitment. He never found Kap's peaceful protest offensive because he and I both know what's right is right and what's wrong is wrong! God bless you.[4]

DOI: 10.4324/9781003250906-7

Jenkins expressed that he was "hurt" by Brees' comments, because they were "extremely self-centered." Jenkins' video response made it clear that he thought Brees, as a white person did not understand the plight of communities of color regarding Floyd's murder:

> Our communities are under siege, and we need help. And what you're telling us is don't ask for help that way. Ask for it a different way. I can't listen to it when you ask that way. We're done asking, Drew. And people who share your sentiments, who express those and push them throughout the world, the airwaves, are the problem. And it's unfortunate because I considered you a friend. I looked up to you. You're somebody who I had a great deal of respect for. But sometimes you should shut the f— up.[5]

Jenkins said that Brees reached out to him shortly thereafter. Jenkins decided to delete the video and engage in dialogue with Brees. Within a few months, ESPN reported that "teammates have praised Brees for his sincere effort to become an ally for the Black community in its fight for racial equality and social justice." Jenkins said of his conversations with Brees that

> obviously the dialogue that he and I had to have publicly, but also privately, I think was important for the country to do and important for us to do. And I think that even moving past that moment, it's gonna be ongoing. But as far as a friendship, the willingness for both of us to engage in that dialogue has been cooperative and been encouraging.[6]

In addition, Jenkins argued that "I think my interaction with Drew is a microcosm to what we need to do as a country."[7]

According to Jenkins' account, what he and Brees did was disagree, communicate, listen, and understand. Jenkins explained afterward that

> we try to move to a post-racial type of society and move on from our past without actually addressing the history and the way that our past pretty much paints the present, and until we change the direction that we're going, until we change the systems that were put in place in the past, we'll always be tethered to that. And I think that starts with truth.[8]

Brees' ability to understand the truth as Jenkins saw it, depended upon an understanding of the past.

The ephemeral public discourse between Brees and Jenkins was emblematic of critical theorists contention that critical thinking necessitates an analysis of the power-dynamics that shape knowledge.[9] The patterns of dominance and asymmetrical power relations that shape interpretations of knowledge are best explained through an examination of the socio-cultural context in which they occur and operate. A **socio-cultural context** refers to the immediate physical and social setting in which someone lives or events occur, which includes the customs, life-styles, and values that characterize a society or group. Brees' interpretation was shaped in a socio-cultural context that differed from Jenkins.

Critical Theory and Knowledge

Critical thinking includes the use of **critical theory**, which "is a scholarly approach that analyzes social conditions within their historical, cultural, and ideological contexts."[10] Critical theory helps us understand the ways in which power systematically shapes our lived experience.[11] Catherine D'Ignazio and Lauren Klein define power as the

> current configuration of structural privilege and oppression, in which some groups experience unearned advantages – because various systems have been designed by people like them and work for people like them – and other groups that experience systematic disadvantages – because those same systems were not designed by them or with people like them in mind.[12]

They explain that **oppression**

> involves the systematic mistreatment of certain groups of people by other groups. It happens when power is not distributed equally – when one group controls the institutions of law, education, and culture and uses its power to systematically exclude other groups while giving its own group unfair advantages or simply maintaining the status quo.[13]

Patricia Hill Collins developed the four domains of the matrix of domination to explain the configuration of power and oppression. Collins explains that "the term **matrix of domination** describes this overall social organization within which intersecting oppressions originate, develop, and are contained."[14] The structural domain organizes oppression through law and politics. There are many examples of these types of laws in U.S. history such as those that prevented women from voting until 1920, and those that classified African Americans as slaves until the 19th century. The disciplinary domain administers and manages oppression by enforcing laws and rules such as law enforcement. The interpersonal domain refers to the individual experiences of oppression where individuals feel and are reminded of their marginalization.[15] The hegemonic domain circulates oppressive ideas and ideologies that are expressed in culture and media.

Ideology refers to "a systematically distorted or false picture of reality, one that benefits one group's interests over another's."[16] Historian Greg Grandin has argued that the socially constructed knowledge around Columbus fed what would be known as the frontier thesis, where progress depended upon never ending expansion and growth, and the victims are necessary casualties of the human story of progress.[17] According to Grandin, the idea of the frontier was both a diagnosis that explains the power and wealth of the United States as well as a legitimization of expansionist ideology which sought to extend the power and wealth of the U.S. In *Capital and Ideology*, Thomas Piketty explains that dominant ideologies are necessary because "every human society must justify its inequalities: Unless reasons for them are found, the whole political and social edifice stands in danger of collapse."[18] **Dominant ideologies** are the "belief systems, promulgated by and for the dominant classes, which make palatable to them, and in varying degrees to subordinate classes, the large inequalities in the social distribution of power and wealth."[19]

As Collins explains, in the hegemonic domain, dominant ideologies are spread through culture. **Culture** "refers to the ideas, language, beliefs, values, and behavioral norms that are shared by the members of a group, community, society, etc."[20] Marxist intellectual and foundational figure in critical theory, Antonio Gramsci, explained the ways in which dominant classes use their **cultural hegemony** to normalize their ideology:

> the 'spontaneous' consent given by the great masses of the population to the general direction imposed on social life by the dominant fundamental group; this consent is 'historically' caused by the prestige which the dominant group enjoys because of its position and function in the world of production.[21]

Critical scholars contend that cultural hegemony empowers a few people to obtain others' consent — which traditionally denotes the voluntary agreement to a proposal or desire — through coercion — which refers to the use of fear, violence, or intimidation to influence or control human behavior — to organize society in a way that exploits the majority of the population.[22] Cultural hegemony allows the few to spread and normalize the dominant ideologies. Knowledge is constructed within these systems of power. As a result, one must understand the power that shapes culture to understand its influence on the production of knowledge.

The Origins of Critical Theory

Critical theory enables an examination of the ways in which power shapes knowledge. Critical theory asks questions of power, such as for whom does the system work? Who is pushed out of the system? Whose priorities get turned into products? Whose priorities are overlooked? To illustrate this point, Ozlem Sensoy and Robin DiAngelo use the example of the Christopher Columbus. By the 15th century, it was commonly believed in Europe that the Earth was flat. Since Columbus arrived in the Americas it became common knowledge that he "discovered" that the world was round. However, in reality, many other cultures knew the world was round, but the hegemony of Western culture was able to privilege Columbus' interpretation while hiding or ignoring other cultures and their intellectual contributions.

As D'Ignazio and Klein contend, societies are structured in a way where oppression is a feature, not a bug of the system. Sensoy and DiAngelo utilize the story of Columbus to illustrate the relationship between power, knowledge, and oppression noting that

> if we believe that Columbus was simply an explorer and trader, we reinforce the idea of discovery as outside of political and ideological interests. The promotion of this idea has allowed dominant culture to ignore the genocide of Indigenous peoples and the transatlantic slave trade that his 'discoveries' set in motion.[23]

Critical theory assesses and critiques society and culture for the purpose of revealing and challenging systems of power. It challenges the idea that knowledge is objective or neutral; promotes self-reflection of knowledge producers; and identifies and critiques dominant ideology.[24] Where theory seeks to understand the world as it is, ideology explains the world as its adherents desire it to be. A **theory** acts as a net, capturing the phenomena we experience, and organizes it in a way to help us understand an unfamiliar environment.[25] Theory is not an **opinion**, which is a judgment of the facts. A theory is grounded in evidence, and tested repeatedly for accuracy and applicability.[26]

Critical theory derives from a bricolage of theorists including Karl Marx and Friedrich Engels' **social conflict theory**, which posits that capitalism as a system engendered an arrangement of social classes that engage in conflict rather than compromise over the allocation of material and non-material resources;[27] scholars of the **Frankfurt School**, which was not a physical school, proposed that the ruling elite maintained their power through cultural hegemony;[28] and the **Birmingham School**, which expanded the analysis of culture and political ideology to include such identities as race and gender.[29] Critical thinking necessitates an understanding of how power obfuscates the thinking process. Critical theorists contend that the privileges people derive from contemporary power relations blind them to the ways in which power shapes knowledge. This does not mean that everyone with privilege lacks empathy or sympathy, nor does it mean that every woman understands patriarchy or every person of color understands racism. It means that those with privilege have to be self-reflective about their blind spots, and utilize theoretical frameworks to mitigate them as best they can. To be privy to these types of analyses, and understand these forms of oppression and control, is what people refer to as being **woke**.

Critical theorists argue that colonizers' hegemony over culture and knowledge results in the majority of people being blind to systems of oppression and exploitation. Using an interdisciplinary approach of biology and sociology, Marina Fischer-Kowalski and Helmut Haberl define **colonization** as the "treatments of natural environments that purposively change some components to render better exploitability."[30] As historians have noted, colonization has been practiced by Western nations from the continents of Europe and North America, on continents such as Asia, Africa, and Latin America.[31] Scholars note that colonialism was justified by arguments of **ethnocentrism**, which is the assumption than one's nation and ethnicity are superior to another.[32] Critical scholars not only look at the way that colonialism shapes knowledge, but its legacy. This field of inquiry is known as **postcolonialism**, which investigates the cultural legacy and human consequences of the colonial control and exploitation.[33] This approach looks at **colonial mentalities**, which are the internalized attitudes about the inferiority of people that colonized people adopt including about them.[34] The study of coloniality contends that social structures and forms of knowledge continue to serve colonizers and marginalize the colonized in post-colonial societies.[35] Critical thinkers seek to resist power-inequities by decolonizing their thinking. **Decolonization** refers to the withdrawing of colonial power and subsequent restoration of political, economic, and cultural autonomy for the previously colonized.[36]

Critical Theory

The case of Jenkins and Brees is a reminder that just as evidence, inference, and logic matter to argumentation, so too does identity. Effective communication depends upon the recognition that identities are expressions of power. Colonialist ideology has constructed identities – such as class, race, and gender – that justify subjugation, and produce power-inequities that reverberate today.[37] Critical theorists contend that identity and privilege can blind participants to systematic realities of oppression that define the lives of those who share a differing identity. They argue that theoretical lenses can be a liberatory force that illuminate the ways in which systems of power operate to justify and normalize dominant ideology. Some of these lenses include:

- **Class:** Karl Marx and Friedrich Engels argued that dominant ideology blinded the working class from attaining class consciousness about the systematic oppression of the working class. **Class consciousness** refers to "the awareness of the individuals about their personal interests as well as the common interest" of their class.[38] Marx and Engels contend that dominant ideologies normalized a class-based system that served the wealthy – which they referred to as the bourgeoisie – by justifying class inequities under the ideology of capitalism.[39] The ideological justifications for class inequities would undergo many iterations, but are expressed most recently in the dominant ideology of **neoliberalism,** which is refers to "the capitalist restructuring that has occurred around the globe since the 1970s in the name of a post-Cold War, post-welfare state model of social order that celebrates unhindered markets as the most effective means of achieving economic growth and public welfare."[40]

- **Critical race theory** (CRT): Stemming from legal studies, critical race theory seeks to understand the systematic nature of white supremacy and its subordination of people of color by exploring systemic racial exclusion and privilege in the U.S.[41] **White supremacy** refers to "the centuries-old racialised social system comprising the totality of the social relations and practices that reinforce white privilege."[42] **Race** "is a social construct, forged through oppression, slavery, and conquest, whereby self-defined racially dominant groups benefit economically, socially, and politically from their legally and/or socially sanctioned exploitation and oppression of those they brand as racially inferior."[43] A **social construct** refers to "a phenomenon or category created and developed by society through its cultural and social practices."[44] Emerging from legal studies, CRT argues that white supremacy is the dominant ideology that centers the interests and perceptions of white people as normal, neutral, and objective.[45] Critical race theory introduces investigates the progenitors of racism, while utilizing a structural analysis to situate culture in the context of unequal power relations.[46] The five tenants of CRT are counter-storytelling, a critique of liberalism, interest convergence, the permanence of racism, and whiteness as property.[47] CRT's analysis is rooted in a Marxist analysis of class expressed in racial capitalism, which argues that capitalism served to perpetuate racial oppression – such as slavery, violence, and genocide – by extracting social and economic value from people of color.[48]

- **Feminist theory:** Feminist theorists seek to illuminate the ways in which the dominant ideology of sexism normalizes systems of patriarchy.[49] **Sexism** naturalizes our belief in sex differences as a way of justifying patriarchal social arrangements by making them seem inevitable and resistance is futile.[50] **Patriarchy** refers to "a set of social institutions that deny women the opportunity to be self-supporting, thereby making them dependent on male relatives for survival, and that otherwise favor men in the intrafamilial allocation of resources and power."[51] Patriarchy consists of largely uneven gendered practices that target girls and women for actual, perceived, or representative challenges to or violations of applicable patriarchal norms and expectations.[52] **Gender** refers to "the array of socially constructed roles and relationships, personality traits, attitudes, behaviors, values, relative power and influence that society ascribes to the two sexes on a differential basis."[53] Feminists maintain that **misogyny** upholds patriarchy by enforcing gender conformity for both men and women.[54] Misogyny is different than sexism, which feminists argue is "the justificatory branch of a patriarchal order, which consists and ideology that has the overall function of rationalizing and justifying patriarchal social relations."[55] Sexism is maintained in part through the communication of assumptions, beliefs, theories, stereotypes, and broader cultural narratives the make important distinction between men and women as a way to rationalize patriarchal social arrangements.[56]

- **Queer theory:** Building upon the work of feminist studies, scholars in the late 20th century developed queer theory.[57] Queer theorists argue that the ideology of heteronormativity normalizes a hegemonic system that mismatches sex, gender, and desire.[58] **Heteronormativity** "refers to norms related to gender and sexuality that seek to reinforce existing power structures and ideologies such as patriarchy and compulsory heterosexuality."[59] The privileges afforded to heterosexuals are evident in laws such as the Defense of Marriage Act which defined marriage as being between a man and woman, and the tax code which until fairly recently only offered economic benefits to married heterosexual couples.[60] Queer theory seeks to emancipate identities from rigid sexual structures by broadening the scope of sexual identity to include lesbian, gay, bisexual, transgender, queer and/or questioning, intersex, and asexual among others. As Southampton Solent University's Nick Rumens, notes "Queer theorists then, like the characteristics associated with queer theories, are diverse and sometimes contradictory, often causing confusion and frustration as to whether queer theory refers to an attitude, particular groups of people, an identity, politics, theory or position."[61]

- **Critical disability theorists:** More recently, Critical disability theory (CDT) has emerged, studying the ways ableist assumptions have systematically privileged the abled.[62] CDT sees the world as privileging the able bodied, and as a result argues that "disability is not fundamentally a question of medicine or health, nor is it just an issue of sensitivity and compassion; rather, it is a question of politics and power(lessness), power over, and power to."[63] Indeed, CDT was behind the successful movement to pass The Americans with Disabilities Act of 1990 (ADA), which prohibits discrimination based on disability.

- **Intersectionality:** This term was coined in 1989 by feminist scholar Kimberlé Crenshaw,[64] and refers to "the interlocking relations of dominance of multiple social, political, cultural and economic dynamics of power that are determined simultaneously by identity categories of race, gender, class, sexuality, disability, and others."[65] The idea germinated when Crenshaw was in law school reading about the case of DeGraffenreid v. General Motors Assembly Division, which focused on a black woman, Emma DeGraffenreid, who sued over discrimination in their seniority policy. The course ruled against DeGraffenreid because GM had a history of hiring black men and white women. Crenshaw noted that the court's analysis ignored the intersection of discrimination on the basis of race *and* gender.[66]

Critical scholars argue that theoretical lenses help illuminate the invisible dominant ideologies that shape knowledge and discourse. Some examples of how colonization, the establishment of control, or appropriation of various spaces physical or intellectual, is reflected in language include:

- **Conflating discussions of consciousness with an -ism:** Critical scholarship has concluded that social constructed identity groups were created to maintain power relations.[67] Thus, only those with power can exert racism, sexism, and classism. It is logically unsound to say a woman is sexist against men or a person of color is racist against whites. They can have prejudicial attitudes towards those groups because they lack the power to exert an -ism. If they had that power, it would be sexism and racism respectively.
- **Conflating "colorblindness" with the absence of racism:** Critical scholars point out that discourses which try and avoid race by pretending it does not exist, such as declaring "I do not see color," are misleading. Racism is a product of the white supremacist system and pretending it does not exist does not mean it will go away.[68] It is analogous to thinking that it is not raining outside because I choose not to see water.
- **Fragility:** Those with privilege demonstrating fragility through discomfort or anxiety when it comes to sexism, racism, or homophobia. In response, they may change the subject or attempting to find another explanation other than race for the issue at hand. The

dismissal of the influence of identity is demonstrative of the colonial mentality.

- **Interrupting and talking over people:** Critical scholars contend that when people of privilege interrupt or talk over an under-privileged person they are expressing their feeling of superiority to that person. Indeed, feminist scholars have long noted that patri-archal practices would prefer women not to talk at all. As a result, misogynistic enforcement mechanisms such as talking over or inter-rupting women are used to dismiss and silence the voices of women.[69]

- **Talking first or most often:** Critical scholars also note that those with privilege are socialized to believe they should and need to be heard, where underprivileged groups are socialized to be submissive and less forthcoming in conversation.[70] Thus, when people of privi-lege talk first or most often compared to an underprivileged person they are expressing their feeling of superiority to that person.

- **Mansplaining:** This refers to "how men feel the need, based upon their privilege, to explain something to women and those with less privilege in society because they know better."[71]

- **Manterruption:** Refers to men silencing women speakers by inter-rupting them with greater frequency than they would with other men.[72]

- **Implicit bias:** "the underlying attitudes and stereotypes that are involuntary and subconscious."[73] Critical schools contend that the subconscious ideas of people of privilege result in the adoption of negative assumptions and reactions to members of underprivileged groups. (This was addressed in Chapter 3.)

- **Microaggressions:** These are "subtle forms of discrimination in which brief, daily, behavioral, verbal, or environmental injustices" that may be intentional or in error.[74]

There are certainly critics of critical theory and its many lenses. It is important to consider these perspectives to broaden the frame of discus-sion and recognize when, where, why, and how differences of perspectives may occur.

Critiques of Critical Theory

Many critics of critical theory, though not all, come from the right, challenging the overall efficacy and new widespread acceptance of and popularity of critical theory. Conservative journalists and commentators like Thomas Sowell and George Will decry it for a lack of objectivity, a betrayal of enlightenment traditions, and emphasis on personal experience over empirical evidence. More conservative critiques from think-tanks like the Heritage Foundation claim that critical theory is a flawed leftist ideology that infuses intersectional tensions into political, economic, and social arrangements and affairs rather than looking at other historical and economic factors for inequalities. They claim that it represents a shift away from traditional western family values. Heritage Visiting Fellows like Christopher Rufo claim critical race theory in particular would not solve racial inequality, it would deepen it, while others like Ellie Krasne claim "Leftists' Critical Race Theory Poisons Our Discussion of Racism."[75] These critics further claim so-called Social Justice Warriors (SJW), activists promoting various offshoots of critical theory, project past tensions onto the present and participate in mass historical revisionism in the process to suit and promote their contemporary ideologies.

Public debates about CRT are complicated by the conflation of discourses on race and racism with CRT. A CRT analysis centers on race and systems of power, but not every study of race conforms to that analysis. In short, not everything about race is CRT. This was lost in much of the discourse regarding the conflicting historiographic approaches of the "1619 Project," developed by Nikole Hannah-Jones, working with the *New York Times* and *New York Times Magazine* for the 400th anniversary of the first African Americans brought to the Virginia colony; and "1776 Unites," a project by African American scholars at the Woodson Center working with the conservative *Washington Examiner* newspaper, which are examples of this tension. The former "aims to reframe the country's history by placing the consequences of slavery and the contributions of Black Americans at the very center of the United States' national narrative."[76] The latter arose out of the desire of more traditional and conservative academics to counter what they saw as a revisionism based on critical race theory coming from the "1619 Project." The "1776 Unites" project led to a "1776 Commission" formed by the Trump Administration that aimed to showcase African Americans as a self-determined people who succeeded in overcoming slavery from the early republic, not as victims of it. The "1619 Project" is clearly influenced by tenets of critical theory, while "1776 Unites" is highly dubious of critical race theory in particular, and its influence on the very historiographic frame of 1619.[77] Proponents of "1776 Unites" claimed they wanted to pursue a "patriotic education," implying critical race theory perverted the integrity of American institutions and their history. Even prominent, establishment American historians like Sean Wilentz, Gordon Wood, and James McPherson challenged the accuracy of the "1619 Project" from yet another perspective, adding to the controversy, which like the study of the past itself, is ongoing.[78]

Other academics, like Canadian clinical psychologist Jordan Peterson, have pointed out the irony of a theory based on criticism that fails to critique itself, whose proponents often refuse to engage in debate with detractors and accuse them of being witless accomplices to oppression. Further, Peterson contends that many who now champion social justice pedagogy, which is rooted in critical theory, fail to examine the leadership roles of many of its practitioners who now play roles in elite societal institutions from the government to education, and even in the private corporate sector where the rhetoric of critical theory has been widely adopted by many in the professional managerial classes, if not the actual practices. According to critics like Peterson, this has created a new bourgeoisie, comprising those imposing their preferred interpretations of how they think the society ought be reorganized, seen through a leftist critical theory lens.

Co-optation

Some argue that Peterson's analysis misses that these actions are being taken not by critical theorists, but bad-faith actors who have co-opted the language of critical theory to further ensconce neoliberal ideology and cement current social relations. If critical theory challenges power structures and hierarchy, many of its critics wonder why so many of its adherents seem to be running university social justice task forces, equity councils, and mandatory diversity and tolerance trainings on campuses and in board rooms – not because those are bad things in and of themselves, but because they have now taken on the hierarchical role of controlling production of knowledge and social order, a new concentration of power once at the center of the ire and suspicion of the critical theorists.[79]

The famous summary of Eric Hoffer's quote "every great cause begins as a movement, becomes a business, and eventually degenerates into a racket" describes the utilization of critical theory for some critics.[80] They contend that the well-founded origins of critical theory have been co-opted and re-appropriated for nefarious purposes that serve those in power. **Co-optation** involves a deliberate appropriation of a concept or movement for means contrary to the original intention, often in maintenance of those in power to control opposition and dissent. Some critics contend that critical theory has been co-opted to perpetuate rather than ameliorate inequities and oppression. Catherine Liu, Professor of Film and Media Studies at the University of California, Irvine, refers to these people as the **professional managerial class** (PMC). PMCs posit themselves as people who once fought for progressive causes, although as a class they have not seemed to have acted much upon them since the mid 20th century. Liu writes:

> They still believe themselves to be the heroes of history, fighting to defend innocent victims against their evil victimizers, but the working class is not a group they find worth saving, because by PMC standards, they do not behave properly: they are either disengaged politically or too angry to be civil.[81]

In late 2020 on *Rising,* Krystal Ball explored this phenomenon, noting that it was sexist for conservatives to mock Dr. Jill Biden's use of the doctoral title, but noted that elite liberals only feigned to care about feminism because they could relate to having a title they feel entitled to being disrespected. According to Ball, the story revealed the ways in which elite culture co-opts feminist language to perpetuate power inequities.[82]

According to Liu, PMCs have a grip on electoral politics because they have co-opted identity politics to divide the electorate. **Identity politics** describes people's tendency to privilege political alliances driven by identity over traditional broad based political parties. It is also used as a prerogative to disregard political arguments centered on identity. Liu explains that PMC's have co-opted the language of identity politics to reduce individuals to one aspect of their identity and conflate any critique of that person with an -ism, which is also known as woke washing. **Woke washing** describes to the process by which political figures' anti-progressive views and polices are ignored because of their identity.[83] Woke washing has been criticized by scholars such as Professor of Media Ecology at New York University, Mark Crispin Miller; Political Science Professor Adolph Reed; and Zhaid Jailalni, a journalist for *The Intercept.* [84] In late 2019, Jimmy Dore mocked the ways in which discourses about the adage of gender progress – *women shattering the glass ceiling* – were woke washed to laud the appointment of Gina Haspel, who helped conceal the Central Intelligence Agency's (CIA) participation in torture, as Director of the Agency: "torturer Gina Haspel broke through the glass ceiling to become the director of the CIA and picked up one of the glass shards and started torturing people."[85] Other critics contend that PMCs' identarian discourses amount to **tokenism,** which refers to the appointment of a person from one group, not to abolish the structures that prevented members of that group from getting the appointment, but to symbolize that those barriers no longer exist. Tokenism enables the outlier to become the rule. For example, the tokenist portrayal of Barack Obama conflated his election to the presidency with a "post-racial" era where racism had been abolished.[86] Keeanga Yamahtta Taylor described the pervasive notion of a "post-racial" society as follows:

> the success of a relative few African Americans is upheld as a vindication of the United States' colorblind ethos and a testament to the transcendence of its racist past. Where there is bad treatment on the basis of race, it is viewed as the product of lapsed personal behavior and morality but it is 'no longer endemic, or sanctioned by law and custom,' as President Obama once suggested.[87]

This is not say that commentators do not view Obama's election as progress in race relations, but they think it is being overblown to ignore the persistence of racism in U.S. society and history.

PMCs assert their moral superiority and commitment to the values of critical theory through **virtue signaling,** which is a pejorative term defined "as symbolic demonstrations that can lead observers to make favorable inferences about the signaler's moral character."[88] Much of this happens in the digital space where users post photos and sign onto letters to display their moral righteousness and cultural superiority. Take the example of masks, which became a hyper-partisan issue with the onset of the COVID-19 pandemic. Online, users signaled their virtue by taking pictures with their masks on. Closely related is the PMC's utilization of **performative wokeness,** which Lizzie Bowes, writing for the University of Cambridge student publication *Varsity*, succinctly defined as "a superficial show of solidarity with minority and oppressed bodies of people that enables (usually white and privileged) people to reap the social benefits of wokeness without actually undertaking any of the necessary legwork to combat injustice and inequality."[89] It is a toxic form of slacktivism – which refers to the practice of showing digital support for a cause with little to no other substantive effort or commitment – that conceals the ways in which the performer is perpetuating the problem. For example, in 2020, Amazon expressed solidarity with people of color by adding a Black Lives Matter banner to its website while it simultaneously was undermining an effort led by a black person to organize a union of Amazon workers.[90]

Other critics argue that the PMC weaponized critical theory to punish the working class for inequities caused by the dominant class.[91] These critics accuse the PMC of normalizing neoliberal ideology with essentialist notions introduced as critical theory. For example, whiteness is introduced by some PMCs as having an essence that is racist. This is expressed in the anti-racism or implicit bias trainings hosted by Robin DiAngelo, the author of *White Fragility*. Some argue that DiAngelo's approach distracts from the systematic nature of oppression, instead treating it like an organic aspect of one's identity. This serves those in power because rather than discussing a system as racist, they argue that it is a problem at the individual level. Regardless, DiAngelo secured a slew of lucrative corporate contracts to perform her trainings after the murder of George Floyd. A June 2020 episode of the podcast *Chapo Trap House* introduced a working-class lens to DiAngelo's PMC anti-racist training. The hosts and their guests, *New Republic's* Jen Pan and *Bad Faith's* Virgil Texas, interpret DiAngelo's work as promoting class inequality under the auspices of furthering racial justice:[92]

JEN PAN: The context in which I encountered *White Fragility* is a few months ago. I was assigned to review it for the *New Republic* in sort of the broader context of the diversity industry. Which you guys are probably aware is this like massive bloated $8 billion industry, which sort of encompasses like anti-racist training sensitivity workshops, cultural competency implicit bias training, and that is incidentally the industry in which this author of *White Fragility*, Robin DiAngelo, works. I think that you know a kind of interesting component to the conversation is the fact that there's kind of been this you know emerging body of literature that talks about how these diversity trainings don't work, they don't reduce people's biases, they don't really make workplaces more diverse, and in some weird cases they even like make people's biases stronger. So I think that's kind of important to keep in mind, when you are thinking about Robin DiAngelo and *White Fragility*, and how her book is basically a documentation of how these trainings don't work.

HOSTS: [*Laughter*]

PAN: She is a diversity trainer, in her case studies in this book, she goes around to people's workplaces and to their schools and talks to them about racism, and her whole thesis is that white people in the room become extremely uncomfortable, they don't like what they're hearing, and they don't react well to her.

AMBER A'LEE FROST: I think that one of the things that kept jumping out at me when I was reading this is that she kept saying like I cannot correct or deprogram my unconscious bias, and feelings of racial superiority. I will always be like this. I will always, you know, walk around with, you know, late in white supremacy, and I'm like then why am I listening to you? Like why are you that the anti-racist trainer? Because she's like every other paragraph, she's like look I know about racism, take it from me, a racist.

HOSTS: [*Laughter*]

FROST: She doesn't do a very good job at justifying her anti-racist credentials, except that she can charge people $10 thousand a session, a speaking session, for two hours, it's better than podcast money, it's amazing.

PAN: Yeah and if you're never done being racist, then all you can do to work on yourself is you know kind of participate in these steps of self-improvement, which of course include buying her book and attending her seminars.

FROST: There's no cure, there's a treatment you have to take all the time always and keep paying her.

WILL MENAKER: I mean I guess what was like sort of sort of weird to me ... if we're in a moment where white people are just, you know, once again perpetually being like "damn there's a lot of racism in this country that's fucked up, like you know what could I do?" It would seem to me, if you were if you like if you wanted to educate yourself ... read any history of the United States. Like or any black author who's written about this, but like this is a white woman. The whole thrust of it is through this kind of corporate HR [human rights] model ...

PAN: Another place in the book she says something like "I just can't understand why these white people would react like this upon getting an opportunity to learn about their racism?" That opportunity, of course as you pointed out Will, is in the workplace. Which of course, is something that she never bothers to not only just interrogate, but doesn't even acknowledge, that you know, the context in which these trainings are unfolding is quite often in her case in the workplace; whereas we all know there are many different power dynamics already at work. The main one of course being between the bosses who organize such workshops and then everyone else.

WILL: [*Interrupting*] Yeah, its mandatory, the idea why are you being open to me the person that your fucking asshole boss paid to yell at you for an hour.

VIRGIL: Is she right? Does she actually never address that?

FROST: Never, not once. She never mentioned that like this is a mandatory school assembly, where your employer is now being invited to like interrogate the most intimate parts of your psyche and brain and experience.

PAN: About a very politically charged topic. Like who the fuck wants their boss talking to them about racism?

HOST: The information certainly will not be put in your file for later use [*laughter from the panel*].

These sentimentalities were shared by others in the podcasting space such as *Useful Idiots* host, journalist Matt Taibbi. To illustrate what he sees as a cynical ploy to mask class warfare as anti-racism, Taibbi compares DiAngelo's use of racial categories as monoliths to Nazi philosophies on race. For example, Taibbi chides DiAngelo for legitimizing negative black stereotypes – such as black people are incapable of arriving to a location on time – by classifying them as cultural aspects whites needed to accept. Furthermore, he accuses DiAngelo of removing talent and agency from famous black Americans such as Jackie Robinson by attributing their success as a product of the will of white men.[93] Taibbi is joined by Krystal Ball of *Breaking Points*, who rebuked DiAngelo for accepting lucrative corporate contracts to lecture the working class on their behavior and attitudes toward race. To Ball, DiAngelo's trainings enabled corporate capitalism – which Ball viewed as a fundamental and contributing factor to the persistence of racism in U.S. society – to shed its culpability and place the blame for racism on squarely on the backs of the some of the least powerful actors in U.S. society: The working class.[94]

The PMC utilizes essentialist notions to dismiss critiques, even when it comes from the underprivileged communities they claim to support. For example, Biden and his vice president Kamala Harris – the first woman of color to hold the position – touted themselves and the Democratic Party has the party of racial justice. When podcast host Charlemagne the God suggested he was not sure if he would vote for Joe Biden in 2020, Biden responded "I tell it if you have a problem figuring out whether you're for me or Trump, then you ain't black."[95] Subsequently, under the auspices of being a supporter of racial equality, Biden told prominent black Americans on a Zoom call in December of 2020, "You guys are going to have to start working more with Hispanics, who make up a larger portion of the population than y'all do!"[96]

From Co-optation to Weaponization?

Still, others argue that critical theory has not only been co-opted, but weaponized. Self-described left-libertarian academic and biologist Bret Weinstein derides critical theory, and critical race theory in particular, and its proponents for having a tendency to be hypocritical and "deeply authoritarian." In 2017, Weinstein, mentioned earlier in this book, was at the center of a controversy at Evergreen College's annual Day of Absence/ Day of Presence event in Olympia, WA, where whites who wanted to participate were asked to not come to campus so as to create a safe space for people of color to discuss race. Weinstein protested what he called "coercive segregation" and called this "an act of oppression," circulated e-mails across campus and penned a widely read op-ed for the *Wall Street Journal*, noting,

> There is a huge difference between a group or coalition deciding to voluntarily absent themselves from a shared space in order to high-light their vital and under-appreciated roles ... and a group or coalition encouraging another group to go away .... On a college campus, one's right to speak—or to be—must never be based on skin color.

A month or so later, 50 students protested his class and demanded his resignation. He noted that the climate on campus shifted from a diversity agenda to an equity one, where one could either accept critical race theory dictates coming from college councils or be branded a racist for wanting to discuss them. Instead, Weinstein sued the college. He and his wife, who taught anthropology there, resigned their positions and settled for $500,000 and the college admitted no wrongdoing.[97]

Another instance involving a one-time leftist academic running at odds with SJW culture happened at New York University (NYU). Michael Rectenwald, a Ph.D. graduate in Cultural Studies from Carnegie Mellon University, and a former Marxist and Professor of Liberal Studies at NYU, decried the rise and prevalence of political correctness and identity politics on college campuses and what he saw as an assault on academic freedom from an anonymous Twitter account (where he was often quite caustic in his remarks). He was later outed by students and his department in 2016 and claimed he was forced out of his position, though the evidence suggests he took a leave of absence and eventually retired in 2019. He described his case and continues his critiques of SJW culture and critical theory as an attack on reason and academic freedom in his books, *Springtime for Snowflakes: Social Justice and its Postmodern Parentage*, and *Beyond Woke*.[98]

Regardless of these critiques, which should be part of an open discussion in a free society, critical theory and its offshoots present important lenses through which one can view the present in historical context. Such criticisms of it, however, illustrate the significance of agreeing to disagree, as while disagreements on these matters may be disparate for some, they can be largely nuanced for others.

Debates Within the Critical Theorist Community

In addition to the critiques from non-critical theorists, there are debates among critical theorists. One centers on the **Oppression Olympics**, which is a dialectical process that characterizes marginalization and ostracization as a competition, based on a comparison of race, gender, socioeconomic status or disabilities, to determine who is most oppressed. Critics contend that the Oppression Olympics is the underprivileged doing the work of the colonizer by critiquing each other rather than uniting for liberation.

This occurs when people engage in **reductionism**, which refers to the practice of dividing the sum into parts. For example, class theorists contend that the material conditions of society as well as the power-dynamics that shape structures of power are best understood through a class lens.[99] Some of them argue that critical race theory engages in a form of **race reductionism**, meaning that it reduces the explanation for inequality to discrimination rather than the class relations that created the structures that discriminate and marginalize people of color disproportionately, but not exclusively. Case in point, some critical scholars argue that the concept of racial capitalism centers on race-based narratives that ignore the historically documented motives and behaviors of capitalists to exploit all working people regardless of their racial identity.[100] Worse, some Marxist scholars contend that race reductionist thinking enables a class war that is framed as anti-racism because it serves to divide the working class along racial lines, which prevents a unified movement to challenge the power of the wealthy class known as the bourgeoisie.[101]

The discourses on reductionism have produced forms of analysis for both division and unity. Critical race theorists counter critiques about race reductionism by accusing class theorists of engaging in **class reductionism**, which refers to "the contention that a focus on class issues reduces all other forms of oppression such as racism, sexism, and homophobia." The division caused by accusations of reductionism are not limited to issues of race and class. There are feminists who argue that reductionism obscures discourses about gender. For example, in 2014, critical scholar Kimberlé Crenshaw criticized Obama's $200 million My Brother's Keeper program, which offered "support to boys and young men of color, most of them African-American or Hispanic" because it did not seek to address the "challenges facing their mothers and sisters."[102] Crenshaw's contention that the race-based policy was aimed at men of color rather than women illustrates the ways in which differing lenses can lead to competing interpretations of the same evidence. Still, there are opponents of reductionism who have argued that there are alternative ways for analyzing identity that are not so divisive. They contend that an intersectional analysis of class, race, gender, sexuality, and ability, allows for theoretical weight and practical solidarity to emerge from the dead-ends of reductionisms.[103] In other words, intersectional analysis should be, at the risk of sounding redundant, intersectional.

Conclusion

The discourses between Jenkins and Brees reveal the centrality and complexity of the ways in which power and identity frame one's lived experience and what they consider knowledge. However, their discourses also revealed the power of constructive dialogue. This chapter introduced critical theorists' contention that critical thinking requires context for analyzing knowledge. The cultural hegemony of dominant classes is rooted in mass communication tools. In order to understand the dominant messages in mass media, critical thinkers decode media messages. The process by which this is achieved is the focus of the academic field of critical media literacy, and is the subject of Part 3 of this book.

Notes

1 Mike Triplett, "'Saints' Drew Brees draws backlash for 'disrespecting the flag' comment," *ESPN*, June 3, 2020, https://www.espn.com/nfl/story/_/id/29262906/saints-drew-brees-says-never-agree-anybody-disrespecting-flag.
2 Ibid.
3 Ibid.
4 Rob Goldberg, "Lakers' LeBron James rips Drew Brees over comments about kneeling in NFL," *Bleacher Report*, June 3, 2020, https://bleacherreport.com/articles/2894659-lakers-lebron-james-rips-drew-brees-over-comments-about-kneeling-in-nfl.
5 Mike Triplett, "'Saints' Drew Brees draws backlash for 'disrespecting the flag' comment," *ESPN*, https://www.espn.com/nfl/story/_/id/29262906/saints-drew-brees-says-never-agree-anybody-disrespecting-flag.
6 Ibid.

7 Michael David Smith, "Malcolm Jenkins: Discussions like I had with Drew Brees are what America needs," *Pro Football Talk,* June 23, 2020, https://profootballtalk.nbcsports.com/2020/06/23/malcolm-jenkins-discussions-like-i-had-with-drew-brees-are-what-america-needs/.

8 Ibid.

9 Max Horkheimer and Theodor W. Adorno, *Dialectic of Enlightenment: Max Horkheimer and Theodor W. Adorono* (New York: Herder & Herder, 1947, 1972); Antonio Gramsci, *Gramsci: Pre-prison Writings* (Cambridge: Cambridge University Press, 1994); Antonio Gramsci, *Prison Notebooks, Volumes 1–3* (New York: Columbia University Press, 2011); Herbert Marcuse, *One Dimensional Man: Studies in Ideology of the Advanced Capitalist Society* (Boston, MA: Beacon Press, 1964); Douglas Kellner, "Cultural studies and social theory: A critical intervention." In *Handbook of social theory*, Edited by George Ritzer and Barry Smart, (London,England: SAGE, 2001): 395–409.

10 Ozlem Sensoy and Robin DiAngelo, *Is Everyone Really Equal?: An Introduction to Key Concepts in Social Justice Education* (New York: Teachers College Press, 2017), 23.

11 Ibid.

12 Catherine D'Ignazio and Lauren Klein, *Data Feminism* (Cambridge, MA: MIT Press, 2020), 24.

13 Ibid., 8.

14 Patricia Hill Collins, "Black feminist thought in the matrix of domination," *Black Feminist Thought:* 227.

15 Patricia Hill Collins, *Black Feminist Thought: Knowledge, Consciousness, and the Politics of Empowerment* (London: Routledge, 2000, 2014).

16 Edward E. Sampson, "Cognitive psychology as ideology," *American Psychologist* 36, no. 7 (1981): 730.

17 Greg Grandin, *The End of the Myth: From the Frontier to the Border Wall in the Mind of America* (New York: Metropolitan Books, 2019).

18 Thomas Piketty, *Capital and Ideology* (Cambridge, MA: Harvard University Press, 2020), 1.

19 Douglas E. Baer and Ronald D. Lambert, "Education and support for dominant ideology," *Canadian Review of Sociology/Revue canadienne de sociologie* 19, no. 2 (1982): 173.

20 Bonnie K. Nastasi, "A model for mental health programming in schools and communities: Introduction to the mini-series," *School Psychology Review* 27, no. 2 (1998): 165–174.

21 Antonio Gramsci, *Selection from the Prison Notebooks* (New York: International Publishers, 1971), 12.

22 Max Horkheimer and Theodor W. Adorno, *Dialectic of Enlightenment: Max Horkheimer and Theodor W. Adorono* (New York: Herder & Herder, 1947, 1972); Antonio Gramsci, *Gramsci: Pre-prison Writings* (Cambridge: Cambridge University Press, 1994); Antonio Gramsci, *Prison Notebooks, Volumes 1–3* (New York: Columbia University Press, 2011); Herbert Marcuse, *One Dimensional Man: Studies in Ideology of the Advanced Capitalist Society* (Boston, MA: Beacon Press, 1964).

23 Ozlem Sensoy and Robin DiAngelo, *Is Everyone Really Equal?: An Introduction to Key Concepts in Social Justice Education* (New York: Teachers College Press, 2017), 25.

24 Sensoy and DiAngelo, *Is Everyone Really Equal,* 29.

25 Em Griffin, Andrew Ledbetter, and Glenn Sparks, *A First Look at Communication Theory* (New York: McGraw-Hill, 2019).

26 Ibid., 3.

27 Jan McArthur, *Rethinking Knowledge Within Higher Education: Adorno and Social Justice* (New York: Bloomsbury, 2013).

28 See the works of Erich Fromm, Herbert Marcuse, Theodor W. Adorno, Max Horkheimer, and Walter Benjamin.

29 See the work of Charlotte Brunsdon, Iain Chambers, John Clarke, Richard Dyer, Michael Green, Stuart Hall, Dick Hebdige, Dorothy Hobson, Tony Jefferson, Richard Johnson, Angela McRobbie, David Morley, Chris Weedon, Paul Willis, and Judith Williamson.

30 Marina Fischer-Kowalski, and Helmut Haberl, "Metabolism and colonization. Modes of production and the physical exchange between societies and nature," *Innovation: The European Journal of Social Science Research* 6, no. 4 (1993): 415–442.

31 Lynn Hunt, Thomas R. Martin, Barbara H. Rosenwein, and Bonnie G. Smith, *Making of the West, Combined Volume: Peoples and Cultures*, 4th ed. (New York: Bedford/St. Martin's Publishing, 2012).

32 James T. Tedeschi, Peter Christiansen, Joann Horai, and James P. Gahagan, "Mythological ethnocentrism as a determinant of international attitudes," *The Journal of Social Psychology* 80, no. 1 (1970): 113–114.

33 Henry Schwarz and Sangeeta Ray, eds, *A Companion to Postcolonial Studies* (Oxford: John Wiley & Sons, 2000, 2005).

34 James R. Ryan, "Postcolonial geographies," in *A Companion to Cultural Geography*, eds James Duncan, Nuala C. Johnson, and Richard H. Schein (Oxford: Blackwell Publishing, 2004), 469–484.

35 See the work of Anibal Quijano, Walter Mignolo, Arturo Escobar, Enrique Dussel, and Nelson Maldonado-Torres.

36 Mel Gray, John Coates, Michael Yellow Bird, and Tiani Hetherington, "Conclusion: Continuing the decolonization agenda," in *Decolonizing Social Work,* eds John Coates and Tiani Hetherington (New York: Routledge, 2016), 323.

37 Brenda J. Allen, *Difference Matters: Communicating Social Identity* (Long Grove, IL: Waveland Press, 2010).

38 Fatih Irmak and İdris Güçlü, "Revisiting Marx and Dahrendorf on social exclusion and inclusion," *Journal of Human Sciences* 9, no. 2 (2012): 1504.

39 Ibid.

40 Kirsten Bell and Judith Green, "On the perils of invoking neoliberalism in public health critique," *Critical Public Health* 26, no. 3 (2016): 239.

41 Kimberlé Crenshaw, Neil Gotanda, Gary Peller, and Kendall Thomas, eds, *Critical Race Theory: The Key Writings that Formed the Movement* (New York: The New Press, 1996); Derrick A. Bell Jr., "Brown v. Board of Education and the interest-convergence dilemma," *Harvard Law Review* (1980): 518–533.

42 Helena Liu and Ekaterina Pechenkina, "Staying quiet or rocking the boat? An autoethnography of organisational visual white supremacy," *Equality, Diversity and Inclusion: An International Journal* 35, no. 3 (2016): 186–204.

43 Nancy Krieger, "Refiguring 'race': Epidemiology, racialized biology, and biological expressions of race relations," *International Journal of Health Services* 30, no. 1 (2000): 211.

44 Lars D. Christiansen and Nancy L. Fischer, "Working in the (social) construction zone," *Introducing the New Sexuality Studies,* eds Nancy L. Fischer and Stephen Seidman (New York: Routledge, 2016), 5.

45 Richard Delgado and Jean Stefancic, *Critical Race Theory: An Introduction* (New York: New York University Press, 2017); Eduardo Bonilla-Silva, *Racism Without Racists: Color-Blind Racism and the Persistence of Racial*

Inequality in the United States (Lanham, MD: Rowman & Littlefield Publishers, 2006).

46   Christine E. Sleeter, "An agenda to strengthen culturally responsive pedagogy," *English Teaching: Practice and Critique* 10, no. 2 (2011): 7–23.

47   Lorenzo DuBois Baber, "Beyond the 'tenets': Reconsidering critical race theory in higher education scholarship," in *Critical Race Theory in Education*, eds Laurence Parker and David Gillborn (Abingdon, UK: Routledge, 2016), 182–199; GerDonna J. Ellis, "Critical race theory and the impact of oppression narratives on the identity, resilience, and wellness of students of color," Master of Arts in Communication Boise State University (2020); Gloria Ladson-Billings, "Just what is critical race theory and what's it doing in a nice field like education?" *International Journal of Qualitative Studies in Education* 11, no. 1 (1998): 7–24; Gloria Ladson-Billings and William F. Tate, "Toward a critical race theory of education," *Teachers College Record* 97, no. 1 (1995): 47–68; Richard Delgado and Jean Stefancic, *Critical Race Theory: An Introduction* (New York: New York University Press, 2001).

48   Cedric J. Robinson, *Black Marxism: The Making of the Black Radical Tradition* (University of North Carolina Press, 1983, 2020); Robin D.G. Kelley, "What did Cedric Robinson mean by racial capitalism?" *Boston Review* 12 (2017).

49   Dawn M. Szymanski, "Relations among dimensions of feminism and internalized heterosexism in lesbians and bisexual women," *Sex Roles* 51, no. 3–4 (2004): 145–159; Catherine D'Ignazio and Lauren Klein, *Data Feminism* (Cambridge, MA: MIT Press, 2020),

50   Kate Manne, *Down Girl: The Logic of Misogyny* (New York: Oxford University Press, 2018, 2019).

51   Anju Malhotra, Reeve Vanneman, and Sunita Kishor, "Fertility, dimensions of patriarchy, and development in India," *Population and Development Review* (1995): 284.

52   Kate Manne, *Down Girl: The Logic of Misogyny* (New York: Oxford University Press, 2018, 2019).

53   Carol Vlassoff, "Gender differences in determinants and consequences of health and illness," *Journal of Health, Population, and Nutrition* 25, no. 1 (2007): 47.

54   Kate Manne, *Down Girl: The Logic of Misogyny* (New York: Oxford University Press, 2018, 2019).

55   Ibid., 79.

56   Manne, *Down Girl*.

57   Michael Warner, "Introduction: Fear of a queer planet," *Social Text* (1991): 3–17.

58   Annamarie Jagose, *Queer Theory: An Introduction* (New York: New York Universality Press, 1996).

59   Jaya Sharma, "Reflections on the Construction of Heteronormativity," *Development* 52, no. 1 (2009): 52–55.

60   Jagose, *Queer Theory: An Introduction*.

61   Nick Rumens, "Sexualities and accounting: A queer theory perspective," *Critical Perspectives on Accounting* 35 (2016): 111–120.

62   "Critical disability theory," *Stanford Encyclopedia of Philosophy*, Sep 23, 2019. https://plato.stanford.edu/entries/disability-critical/; Sami Schalk, "Critical disability studies as methodology," *Lateral* 6, no. 1 (2017).

63 Jennifer Gillies, and Sherry L. Dupuis, "A framework for creating a campus culture of inclusion: A participatory action research approach," *Annals of Leisure Research* 16, no. 3 (2013): 193–211.

64 Kimberlé Crenshaw, "Demarginalizing the intersection of race and sex: A black feminist critique of antidiscrimination doctrine, feminist theory and antiracist politics," *The University of Chicago Legal Forum* (1989), 139–167.

65 Amanda Gouws, "Feminist intersectionality and the matrix of domination in South Africa," *Agenda* 31, no. 1 (2017): 19.

66 Catherine D'Ignazio and Lauren Klein, *Data Feminism* (Cambridge, MA: MIT Press, 2020).

67 Chandra L. Ford, and Collins O. Airhihenbuwa. "Critical race theory, race equity, and public health: Toward antiracism praxis," *American Journal of Public Health* 100, no. S1 (2010): S30–S35.

68 Ibid.

69 Kate Manne, *Down Girl: The Logic of Misogyny* (New York: Oxford University Press, 2018, 2019).

70 Ibid.

71 Black English and Uncensored Mode, "A note on language," in *Hip Hop Beats, Indigenous Rhymes: Modernity and Hip Hop in Indigenous North America*, ed. Kyle T. Mays (New York: University of New York Press, 2018).

72 Imogen Clark, and Andrea Grant, "Sexuality and danger in the field: Starting an uncomfortable conversation," *Journal of the Anthropological Society of Oxford* 7, no. 1 (2015): 5.

73 Kimberly G. Kallianos, Emily M. Webb, Christopher P. Hess, Jason Talbott, and Matthew D. Bucknor, "Use of the implicit association test to improve diversity in radiology," *Journal of the American College of Radiology* 16, no. 7 (2019): 976.

74 Tiffany K. Chang and Y. Barry Chung, "Transgender microaggressions: Complexity of the heterogeneity of transgender identities," *Journal of LGBT Issues in Counseling* 9, no. 3 (2015): 217–234.

75 Christopher Rufo, "Critical race theory would not solve racial inequality: It would deepen it," The Heritage Foundation, March 23, 2021, https://www.heritage.org/progressivism/report/critical-race-theory-would-not-solve-racial-inequality-it-would-deepen-it; Ellie Krasne, "How leftists' critical race theory poisons our discussion of racism," The Heritage Foundation, June 29, 2020, https://www.heritage.org/civil-society/commentary/how-leftists-critical-race-theory-poisons-our-discussion-racism.

76 1619 Project, https://www.nytimes.com/interactive/2019/08/14/magazine/1619-america-slavery.html.

77 1776 Unites, https://1776unites.com.

78 Ibid. See also, Adam Serwer, "The fight over the 1619 Project is not about the facts," *The Atlantic*, December 23, 2019, https://www.theatlantic.com/ideas/archive/2019/12/historians-clash-1619-project/604093/.

79 Uri Harris, "Jordan B. Peterson, critical theory, and the new bourgeoisie," *Quillette*, January 17, 2018, https://quillette.com/2018/01/17/jordan-b-peterson-critical-theory-new-bourgeoisie/; Michael Liccione, "'Critical theory' needs a good critique," *Intellectual Takeout*, Charlemagne Institute, January 26, 2018, https://www.intellectualtakeout.org/article/critical-theory-needs-good-critique/.

80 George Packer, "The new liberalism," *Ariz. L. Rev.* 51 (2009): 543–557, 547.

81 Catherine Liu, *Virtue Hoarders: The Case Against the Professional Managerial Class* (Minneapolis, MN: University of Minnesota Press, 2021), 1.

82   *Rolling Stone*, "Useful Idiots with Matt Taibbi and Katie Halper," *Apple*, January 2021, https://podcasts.apple.com/us/podcast/useful-idiots-with-ma tt-taibbi-and-katie-halper/id1476110521.

83   Staff, "Biden apologists are 'wokewashing' his awful team," *YouTube*, November 23, 2020, https://www.youtube.com/watch?v=J-vsVguhrJE.

84   *Rolling Stone*, "Useful Idiots with Matt Taibbi and Katie Halper,"; "The Katie Halper Show," *Google Podcasts,* June 17, 2016, https://podcasts.google.com/ feed/aHR0cHM6Ly9mZWVkcy5zb3VuZGNsb3VkLmNvbS91c2Vycy9zb3Vu ZGNsb3VkOnVzZXJzOjU0Mzc5Njg0L3NvdW5kcy5yc3M/episode/dGFnO NvdW5kY2xvdWQsMjAxMDp0cmFjazMvMjY5NjI2ODAz?sa=X&ved=2ah UKEwjI9MrUn7LtAhU6uFkKHbOxDakQkfYCegQIARAF.

85   *The Hill*, "Rising: Jimmy Dore rips Democrats on impeachment," *YouTube*, October 8, 2019, https://www.youtube.com/watch?v=fa0kDY4VE9c&fea ture=emb_logo.

86   Richard Delgado and Jean Stefancic, *Critical Race Theory: An Introduction* (New York: New York University Press, 2017), 26; Michael Eric Dyson, *The Black Presidency: Barack Obama and the Politics of Race in America.* (Boston, MA: Houghton Mifflin Harcourt, 2016); Eddie S. Glaude Jr, *Democracy in Black: How Race Still Enslaves the American Soul* (New York: Broadway Books, 2016); Cornel West, "Pity the sad legacy of Barack Obama," *Guardian*, January 9, 2017, https://www.theguardian.com/comm entisfree/2017/jan/09/barack-obama-legacy-presidency.

87   Keeanga Yamahtta Taylor, *From Black Lives Matter to Black Liberation* (Chicago: Haymarket Books, 2016), 4.

88   Ekin Ok, Yi Qian, Brendan Strejcek, and Karl Aquino, "Signaling virtuous victimhood as indicators of Dark Triad personalities," *Journal of Personality and Social Psychology*, July 2, 2020, http://dx.doi.org/10.1037/pspp0000329.

89   Lizzie Bowes, "Performative wokeness needs to stop," *Varsity*, December 21, 2017, https://www.varsity.co.uk/profile/lizzie-bowes.

90   Kari Paul, "Amazon says 'Black Lives Matter'. But the company has deep ties to policing," *Guardian,* June 9, 2020, https://www.theguardian.com/ technology/2020/jun/09/amazon-black-lives-matter-police-ring-jeff-bezos.

91   Catherine Liu, *Virtue Hoarders: The Case Against the Professional Managerial Class* (Minneapolis, MN: University of Minnesota Press, 2021), 1.

92   *Chapo Trap House*, "No Crying in Raceball feat. Jen Pan: Chapo Trap House, Episode 428," *YouTube*, June 16, 2020, https://www.youtube.com/ watch?v=SOy60-pfiRU.

93   *Rolling Stone*, "Useful Idiots with Matt Taibbi and Katie Halper," *Apple*, January 2021, https://podcasts.apple.com/us/podcast/useful-idiots-with-ma tt-taibbi-and-katie-halper/id1476110521.

94   Staff, *The Hill,*" *YouTube*, February 5, 2021, https://www.youtube.com/cha nnel/UCPWXiRWZ29zrxPFIQT7eHSA.

95   Staff, "Joe Biden faces backlash after comments on popular black radio show," *NPR,* May 22, 2020, https://www.npr.org/transcripts/861321203.

96   Ruben Navarrette, "Column: Biden tells civil rights leaders where they went wrong," *Yakima Herald,* January 25, 2021, Comments, https://www. yakimaherald.com/opinion/columnists/column-biden-tells-civil-rights-leader s-where-they-went-wrong/article_07e380b6-e5a2-5ccc-9527-bfc69ad24180 .html.

97   Abspegman, "Evergreen settles with Weinstein, professor at the center of campus protests," *The Olympian*, September 16, 2017, https://www.theo lympian.com/news/local/article173710596.html; Bret Weinstein, "The

campus mob came for me—and you, professor, could be next," *Wall Street Journal*, May 30, 2017, https://www.wsj.com/articles/the-campus-mob-cam e-for-meand-you-professor-could-be-next-1496187482.

98   Michael Rectenwald, *Springtime for Snowflakes: Social Justice and Its Postmodern Parentage* (Nashville, TN: New English Review Press, 2018); Michael Rectenwald, *Beyond Woke* (Nashville, TN: New English Review Press, 2020).

99   Touré Reed, *Toward Freedom: The Case Against Race Reductionism* (New York: Verso Books, 2020).

100   Adolph Reed Jr, "Response to Backer and Singh: How should we think about race in relation to class formation on the left?" *Verso*, October 10, 2018, https://www.versobooks.com/blogs/4073-response-to-backer-and-singh.

101   Hope Reese, "Adolph Reed Jr.: The perils of race reductionism. The political scientist Adolph Reed Jr. on the Black Lives Matter movement, the 'rich peoples' wealth gap,' and his Marxism," *JStor*, April 28, 2021, https://daily.jstor.org/adolph-reed-jr-the-perils-of-race-reductionism/; Park Center for Independent Media, "Recognize race reductionism with scholars of sociology, history," May 16, 2021, *YouTube,* https://www.youtube.com/wa tch?v=nwCSs0T5Tbk&t=5267s; Touré Reed, *Toward Freedom: The Case Against Race Reductionism* (New York: Verso Books, 2020); Adolph Reed Jr., "The myth of class reductionism: The fight for racial and gender justice has always been about economic inequality, too," *The New Republic,* September 25, 2019, https://newrepublic.com/article/154996/myth-class-reductionism; Cedric Johnson, "Black political life and the Blue Lives Matter presidency," *Jacobin,* February 17, 2019, https://jacobinmag.com/2019/02/black-lives-ma tter-power-politics-cedric-johnson.

102   Kimberlé Williams Crenshaw, "The girls Obama forgot," *New York Times,* July 29, 2014, https://www.nytimes.com/2014/07/30/opinion/Kimberl-William s-Crenshaw-My-Brothers-Keeper-Ignores-Young-Black-Women.html.

103   Patricia Hill Collins, "The difference that power makes: Intersectionality and participatory democracy," in *The Palgrave Handbook of Intersectionality in Public Policy*, eds Olena Hankivsky and Julia S. Jordan-Zachery (Cham, Switzerland: Palgrave Macmillan, 2019), 167–192.

Part III

Critical Media Literacy

"Whatever is your first priority, whether it is women's rights or saving wildlife, your second priority has to be media reform. With it you at least have a chance of accomplishing your first priority. Without it, you don't have a prayer" argues the former Federal Communication Commission (FCC) Commissioner Nicholas Johnson.[1] Johnson's statement notes the centrality of media as tools for communication, and mass media as the dominant story tellers and opinion makers who shape culture, disseminate information, and set the national agenda.

Studies reveal that contemporary media are shaping divisive discourses that are antithetical to constructive dialogue. For example, journalist Matt Taibbi argues in *Hate Inc.* that the news media's business model shifted in the 1990s to one that seeks to capture select demographics by making them fear and hate citizens with competing ideologies.[2] Similarly, studies about social media have revealed that the platforms are designed in a way that curtail constructive dialogue because they confirm users' beliefs, whether they are true or not, and privilege division among users.[3] All of these observations point to the need for a more critically media literate public.

The third part of this text explores these concepts further, and applies the critical thinking skills and theory to media analysis for the purpose of fostering constructive dialogical strategies.

In Chapter 5: Investigate and Evaluate Mass Media, we delve into the world of critical media literacy and unpack mass media systems, advertising and public relations, ideology and representation, and the power of becoming an active user rather than passive consumer of information. We then address in Chapter 6: Critique Content: "Fake News" and Ethical Journalism, the epistemic crisis we face in a supposedly "post-truth" world. We explore how to deconstruct and understand propaganda, call out fake news stories, and develop healthier relationships with our information ecosystems. Chapter 7: Assess and Analyze Digital Media Use and Abuse outlines challenges around social media and reminds readers why

DOI: 10.4324/9781003250906-8

being mindfully engaged with these new media platforms matters, particularly in this digital era we now inhabit.

In all, this section instructs on how to be more responsibly informed about the world. Media users need to think critically and carefully before they click, like, and share their way across the internet. Whether it be the George Floyd video or former president Donald Trump's tweets, much of what constitutes evidence in contemporary discourse derives from media. Citizens cannot begin to engage in dialogue without a shared understanding of evidence, and they cannot properly assess and evaluate media content until they are media literate. The subsequent chapters introduce critical media literacy for the purposes of fostering constructive dialogue.

Chapter 5

Investigate and Evaluate Mass Media

I first heard about Robert White when I was a teenager, and then I later met him. I met him just a month after he got out of prison. He was in prison, serving a sentence for assault with intent to murder two black men, with a shotgun, and another sentence – conspiring to bomb a synagogue in Baltimore. Now, I am a professional musician. I tour all over this country and around the world, playing music. So how do I end up with a policeman's uniform? He worked for the police department by day. But he also had another job, which required a different kind of uniform. He was the grand dragon of the Ku Klux Klan for the State of Maryland. This is his robe. This is what he wore when he conspired to bomb the synagogue and when he made plans to kill two black men, with a shotgun.[4]

So explains Daryl Davis as he holds up both uniforms for the Naperville, Illinois audience to see. Davis is an African American and anti-racist speaking to an audience attending his Ted Talk. Davis' talk centers on his experiences with the Ku Klux Klan (KKK).

In the auditorium, Davis recounts that his earliest memory of racism was when he was hit by bottles and other debris from whites who were angry to see him, the only black kid, in a 1958 Boy Scout march. He said after numerous subsequent incidences his parents finally sat him down to explain the concept of racism. He remembered,

It was inconceivable to me that someone who had never laid eyes on me, never spoken to me, knew absolutely nothing about me would want to inflict pain upon me for no other reason than this: the color of my skin. So I did not believe my parents. But more and more incidents began happening, and I realized my parents had told me the truth. I didn't know why people felt that way, but I realized that there were some people who did. So at the age of 10, I formed a question in my mind. That question was 'How can you hate me when you don't even know me?'[5]

DOI: 10.4324/9781003250906-9

This question would drive Davis' life work. For years, Davis read numerous texts about Nazi and white supremacist ideology but none of it provided the answers he sought. So in his adult years, now a professional musician, he had his secretary, Mary, book an appointment with Roger Kelly, an Imperial Wizard in the KKK. However, she neglected to mention that Davis was black. Davis said that once Kelly agreed to a meeting,

> We reserved a motel room. Mary and I got there early. Right on time, to the minute ... In walks Mr. Kelly and his bodyguard. The bodyguard was armed with a sidearm right here on his hip. When they saw me, they just kind of like froze because they were expecting a white guy. I stood up and went like this to show I had nothing in my hands, and I approached. I said, 'Hi, Mr. Kelly, I'm Daryl Davis.'... And we conversed – agreed on some things, disagreed on other things. But he let me know – he let me know that I was not his equal. I was inferior; he was superior. And this was justified and determined by the color of my skin. I wasn't there to fight him; I was there to learn from him: where does this ideology come from? Because once you learn where it comes from, you can then try to figure out how to address it and see where it's going. So we continued conversing ... I would invite Mr. Kelly to my home. He would come to my home. He'd bring his bodyguard, who would sit on the couch next to him ... I would invite over some of my other friends – my Jewish friends, my black friends, my white friends, other people – just to engage in conversation with Mr. Kelly. Other than me, I wanted him to experience different people. This went on for a couple years. He did not invite me to his home, but he would have dinner or lunch at my table with me – this inferior person that he deemed not his equal. After a couple years, he began coming down to my house by himself – a national leader in the Ku Klux Klan. And then he began inviting me to his house. I would see his Klan den, and I would take pictures and take notes for my own knowledge and things. Then he began inviting me to Klan rallies. I'd go to these Klan rallies ... And there's a rally with the cross on fire. Now, they would give speeches. I would take more notes and try to absorb and try to understand – not that I'm believing in what they're preaching, but I'm trying to learn and understand what is the impetus for it?[6]

Describing the dialogue with Kelly, Davis explained that

> respect is the key. Sitting down and talking – not necessarily agreeing – but respecting each other to air their points of view. Because of

that respect and my willingness to listen and his willingness to listen to me, he ended up leaving the Klan, and there's his robe right there.[7]

In fact, Davis would reportedly go on to attain over 200 robes from ex-Klansman he convinced to leave the organization.[8]

Kelly would later say of Davis:

> I'd follow that man to hell and back because I believe in what he stands for and he believes in what I stand for. We don't agree with everything, but at least he respects me to sit down and listen to me, and I respect him to sit down and listen to him.[9]

Davis explains that anyone can do what he does, noting:

> I am a musician, not a psychologist or sociologist. If I can do that, anybody in here can do that. Take the time to sit down and talk with your adversaries. You'll learn something; they'll learn something. When two enemies are talking, they're not fighting – they're talking. It's when the talking ceases that the ground becomes fertile for violence. So keep the conversation going.[10]

The difficult and often dangerous work of Davis reveals the importance of dialogue and respect. However, what Davis' story does not explain is how people come to adopt and normalize ideologies such as white supremacy. Through his multiple interactions Davis came to believe that hate derived from fear, including fear of the unknown. Although it is true that KKK members may now *know* people of color, they still have a fallacious conception of them. Where does that conception come from? Part of the answer is mass media. Mass media's awesome communicative power and influence enables them to promulgate and normalize select ideologies that shape American attitudes and discourse, including white supremacy. This chapter examines how mass media represent people and ideologies in their content.

Mass Media as Popular Culture

On average, American adults spend over 10 hours a day consuming media (TV, video games, radio, tablet, smartphone, and computer).[11] A majority of American adults own a combination of laptop or desktop computer, tablet, or smartphone.[12] Much of what they use is mass media. **Mass media** refers to the wide range of media technologies – such as print, broadcast, and digital – that reach a large audience via mass communication. In the U.S., roughly six corporations dominate **legacy mass**

media: Comcast/NBC Universal, Disney, CBS, Viacom, News Corpora-tion, and AT&T.[13] **Legacy media** refers to media outlets that were established in the pre-digital era. We will discuss the digital era mass media in Chapter 7. This tiny number of media corporations are able to shape popular culture in the U.S. and around many parts of the globe. **Popular culture,** which refers to "the cultural process whereby people create or ascribe meaning to their activities and artifacts."[14] Popular cul-ture is best understood as an act of **symbolic representation and inter-pretation,** which refers to the process by which humans assign ideas, qualities, and other forms of meaning to symbols that differ from their literal sense.[15] Mass media facilitate the process by which audiences assign meaning.

All media have some message, but as the communication thinker Marshall McLuhan's famous "the medium is the message" phrase notes, that is characterized by the content and the medium.[16] That is to say that media are not neutral, they communicate messages. Consider the litany of photos shared in social media and text messaging. They are commu-nicating a message. For example, if a picture is taken with bright light it communicates something different than if it is taken in the dark. The same is true for images that are taken close up or far away. Audio is another way in which media communicate messages. For example, tele-vision and radio have long used laugh tracks to subtly tell audiences when they are supposed to laugh. Similarly, film relies on sound effects and carefully composed soundtracks. Think of the jarring high-pitch sound when you are looking at a dark screen. Chances are it is a horror film, and the uncomfortable sound coupled with the feeling of being able to see nothing channels emotions of fear in the audience. Video games are no different, relying on faster music to provide a sense of urgency or importance to something that has transpired in the game. Finally, pod-casters will use additional sounds such as crunching leaves to demonstrate that they are walking in a wooded area. Podcasters can also make the audience feel the distance between the program's hosts if they muffle and drop the audio on one person's voice to make them sound further away. This provides the illusion that the audience and the one host are closer and everyone else is further away.

McLuhan's famed quote explains that each medium's content takes the form of the message, but the character of the medium is an entirely dif-ferent yet influential message that is overlooked. For example, the advent of the print media enabled knowledge and news to reach an audience previously thought impossible. Similarly, the advent of the internet saw the fragmentation of shared experience and culture into sub-cultures. These are powerful phenomena made possible by the medium regardless of messages invested in the individual pieces of content. More formerly, McLuhan's statement points to semiotics theory, which contends that "each medium has its own language with specific grammar and semantics."[17] Because this language can be complex, critical scholars decode the medium and the message. To **decode** is to convert complex ideas or information into digestible or understandable language.

Media messages are given meaning through the use of codes and conventions that comprise genres that are unique to each medium. In a media context, **genre** refers to "a distinctive type of text that is known and used by members of a community or social group as a routinized linguistic practice to achieve recurrent and socially recognized communicative tasks."[18] Each media genre is defined by a select set of features and is unique to a particular medium. Each genre has its own codes and conventions which are the language of media. In terms of media, **codes** refer to "a set of practices familiar to users of the medium operating within a broad cultural framework and it is a basic element of communication "activated in various communication acts."[19] Media **conventions** are the traditional or agreed upon practices for media production in a particular medium. They are how media producers organize and utilize codes to communicate and influence audiences' interpretation of their content.[20] Therefore, by identifying the genre of a media text, users can analyze the codes more easily. Once users recognize the movie that they are watching is a horror genre, then they are less likely to expect to laugh or believe that it is real.

Scholars have long argued that mass media representations are not neutral entertainment, but influential messaging.[21] As George Gerbner's **cultivation theory** explains, our perception of the world is framed by the media we consume. Indeed, relying on the dominant medium of his time, he argued that the more television viewers watch the more they see the actual or "real world" through the lens of the television.[22] He noted the power of television did not influence the individual, but the larger culture. According to Gerbner, television cultivated a homogenous view of the world among a diverse audience, something he referred to as "mainstreaming." Mainstreaming is best understood as "the blurring, blending, and bending process by which heavy TV viewers from disparate groups develop a common outlook through constant exposure to the same images and labels."[23] According to Gerbner, mass media procure a "mean world syndrome" in audiences, where they develop a "cynical mindset of general mistrust of others …"[24] The more that mass media convinces audiences that its representations are the real world, the more likely audiences are to succumb to mass media messaging.[25] Scholar and cultural critic Henry Giroux has referred to this as Hollywood's public pedagogy.[26] He explains that:

> by defining itself almost exclusively as entertainment, the movie industry conceals the political and ideological nature of the pedagogical work it performs …. As forms of public pedagogy, films must

be understood in terms of their political and educational character and how they align with broader social, racial, economic, class, and institutional configurations.[27]

Giroux illuminates the ways in which the public's understanding of their world is shaped by media.

Mass media have longed served to calcify racism through the spread of racist stereotypes. From the 1915 *Birth of a Nation*, which celebrated the KKK for suppressing black equality and civil rights, to the 1933 film *King Kong*, which was a racist analogy for demeaning black masculinity and interracial relationships. Further, late 20th century television shows like *Cops* narrowly defined blacks as criminals, and well into the 21st century, crime drama programs on Netflix, NBC and ABC overwhelmingly reduced people of color to depictions of criminals.[28] Among other factors, these disquieting messages perpetuate and normalize racism. In order to effectively engage in critical thinking and constructive discourse, we must share common evidence even if we disagree on what the evidence means. This involves investigating the evidence. In terms of media text, users must consider the process behind the production and dissemination of content.

Critical Media Literacy

Rather than, refrain from engaging with media, scholars argue that citizens can become more responsible media users and creators when they are media literate. Starting in 1993, the U.S. defined media literacy as "the ability to access, analyze, evaluate, create, and act using all forms of communication."[29] The four approaches to media literacy include:[30]

- **Protectionist approach:** This emerged out of a fear of media, and aims to protect or inoculate audiences, especially children, against the dangers of media content such as pornography and violence, A protectionist approach posits that audiences are powerless against media manipulation and addiction. It is criticized for discussing media audiences as passive victims rather than active participants because this implies that audiences have no power.

- **Arts education approach:** Values the aesthetic qualities of media and the arts; encourages creativity and self-expression through creating art and media; and integrates pleasure and popular culture into media analysis. However, it is criticized for being too technical and lacking critical analysis.

- **Media education approach:** Expands audiences' understanding of how they communicate and engage with media, but seeks political neutrality. As a result, it is criticized for mitigating the transformative potential of media literacy to become a powerful tool to challenge oppression and strengthen democracy.

- **Critical media literacy (CML) approach:** Applies critical theory to media literacy. It examines the representations and ideologies that shape media messages.[31] The goal of critical scholars is to liberate audiences from dominant messaging to achieve social justice.[32]**Social justice** refers to "the minimization of social and economic conditions that adversely affect the health of individuals and communities."[33] CML emerged from a blend of critical theory in education and the field of cultural studies.[34] As a scholarly discipline, **cultural studies** is useful in helping audiences understand the power-dynamics vested in mass media and popular culture because it reveals the political dynamics, historical origins, and defining characteristics of contemporary culture.[35] The steering committee of the 2021 Critical Media Literacy Conference of the Americas defined CML by stating:

> The goal of critical media literacy is to engage with media through critically examining representations, systems, structures, ideologies, and power dynamics that shape and reproduce culture and society. It is an inquiry-based process for analyzing and creating media by interrogating the relationships between power and knowledge. Critical media literacy is a dialogical process for social and environmental justice that incorporates Paulo Freire's (1970) notion of praxis, "reflection and action upon the world in order to transform it" (p. 36). This pedagogical project questions representations of class, gender, race, sexuality and other forms of identity and challenges media messages that reproduce oppression and discrimination. It celebrates positive representations and beneficial aspects of media while challenging problems and negative consequences, recognizing media are never neutral. Critical media literacy is a transformative pedagogy for developing and empowering critical, caring, nurturing, and conscientious people.[36]

As noted earlier, critical theory is a central component of critical thinking because it allows for an analysis of how systems of power shape knowledge. It is true that media texts are carefully produced by teams of people. However, CML reminds users that they do not have to agree with, believe, or even fully understand those messages. The power of audiences of interpret messages and create their own meaning is best understood through the process of encoding/decoding.

The encoding/decoding model was first proposed by British media scholar Stuart Hall in the early 1970s.[37] Hall, who was mostly focused on television, argued that texts were embedded with particular messages as part of their production, and audiences could decode those messages to make sense of them. In addition to understanding the message from the media producer (**encoding**), Hall argued that individual audience members could and do bring their own meaning to media texts (**decoding**). Audiences have the power to believe, accept, reject, or reinterpret the intended meaning of a media message. Hall's encoding/decoding model stands in stark contrast to the protectionist model, which contends that audiences are unable to resist media messages.

A protectionist approach runs antithetical to critical thinking because it ignores an audiences' ability to decode messages. Although they share an appreciation for the beauty and limited utility of media, the arts and education and media literacy movement approaches do not adequately explore the power ensconced in media. A critical approach allows users to not only investigate the power dynamics invested in mass media, but explore their own power to negotiate their relationship with and the influence of mass media. As a result, CML is the most conducive media literacy approach for critical thinkers. The remainder of this text will use a CML approach to analyzing mass media and popular culture.

Critically Thinking About Media, Marketing, and Public Relations

Most media are commercial, even media that seem to be free such as radio or Google, and that is why it is important to analyze the relationship between marketing and media. **Marketing** is the process of planning, conceiving, executing, and pricing of ideas, goods, and services.[38] Marketing can be direct or indirect. **Direct marketing** refers to "direct communications with carefully targeted individual customers to obtain an immediate response and to cultivate lasting customer relationships."[39] Some examples of direct marketing include mail, telemarketing, email marketing, and text (SMS) marketing. **Indirect marketing** refers to promotions that associate the product with another product or activity.[40] For example, a product can be introduced to a sports audience during a sports contest so the audience will associate their positive feelings about sports with the product. Commonly, celebrity endorsements are used where the audiences' warm perception of the celebrity is linked to the product that the celebrity is endorsing. The advent of online marketing moved marketing techniques beyond newspapers, radio, television, magazines, and signs into social media, GPS, customer reviews, and mobile apps. The digital era has allowed for the proliferation of **influencer marketing**, which relies on product endorsements and placement from people, often celebrities, and organizations who possess social influence over users.[41]

The marketing industry convinces audiences to purchase their product or service through advertising. **Advertisements** are considered "any paid form of non-personal presentation and promotion of ideas, goods, or services by an identified sponsor."[42] In order to procure a purchase form an advertisement, Vance Packard's 1957 *The Hidden Persuaders* drew upon Abraham Maslow in his 1943 hierarchy to identify human needs that advertisers exploit or excite: Creative outlets, ego-gratification, emotional, love, objects, reassurance of worth, security, sense of power, sense of roots, and immortality.[43] A few of the techniques that advertisers use to compel these needs are:

- **Anthropomorphism** – non-humans, beings or things being portrayed as having human qualities or characteristics.
- **Anti-consumerism or anti-advertising** – where the advertiser makes the viewer feel they are not being advertised to.
- **Misleading visuals** – portray a product such as food or a resort in a way that differs from its actual appearance.
- **Native advertising** – or sponsored content, occurs when an advertisement is constructed in a way that adheres to a platform so that users conflate the advertisement for platform content.
- **Social proof** – occurs when the popularity of the company or product is said to be proof of its effectiveness.
- **Suggested sex appeal** – occurs when advertisers insinuate that buying a product increases potential for sexual activity.

CML scholars contend that audiences are not beholden to media producer's messages. Yes, audiences are often influenced by ads, in fact that is why advertisers spend billions of dollars on advertisements annually. However, humans have agency and can resist any media messages. Marketing messages are not all powerful, nor are they without any influence. Audiences have the power to interpret the content for what it is: Marketing. However, this requires asking a series of investigative questions provided by the University of Massachusetts, Amherst, Media Education Foundation's "Deconstructing An Advertisement" concerning:[44]

- Aesthetics;
- the representation and depiction of people and their behavior and attitudes;
- the representation and depiction gender, race, class, age, and other identities;
- camera angles in terms of close versus far, down versus up;
- the use of natural and artificial lighting;
- the use of brightness and darkness;
- the color choices;
- the use of shadows;
- the font and word choices.

Then look deeper than its effort to sell a product or promote a policy. You can attain a comprehensive understanding if you consider:

- What is being sold or promoted?
- Do you find the person, policy, or product appealing?
- Who is the target audience for this content?
- What feelings or emotions is the ad trying to associate with the content? Did it work? How do I feel?

After making these observations consider why these choices were made by evaluating the **assumptions** – which refers to something that is accepted as true or as certain without proof – made in the content by asking:

- What assumptions does the content make about gender, race, class, age, and other identities?
- Are these assumptions realistic? Why or why not?
- Do these assumptions reinforce or challenge power structures?
- What ideologies are expressed in the content?
- Do those ideologies reflect or contradict your lived experience?

Marketers have to purchase time or space for their advertisement in mass media platforms. Rather than rely on buying time or space, **public relations** (PR) seeks to influence media makers to adopt or echo their view point, information, or perspective. It refers to the "communication relationship between organizations and individual or public."[45] This is not a new practice, as noted above, but the degree to which our discourses are influenced by marketing and public relations, what early advertising titans like Sigmund Freud's nephew Edward Bernays literally called propaganda in his 1928 book of the same name, cannot be overstated. Bernays wrote at length on matters relating to the fashioning of public opinion and the engineering of consent and basically pioneered the professional field of public relations itself.[46] PR firms seek to manage the perception of their clients and they constituted a $14 billion industry in 2016.[47] According to sociologist Peter Phillips, the three largest in the U.S. are Omnicom Public Relations Group, WPP, and The Interpublic Group of Companies.[48] They each have hundreds of smaller propaganda firms that work under their corporate umbrella.[49] They represent products and governments to serve the economic and political interests of their clients.[50] There are usually three elements to a PR campaign: Identifying an objective, selecting a message that will achieve that objective, and communicating that message to the suitable audience.[51] The tools used by PR firms include: Press releases, press kits, tip sheets and newsletters, bylined articles, awards, online influencers, special events, trade shows/conferences, and speeches.

Public marketing can be very influential. In fact, an internal study from the oil and natural resource company Exxon in 1977 concluded that climate change was occurring, and that their industry was partially responsible.[52] It would be almost four decades before Exxon (then ExxonMobil) would reveal this study following a report from a climate change investigation. Until then, ExxonMobil spent decades conducting a PR campaign that disseminated misleading and false information that denied the existence of climate change and their industry's contributions to the problem.[53] The goal was not to convince everyone that climate change was false. The actual goal was to plant doubt because when people are in doubt, they remain docile and avoid taking action. Exxon went so far as to set up a front organization in the Heartland Institute, which collected money from libertarian contributors like the Koch Bros. and other titans of the fossil fuel industry in an ongoing attempt to cast doubt that climate change was real, and was related to human activities. Shell Oil was found guilty of a similar practice through the same time period.[54] This practice has been replicated from the corporate playbooks of big tobacco, asbestos and sugar industries, and many more, all documented in scholarly works like *Doubt is Their Product*, and *Merchants of Doubt*. [55]

Just as media has the power to cultivate widespread denial of climate change, users have the power to resist these messages. One of the most famous historical examples are the Yes Men, who use culture jamming as a form of counter public relations. **Culture jamming** refers to

> a symbolic strategy by way of which anti-corporate activists make use of diverse artistic techniques (e.g., appropriation, collage, ironic inversion, juxtaposition) to change the original discourse of corporate advertising by altering corporate symbols (logos, slogans, etc.) visually and thus giving them a new meaning.[56]

In 2010, the Yes Men created a fake webpage that posed as a Chevron corporation website that argued "Oil Companies Should Clean Up Their Messes." The website promised that Chevron would and should take responsibility for the $27 billion clean-up costs stemming from their pollution in Ecuador. The real Chevron Corporation was tied up with litigation, trying to avoid paying for these costs. However, the Yes Men's PR stunt worked as many reported it as coming from the Chevron Corporation.[57] As a result, it forced a discussion about the complacency of these companies regarding ecological disasters into the press. Critically analyzing media is not limited to identifying marketing strategies or fact-checking the veracity of the messages, but investing the power-dynamics that shape these practices.

In a more recent example, Change the Ref, an organization founded by Manuel and Patricia Oliver after their son Joaquin "Guac" was killed in a

2018 school shooting at Marjory Stoneman Douglas High School in Parkland, culturally jammed the National Rifle Association (NRA). The NRA has long been resistant to gun regulation, pitting them at odds with those seeking gun regulation in response to school shootings. In June of 2021, Change the Ref invited David Keene, a former NRA president and current board member of the gun rights group, to give a graduation speech at the James Madison Academy. Keene explained, "An overwhelming majority of you will go on to college, while others may decide their dream dictates a different route to success," said Keene. "My advice to you is simple enough: follow your dream and make it a reality." His speech was actually given to a lot of 3,044 empty chairs, each of which represented the estimated number of children who would have graduated in 2021 had it not been for gun violence.[58]

Ideology and Political Economy of Mass Media

CML scholars Douglas Kellner and Jeff Share explain that "media messages and the medium through which they travel always have a bias and support and/or challenge dominant hierarchies of power, privilege, and pleasure."[59] CML employs intersectional frameworks to look for the ways in which the dominant ideologies of race, class, gender, and sexuality are fortified through media messaging and representation.[60] CML's analysis decodes media by analyzing the message and the medium, the process, representations, the audience, and the political economy to reveal issues of ideology, power, and pleasure in the texts.[61]

A critical approach to media analyzes how dominant ideologies communicated in mass media manifest in popular culture. As a reminder, **ideology** refers to "a systematically distorted or false picture of reality, one that benefits one group's interests over another's."[62] In addition to their invisibility, the process of elucidating ideologies in mass media is further complicated by communication practices of obfuscation. Former Republican political strategist Lee Atwater revealed the ways in which dominant ideologies, in this case white supremacy, are obfuscated in mass media communications. Atwater explained that in the 1960s, commentators, scholars, and critics had decided that racist rhetoric was no longer tolerated. In response, Atwater explains that he worked to spread white supremacist ideology without using directly racist language:

> You start out in 1954 by saying, '[n-word], [n-word], [n-word].' By 1968 you can't say '[n-word]' – that hurts you, backfires. So you say stuff like, uh, forced busing, states' rights, and all that stuff, and you're getting so abstract. Now, you're talking about cutting taxes, and all these things you're talking about are totally economic things and a byproduct of them is, blacks get hurt worse than whites ....'We want

to cut this,' is much more abstract than even the busing thing, uh, and a hell of a lot more abstract than '[n-word], [n-word].'[63]

Atwater's admission revealed the ways in which white supremacist ideology can permeate in media without overtly racist language.

Another earlier example of this, during the presidency of Richard Nixon (which influenced people like Lee Atwater), presidential aide John Ehrlichman revealed the so-called war on drugs was a ruse, a cover for criminalizing minorities and political dissent. He noted to journalist Dan Baum in 1994, later writing for *Harpers*,

> The Nixon campaign in 1968, and the Nixon White House after that, had two enemies: the antiwar left and black people. You understand what I'm saying? We knew we couldn't make it illegal to be either against the war or black, but by getting the public to associate the hippies with marijuana and blacks with heroin, and then criminalizing both heavily, we could disrupt those communities. We could arrest their leaders, raid their homes, break up their meetings, and vilify them night after night on the evening news. Did we know we were lying about the drugs? Of course we did.[64]

Further interests of mass media producers and their political proxies are revealed through an analysis of the political economy of media. **Political economy** refers to "research which attempts to answer simultaneously two central questions: how do institutions evolve in response to individual incentives, strategies, and choices, and how do institutions affect the performance of political and economic systems?"[65] The political economy of media refers to the production and market aspects of media and their relationship with culture, law, and government. The dearth of media owners is accompanied by a homogeneity of racial and gender identities in media ownership. According to the FCC, as late as 2011, 70 percent of media companies, 26.6 were owned in part by a white person, and only 4 percent of media companies were owned by people of color. At the same time, males owned nearly 65 percent of media companies and were co-owners in 28 percent of media companies leaving women to solely own just fewer than 7 percent of media companies.[66]

As cultural studies scholar Stuart Hall notes, in media, ideologies are normalized to the point that they are treated as the objective or normal position because they are introduced as "common sense."[67] This process is illustrated in David Sirota's *Back to Our Future: How the 1980s Explains the World We Live in Now – Our Culture, Our Politics, Our Everything*, which chronicles how contemporary culture reflects the dominant economic and political ideologies invested in 1980s popular culture.[68] Sirota argues that the ideological support for militarism during the War on Terror was aided by war films. He points out that since the makers of blockbuster films such as *Top Gun* and the *Hunt for Red October* worked with the Pentagon in the 1980s, Hollywood will not fund films unless the Pentagon approves them. Their approval results in access to military equipment that attracts movie going audiences, but in exchange the Pentagon edits scripts to make them favorable toward the military's image and militarism.[69]

Sirota also noted, years before Donald Trump was elected president, that 1980s popular culture sought to normalize conservative ideology with shows such as *Family Ties*, which depicted old liberals as weak and anachronistic compared to conservatives who were portrayed as young, hip, and realistic. Advertisements like Nike's "Just Do it" fed into the hedonistic individualism at the center of 1980s conservative ideology. The shift to conservative ideology was made possible, in part, due to mass media re-reframing the 1950s — an era that preceded the social progress of the 1960s — to America's golden era. Movies like *Back to The Future* portrayed the 1950s as the best time in American History despite the red scare and segregation policies of the era. Tapping into the desire to revert to a better time, Ronald Reagan's 1980 presidential campaign phrase was "Let's Make America Great Again." Just as Reagan had done, Trump used the same phrase to perpetuate the mythology of the 1950s.[70]

The popular culture, or entertainment industry, can insidiously infuse erroneous narratives in the minds of its consumers seemingly innocuously, especially if repeating commonly held notions and stereotypes. If movies and shows are to whisk us away from our daily grinds, audiences may not scrutinize the content the same way they may a news article, or obvious argument. However, styles of presentation from the entertainment business have long infiltrated news programs. In the quest of ratings, many news organizations have to resorted to **infotainment** approaches to keep audiences, and thus advertising dollars. Infotainment is informative in content, yet entertaining in content selection and delivery.[71]

Just as there is information, **misinformation** (erroneous information), and **disinformation** (purposely deceptive information), there could be categories of "misinfotainment" and "disinfotainment" applied to popular culture. The former of which may be more a result of feel-good stories buttressing status quo values, historical fiction, for example, which may innocently distort or ignore the actual record to tell another, more popular or "feel-good" story. Disinfotainment is more like propaganda, perpetuating past falsehoods, invoking powerful emotion and mythology, that act to distort and censor the historical factual record, or even rewrite history. **Propaganda**, as defined by communication scholars Garth S. Jowett and Victoria O'Donnell, "means to disseminate or promote particular ideas ... to identify a message as propaganda is to suggest something negative and dishonest."[72] The term is associated with an intent to control messaging in an effort "to alter or maintain a balance of power that advantageous to the propagandist."[73] Jowett and O'Donnell further elaborate on three types of propaganda referred to as White, Black, and Gray. *White* propaganda is from an identifiable source and is accurate in its messaging, though may not be in the fullest context. It aims to appear good, just, and proper, and acts to build credibility with favorable audiences. *Black* propaganda is from a concealed of false/flawed source that peddles disinformation. It fosters "the big lie," which is an untruth that is central to the creation of other untruths.[74] *Gray* propaganda is somewhere in between the two. According to Jowett and O'Donnell, "the source may or may not be correctly identified, and the accuracy of the information is uncertain."[75] It can also be used "to embarrass an enemy or competitor."[76]

Films like *Argo* or *Black Hawk Down* about U.S. foreign policy can serve as forms of Gray propaganda, promoting revisionist historiography by augmenting exceptionalist mythologies, while not being totally false, or biopics like *Christopher Columbus: The Discovery* that largely block out controversial details while highlighting favorable ones, sometimes even fabricating them. Additionally, the entire field of documentary films has exploded over the past decade, which is both welcome and problematic as these films purport to be didactic, nonfictional accounts of real events or people. However, these films can often amount to hagiographic, cherry-picked narratives that reinforce heroic interpretations of otherwise problematic or controversial characters, or turn into hit pieces or screeds designed to cast aspersions or leave audiences with negative impressions. It may not even be the case that material presented in documentaries is false, but it may be one-sided, or partial in its presentation, which is a form of propaganda. It is through these pervasive forms of infotainment that many can be manipulated, or be led to unquestioningly accept things that have not been proven with evidence, to accept prevailing or dominant ideologies and representations that support the status quo. It is important to remember that most Hollywood productions are not historical or journalistic documentaries, and thus, poetic license amounts to historical revisionism in many cases. Entertainment can be powerful propaganda as it appeals to emotions and disarms the critical mind.

Other examples of infotainment as propaganda and distraction include what media scholars Brad Waite and Sara Brooker called **humilitainment**, which they defined as programs designed to showcase human failings, or that find joy in the humiliation of others. The term is somewhat related to "schadenfreude," a German compound discussed earlier, that describes finding joy in others' pain. Examples are TV shows like *The Apprentice*, where Donald Trump took great glee in firing people, or *American Idol*, where poor performances of amateur singers were widely mocked and became viral in media.[77] More recently, Netflix reality TV hits like *Tiger King: Murder, Mayhem, and Madness* captured audiences like a bad accident, one from which people just could not look away. If another type of infotainment transcends this and devolves more into the macabre it would be what British journalist Mick Hume calls "mourning sickness" or "recreational grieving." This is the phenomenon in popular culture where audiences are obsessed with the demise of celebrities of any stripe, especially if their deaths were particularly tragic and controversial. Patrick West, author of the pamphlet *Conspicuous Compassion*, calls it **grief porn**, where public display of mourning for strangers becomes an "enjoyable event, much like going to a football match or the last night of the proms."[78] Examples of such displays include the highspeed paparazzi chase involving Princess Diana, the overdose deaths of Michael Jackson or Anna Nicole Smith (and subsequent anniversaries of those deaths), or bizarre autoerotic asphyxiation "accidental" suicides of actors like David Carradine. Grief porn even extends itself to being infatuated with gruesome details of obituaries written more like gossip columns, and even to anniversaries of celebrity deaths. In short, there is no basement to the debasement in this kind of media, largely designed to capture audiences for advertisers and celebrate the worst in humankind, all on the way to the bank.[79]

Representation

In addition to revealing the ways in which dominant ideologies are normalized through popular culture, critical scholars deconstruct the power-dynamics vested in mass media representations. CML scholars contend that the representation of identity groups in mass media can be an expression of power that solidifies power relations.[80] **Representation** refers to "the way images and language actively construct meanings according to sets of conventions shared by and familiar to makers and audiences."[81] Scholar bell hooks explains that through their representations, mass media convince audiences that the poor, people of color, ethnic minorities, women, and non-heterosexuals have limited value, and are outsiders.[82] hooks refers to this as "White supremacist capitalist patriarchy." Rather than look at representations on a case-by-case basis, hooks argues that the expression of dominant ideologies in media are best understood through an examination of problematic patterns[83] such as the ways that women are over-sexualized in order to placate male fantasies, and black men are often villainized to perpetuate white audiences' fears about black criminals.[84] These representative patterns result in the development of **stereotypes** which are "the attributes that people believe characterize a group of people."[85] Media makers also utilize archetypes to assist audiences in making sense of a story or role. However, these categories are fluid. Audiences will have different interpretations, and one person's archetype is another person's stereotype. An analysis of media patterns reveals the following dominant stereotypes:

Gender/Sexuality Stereotypes

- **Bad boy** – a womanizing macho rogue male.
- **Cat lady** – an eccentric and often old woman who lives alone with many cats.
- **Co-dependent woman** – a woman who is willing to put everything on hold, including her career, because she feels like she needs a man.
- **Damsel in distress** – a gorgeous girl in need of rescue.
- **Dragon lady** – an Asian woman who is domineering and mysterious, but often deceitful as well.
- **Dumb blonde** – a striking blonde-haired young woman who frequently demonstrates her lack of common sense.
- **Farmer's daughter** – a naïve and desirable woman with conservative home values.
- **Femme fatale** – a mysterious and seductive self-interested woman, who's not afraid to hurt, punish, or murder any man that gets in her way.
- **Final girl** – the last woman alive or standing in a horror film after all other characters have been eradicated.
- **Gentle giant** – a large man who induces fear through appearance, but love through their actions.
- **Gentleman thief** – an elegant thief who tries to avoid violence and be well mannered.
- **Girl next door** – a woman with a wholesome demeanor whose appearance is viewed as average or reasonably attractive.
- **Hardboiled detective** – a heavy-drinking detective made bitter and cynical after years of exposure to violence and corruption.
- **Hooker with a heart of gold** – her soul's ability to remain pure, after she sells her body, is made apparent by societal expectations she overcomes to help the protagonist.
- **Hotshot** – a risk-taking and impulsive macho character noted for their recklessness.
- **Housewife** – a mother and wife who is busy with housework.
- **Jock** – a male athlete whose muscular physique came at the expense of intelligence.
- **Materialistic woman** – a woman so obsessed with material goods, such as diamonds or handbags, she will give up anything in return.
- **Mean popular girl** – an attractive girl whose popularity in school is used as a pretext to mistreat and bully others.
- **Mother-in-law** – another character's spouse's mother who is frequently disapproving of her daughter/son-in-law.

- **Mother's boy** – a boy who is so attached to his mother that he spends inordinate amounts of time considering her feelings and desires before he engages in his own pursuits.
- **Nice guy who finishes last** – a genial but modest and selfless character who drops everything to pursue a woman, whom he fails to develop a relationship with.
- **Over-the-top gay man** – a loud and flamboyant sexualized gay character who treats every scene as if it is a Broadway musical.
- **Plain Jane** – an unassuming and homely woman who provides both a comic relief and a warm heart.
- **Prince charming** – a man who rescues the damsel in distress.
- **Schoolma'am** – a modestly dressed young school teacher on the frontier.
- **Sexy female foreigner** – a character who displays a heavy accent, usually from Europe, and is sexually aggressive.

Race/Ethnicity Stereotypes

- **Angry black woman** – an assertive and loud black woman whose overbearing attitude results in nagging and emasculating a male character.
- **Ethnic terrorist** – through appearance, accent, and language, this violent character demonstrates a disdain for the U.S. and a preference for violence.
- **Funny minority** – a non-white background character who provides comedy relief to the white-centered storyline.
- **Immigrant convenience store owner** – a convenience store owner who through appearance, accent, and language demonstrates they are from somewhere outside the U.S.
- **Italian-American mobster** – family-oriented and pasta-loving character who is involved in illegal activity that most often includes the mafia.
- **Latina maid** – Latinx women are often portrayed as maid staff and sometimes act as the funny minority as well.
- **Magical negro** – a black person whose mystical powers end up benefitting a white protagonist.
- **Mammy archetype** – a portly and homely black woman with a positive demeanor.
- **Neurotic Jew** – a Jewish character who talks a lot, is stingy, and is a hypochondriac who is often in therapy.
- **Noble savage** – an "uncivilized" indigenous person who is uncorrupted after their introduction to civilized society.
- **Wise old Asian who's actually really mean** – a character who appears to be wise and comforting, but has a secret and malicious dark side.

Class Stereotypes

- **Antihero** – a protagonist lacking the traditional heroic qualities of bravery, idealism, or morality.
- **Outlaw** – a romanticized crook whose charisma makes them appealing.
- **Preppy** – an upper-class character who displays wealth, intellect, and etiquette in their behavior, attitude, and appearance.
- **Rebel** – a nonconformist loner who rejects societal rule and conventions.
- **Reluctant hero** – a seemingly ordinary person who resists change until circumstances force him to rise to the occasion.
- **Rich old bitch** – a old rich woman who deals with her own unhappiness by spreading it to others.
- **Scrooge** – a wealthy, but stingy old person.
- **Sleazy lawyer** – a corrupt lawyer who relies on technicalities in the law to free obviously guilty individuals from punishment.
- **Sleazy politician** – a politician who will rest at nothing to realize their lust for power.
- **Yokel** – an unsophisticated person from the rural countryside who provides comic relief with their coarse manners and accent.
- **Yuppie** – a young urban professional whose main motivation in life is career and wealth.

Recently, discourses concerning the relationship between representation and power have focused upon the concept of cultural appropriation. **Cultural appropriation** refers to the process by which the dominant or privileged culture borrows or steal aspects of subaltern cultures without their consent, and use it outside its original context to further their self-interests. Some examples of cultural appropriation include:

- The use of chop-sticks in people's hair which is viewed as a cultural appropriation of Asian culture by westerners;
- the use of cornrows by whites, which is viewed as a cultural appropriation of African Americans;
- Halloween costumes such as white people dressing like Native Americans such as Pocahontas;
- sports mascots such as the Atlanta Braves which culturally appropriated Native Americans;
- white people wearing a sombrero to celebrate Cinco de Mayo Day.

Elvis Presley's appropriating of African American inspired blues music was an expression of cultural appropriation in mass media. So too was the long-standing practice of black and yellow face, which refers to whites painting their faces to appear African American and Asian respectively. Famous examples of yellow and black face include the Academy Award winning 1937 film *The Good Earth* and D.W. Griffith's 1915 racially charged *The Birth of a Nation* respectively. More recent accusations of cultural appropriation include:

- Miley Cyrus for hip-hop performances which appropriated African American culture;[86]
- Beyoncé and Cold Play for their "Hymn for the Weekend" music video which appropriated the nation of India;[87]
- Zac Efron for posting an Instagram photo of himself with dreadlocks with the caption "just for fun;"[88]
- Katy Perry for dressing as a geisha during a performance and another time for performing with cornrows;[89]
- J.K. Rowling for introducing Native American culture as synonymous with wizards;[90]
- Pharrell Williams for appearing on a magazine cover in a Native American headdress;
- Victoria's Secret model Karlie Kloss for walking the runway with a leopard print bikini and Native American headdress;[91]
- Selena Gomez for wearing a Hindu bindi during a performance at the 2017 MTV Movie Video Awards;[92]
- Wes Anderson's for perpetuating Asian stereotypes in Isle of Dogs;[93]
- Quentin Tarantino for appropriating black and Asian culture in *Django Unchained* and *Kill Bill* respectively.[94]

Debates persist about cultural appropriation. Some of the debates center on the definition. For example, Fordham University's Susan Scafidi, defined cultural appropriation as "taking intellectual property, traditional knowledge, cultural expressions, or artifacts from someone else's culture without permission ..."[95] Author Lionel Shriver took umbrage with the definition asking:

> However are we fiction writers to seek "permission" to use a character from another race or culture, or to employ the vernacular of a group to which we don't belong? Do we set up a stand on the corner and approach passers-by with a clipboard, getting signatures that grant limited rights to employ an Indonesian character in Chapter Twelve, the way political volunteers get a candidate on the ballot?[96]

Nonetheless, in digital spaces there are a series of articles claiming that one must seek permission from the culture they are appropriating. For example, an article titled "Examples of Cultural Appropriation and How to Avoid It" argues that before an individual engages in an act that could be considered cultural appropriation they should ask themselves "Do people who belong to that culture say it's offensive?"[97]

In response to cultural appropriation critics, on MTV, Franchesca Ramsey responds to common justifications (listed in bold) for cultural appropriation:[98]

1   **You're just looking for something to be offended by. It's just clothing, hairstyles, decorations, whatever … Don't you have something better to worry about?**; it is possible to care about more than one issue at one time. Furthermore, much of what is being appropriated, such as cornrows, has been used to penalize people of color, but is a source of strength for those with privilege.

2   **I'm just showing appreciation for the culture.** If you truly appreciate a culture, you need to have respect and understanding. Stripping culture symbols of their meaning in order to make media or sell products is a lack of respect.

3   **I don't find it offensive, and I asked someone from that culture and they said it was ok.** One person does not speak for an entire community.

4   **Fashion, art, film, music always borrows from other sources. It doesn't hurt anybody.** Cultural exchange does occur, but it has to be mutual and based on respect. When it perpetuates stereotypes, people are hurt.

5   **You're just trying to tell everyone what to think.** Marginalized people cannot force your thoughts or behavior only request changes out of respect.

6   **So because I'm white, I'm automatically racist?** This is not about beating up White people, even people of color can culturally appropriate.

7   **If Chinese people wear blue jeans, aren't they appropriating my culture? Or what about Black girls wearing blond weaves? Or how about speaking English?** No, that is **assimilation** not appropriation. Marginalized people often have to hide their culture and are sometimes forced adopt the dominant culture, assimilate, or risk further ostracization. For example, students have been suspended for speaking Spanish or indigenous language in U.S. schools.[99]

Cultural appropriation is not just about the message, but who has the power to create it. Critical scholars point out that the power dynamics complicate issues of appropriation. For example, the power dynamics are much different when a person of privilege, such as a white male is appropriating an under-privileged person, such as a woman of color, than the reverse. Audiences have the power to interpret representations how they choose, but they also need to question power. Does it also matter who is creating the representation? The same message from someone about their own culture is different than from somebody who is not. These are the layers of complexity that face audiences engaging in a critical analysis of media.

Audience Power

Critical media literacy empowers audiences to recognize the intended meaning of the messages while accounting for multiple contextual factors as they formulate their own interpretation. Critical scholars argue that there are three ways to read a media text: Dominant, alternative, and resistant readings. **Dominant readings** provide the most common and widely accepted interpretations of a given text. An **alternative reading** differs from the dominant reading, but does not challenge the dominant interpretation. Meanwhile, the resistant reading not only is different, but contradicts the dominant reading.[100] Teaching Tolerance, a social justice and anti-bias bastion of educator resources, explains that **resistant reading** requires users to

> analyze the dominant reading of a text and 'resist' it by engaging in alternative readings. Resistant readings scrutinize the beliefs and attitudes that typically go unexamined in a text, drawing attention to the gaps, silences and contradictions .... Resistant Reading combines analysis, synthesis, evaluation and creation. It also develops and assesses comprehension, as students must understand the text to successfully engage in an alternative reading.[101]

Example of resistant readings are:

- Reading Jack and the Bean Stalk as the story of a child, Jack, who trespassed and stole from the Giant, who seemingly has a reason to be angry;
- interpreting the movie *Top Gun* as a homosexual love story.[102]

Audiences have the power and autonomy to utilize critical frameworks to interpret media in a way that differs from the media producer's intended meaning.

However, mass media have the power to produce and disseminate contrived content that appropriate movements to dismantle dominant ideologies in mass media. To appropriate is to take something that belongs to others and make it one's own.[103] When this appropriation occurs for profit-making purposes it is known as **commodification**, which refers to "the process of assigning market value to goods or services that previously existed outside of the market."[104] For example, in 1990, feminist social critics like Camille Paglia, then professor at University of the Arts in Philadelphia, argued that performer and musician Madonna was in fact a true feminist for using her sexuality as she as she saw fit, reclaiming it in an empowering way that made her a cultural icon.[105] However, according to hooks, Madonna established herself as a feminist backlash to patriarchy, but she was commodified by the white supremacist capitalist patriarchy, resulting in her garnering wealth and power for the very system she sought to dismantle.[106] More recently, some have argued that former National Football League (NFL) quarterback Colin Kaepernick's protest, which saw players take a knee during the National Anthem of NFL games in solidarity against police violence against people of color, was appropriated and commodified by the Nike corporation to sell shoes and refurbish their image after human rights scandals and negatively impacted their public image and profit model.[107]

Conclusion

The power and process of mass media production reveal the ways in which dominant ideologies are communicated and normalized through popular culture. They also offer a potential explanation for why people's views of the world, and other humans, divert from reality. One has to wonder what influence these messages have on the Klansmen that Daryl Davis tries to reach. Nonetheless, Davis' story demonstrates that despite their power and influence, mass media have a formidable opponent when it comes to people practicing constructive dialogue. The next two chapters will apply this analysis to social media, advertising, and news content.

Notes

1   Nicholas Johnson, *Your Second Priority: A Former FCC Commissioner Speaks Out* (Morrisville, NC: Lulu Press), i.
2   Matt Taibbi, *Hate Inc: Why Today's Media Makes Us Despise One Another* (New York: OR Books, 2019).
3   Eli Pariser, *The Filter Bubble: How the New Personalized Web is Changing What We Read and How We Think* (London: Penguin, 2011); Siva Vaidhyanathan, *Anti-Social Media, How Facebook Disconnects Us and Undermines Democracy* (New York: Oxford University Press, 2018); Nolan Higdon, *The Anatomy of Fake News: A Critical News Literacy Education* (Oakland, CA: University of California Press, 2020).
4   Daryl Davis, "Why I, as a black man, attend KKK rallies," TEDxNaperville, *YouTube,* December 8, 2017, https://www.youtube.com/watch?v=ORp 3q1Oaezw.
5   Ibid.
6   Ibid.
7   Ibid.

8 Dwane Brown, "How one man convinced 200 Ku Klux Klan members to give up their robes," *NPR*, August 20, 2017, https://www.npr.org/2017/08/20/544861933/how-one-man-convinced-200-ku-klux-klan-members-to-give-up-their-robes.

9 Daryl Davis, "Why I, as a black man, attend KKK rallies," https://www.youtube.com/watch?v=ORp3q1Oaezw.

10 Ibid.

11 Nielson, "The Total Audience Report: Q1 2016," July 27, 2016, http://www.nielsen.com/us/en/insights/reports/2016/the-total-audience-report-q1-2016.html.

12 Leah Christian, Amy Mitchell, and Tom Rosentiel, "Mobile devices and news consumption: Some good signs for journalism," *Pew Research Center,* March 18, 2012, www.journalism.org/2012/03/18/mobile-devices-and-news-consumption-some-good-signs-for-journalism/1-23-percent-of-u-s-adults-get-news-on-at-least-two-digital-devices-300x155/.

13 Nickie Louise, "These 6 corporations control 90% of the media outlets in America," *Tech Startups,* September 18, 2020, https://techstartups.com/2020/09/18/6-corporations-control-90-media-america-illusion-choice-objectivity-2020/.

14 John Alt, "Popular culture and mass consumption: The motorcycle as cultural commodity," *Journal of Popular Culture* 15, no. 4 (1982): 129.

15 Richard Elliott, "Symbolic meaning and postmodern consumer culture," *Rethinking Marketing: Towards Critical Marketing Accountings* (1999): 112–125.

16 Marshall McLuhan, *Understanding Media: The Extensions of Man* (Cambridge, MA: MIT Press, 1964), 1.

17 Douglas Kellner and Jeff Share, *The Critical Media Literacy Guide: Engaging Media and Transforming Education* (Boston, MA: Brill Sense, 2019), 9.

18 Stefan Hauser, "Theoretical and methodological issues of a genre-based approach to contrastive media analysis," in *Contrastive Media Analysis: Approaches to Linguistic and Cultural Aspects of Mass Media Communication*, eds Stefan Hauser and Martin Luginbühl (Philadelphia, PA: John Benjamins Publishing, 2012), 220.

19 Kinga Kowalewska and Marta Koszko, "Social semiotics in visual communication applied in advertisements of banking products and services," *Scripta Neophilologica Posnaniensia* 15 (2015): 109.

20 Julie Coiro, "Exploring literacy on the Internet," *The Reading Teacher* 56, no. 5 (2003): 458–464.

21 Walter Lippmann, *Liberty and the News* (Princeton, NJ: Princeton University Press, 1920); W.W. Biddle, "A psychological definition of propaganda," *The Journal of Abnormal and Social Psychology* 26, no. 3, (1931): 283–295; "Whistleblowers Challenge Official Narrative on Syrian Chemical Weapons Attacks," *Project Censored*, March 29, 2021, https://www.projectcensored.org/whistleblowers-challenge-official-narrative-on-syrian-chemical-weapons-attacks/; Edward S. Herman and Noam Chomsky, *Manufacturing Consent: The Political Economy of the Mass Media* (New York: Pantheon Books, 1988); Christian Fuchs, "Propaganda 2.0: Herman and Chomsky's propaganda model in the age of the internet, big data and social media," in *The Propaganda Model Today: Filtering Perception and Awareness,* eds Joan Pedro-Carañana, Daniel Broudy, and Jeffery Klaehn (London: University of Westminster Press, 2018).

22 Em Griffin, Andrew Ledbetter, and Glenn Sparks, *A First Look at Communication Theory* (New York: McGraw-Hill, 2019), 359.

23   Ibid., 361.

24   Ibid., 364.

25   Ibid.

26   Henry A. Giroux, "Hollywood film as public pedagogy: Education in the crossfire," *Afterimage* 35, no. 5 (2008): 7.

27   Ibid.

28   Gail Dines, "King Kong and the white woman: Hustler magazine and the demonization of black masculinity," *Violence Against Women* 4, no. 3 (1998): 291–307; Paul McEwan, "Racist film: Teaching The Birth of a Nation," *Cinema Journal* 47, no. 1 (2007): 98–101; Paul G. Kooistra, John S. Mahoney, and Saundra D. Westervelt. "The world of crime according to cops," *Entertaining Crime: Television Reality Programs* (1998): 141–158; "Normalizing injustice: The dangerous misrepresentations that define television's scripted crime genre. A comprehensive study of how television's most popular genre excludes writers of color, miseducates people about the criminal justice system, and makes racial injustice acceptable," report by Color of Change and The USC Annenberg Norman Lear Center, January 2020, https://hollywood.colorofchange.org/crime-tv-report/.

29   Patricia Aufderheide, *Media Literacy. A Report of the National Leadership Conference on Media Literacy* (Aspen Institute, Communications and Society Program, 1755 Massachusetts Avenue, NW, Suite 501, Washington, DC 20036, 1993).

30   Nolan Higdon, Allison Butler, and J.D. Swerzenski, "Inspiration and motivation: The similarities and differences between critical and acritical media literacy," *Democratic Communique* 30, no. 1 (2021): 1.

31   Douglas Kellner and Jeff Share, *The Critical Media Literacy Guide: Engaging Media and Transforming Education* (Boston, MA: Brill Sense, 2019).

32   Ibid.

33   Dilworth-Anderson, Peggye, Geraldine Pierre, and Tandrea S. Hilliard. "Social justice, health disparities, and culture in the care of the elderly," *The Journal of Law, Medicine & Ethics* 40, no. 1 (2012): 27.

34   Douglas Kellner and Jeff Share, *The Critical Media Literacy Guide: Engaging Media and Transforming Education* (Boston, MA: Brill Sense, 2019), 8–9.

35   Kuan-Hsing Chen and David Morley, eds, *Stuart Hall: Critical Dialogues in Cultural Studies* (London: Routledge, 2006).

36   Critical Media Literacy of the Americas Steering Committee, "Call for proposals," *Critical Media Project*, 2021, https://criticalmediaproject.org/cmlca 2021proposals/.

37   Stuart Hall, "Encoding/decoding," in *Culture, Media, Language*, eds Stuart Hall, Dorothy Hobson, Andrew Lowe, and Paul Tillis (London: Hutchinson, 1980), 128–138.

38   Mawutor K. Glover, Joyce Obubuafo, Mathew O. Agyeman-Duah, Grace D. Doku, and Edinam K. Glover, "Constraints associated with the marketing channel of lettuce and cabbage trade in Ghana," *Journal of Agriculture and Sustainability* 10, no. 2 (2017).

39   Philip Kotler, Gary Armstrong, John Saunders, and Veronica Wong, *Principles of Marketing*, 4th European ed. (Harlow, UK: Pearson Education Limited, 2005), 829.

40   Dainora Grundey, "Global marketing ethics: Social and emotional-psychological issues in advertising to children," *Transformations in Business & Economics* 6, no. 2 (2007).

41   Xin Jean Lim, Aifa Rozaini bt Mohd Radzol, Jun-Hwa Cheah, and Mun Wai Wong, "The impact of social media influencers on purchase intention

and the mediation effect of customer attitude," *Asian Journal of Business Research* 7, no. 2 (2017): 19–36.

42 Jörg Müller, Florian Alt, and Daniel Michelis, "Pervasive advertising," in *Pervasive Advertising* (London: Springer, 2011), 1–29.

43 Chris Hackley, "Marketing psychology and the hidden persuaders," *The Psychologist* 20, no. 8 (2007): 488.

44 Media Education Foundation, "Deconstructing an advertisement," Media Education Foundation, 2005, https://www.mediaed.org/handouts/DeconstructinganAd.pdf.

45 G.A.O. Yan-bing, "Basic effect of public relations on college students' professional development," *Journal of Chengde Petroleum College* 2 (2010): 28.

46 Edward Bernays, *Crystalizing Pubic Opinion* (New York: Boni and Liveright, 1923); Edward Bernays, *Propaganda* (New York: Horace Liveright, 1928); Edward Bernays, *Public Relations* (Boston: Bellman, 1945); Edward Bernays, *The Engineering of Consent* (Norman, OK: University of Oklahoma Press, 1955).

47 USC Annenberg Center for Public Relations, "Global Communications Report Executive Summary," *USC Annenberg,* 2016, https://annenberg.usc.edu/sites/default/files/USC_REPORT_New.pdf.

48 Peter Phillips, *Giants: The Global Power Elite* (New York: Seven Stories Press, 2018).

49 Ibid.

50 Ibid.

51 John Lister, "Three characteristics of a public relations campaign small business," *Small Business,* March 12, 2019, https://smallbusiness.chron.com/three-characteristics-public-relations-campaign-24956.html#:~:text=Ultimately%20a%20public%20relations%20campaign,message%20to%20the%20appropriate%20audience.

52 Shannon Hall, "Exxon Knew about climate change almost 40 years ago: A new investigation shows the oil company understood the science before it became a public issue and spent millions to promote misinformation," *Scientific American,* October 26, 2015, https://www.scientificamerican.com/article/exxon-knew-about-climate-change-almost-40-years-ago/.

53 Ibid.

54 Damian Carrington and Jelmer Mommers, "'Shell knew': Oil giant's 1991 film warned of climate change danger," *The Guardian,* February 28, 2017, https://www.theguardian.com/environment/2017/feb/28/shell-knew-oil-giants-1991-film-warned-climate-change-danger.

55 Naomi Oreskes and Erik M. Conway, *Merchants of Doubt: How a Handful of Scientists Obscured the Truth on Issues from Tobacco Smoke to Climate Change* (New York: Bloomsbury, 2010); David Michaels, *Doubt is Their Product: How Industry's Assault on Science Threatens Your Health* (New York: Oxford University Press, 2008).

56 Eduardo Romanos Fraile, "Humor in the streets: The Spanish indignados," *Perspectives on Europe* 43, no. 2 (2013): 18.

57 David Zax, "Chevron's new ad campaign is a slick Yes Men hoax [Update] Part of the genius of the Yes Men is that they really know when to pull the trigger on a good prank. We bit," October 18, 2010, *Fast Company,* https://www.fastcompany.com/1695892/chevrons-new-ad-campaign-slick-yes-men-hoax-update.

58 Amber Jamieson, "A Parkland victim's dad tricked a former NRA President into speaking at a fake graduation," *BuzzFeed,* June 23, 2021, http

s://www.buzzfeednews.com/article/amberjamieson/nra-president-graduation-speech.

59 Douglas Kellner and Jeff Share, *The Critical Media Literacy Guide: Engaging Media and Transforming Education* (Boston, MA: Brill Sense, 2019), 8–9.

60 Ibid.

61 Douglas Kellner and Jeff Share, "Critical media education and radical democracy," in *The Routledge International Handbook of Critical Education,* eds Michael W. Apple, Wayne Au, and Luis Armando Gandin (New York: Routledge, 2009), 281–295.

62 Edward E. Sampson, "Cognitive psychology as ideology," *American Psychologist* 36, no. 7 (1981): 730.

63 Rick Perlstein, "Exclusive: Lee Atwater's infamous 1981 interview on the Southern Strategy. The forty-two-minute recording, acquired," *The Nation,* November 13, 2012, https://www.thenation.com/article/archive/exclusive-lee-atwaters-infamous-1981-interview-southern-strategy/.

64 Dan Baum, "Legalize it all," *Harper's Magazine,* April 2016, https://harpers.org/archive/2016/04/legalize-it-all/.

65 James E. Alt, and Alberto Alesina, "Political economy: An overview," *A New Handbook of Political Science* (1996): 645.

66 Chief of Media Bureau for the Federal Communications Commission, *Before the Federal Communications Commission,* Washington, D.C. 20554, November 14, 2012, transition.fcc.gov/Daily_Releases/Daily_Business/2012/db1114/DA-12-1667A1.pdf.

67 Stuart Hall, "The whites of their eyes," in *Gender, Race, and Class in Media: A Text-Reader,* eds Gail Dines and Jean M. Humez, 2nd ed. (London: Sage Publications, 2003), 89–93.

68 David Sirota, *Back to Our Future: How the 1980s Explains the World We Live in Now – Our Culture, Our Politics, Our Everything* (New York: Ballantine Books, 2011).

69 Ibid.

70 Ibid.

71 Mickey Huff and Andy Lee Roth, eds, *Censored 2013: Dispatches from the Media Revolution* (New York: Seven Stories Press, 2012), 153.

72 Garth S. Jowett and Victoria O'Donnell, *Propaganda and Persuasion,* 4th ed. (London: Sage Publications, 2006), 2.

73 Ibid., 3.

74 Ibid; Katherine A. Elder, "Propaganda for Kids: Comparing IS-Produced Propaganda to Depictions of Propaganda in The Hunger Games and Harry Potter Film Series." International Journal of Communication 12 (2018): 19.

75 Jowett and O'Donnell, 20.

76 Ibid.

77 Sarah Booker and Brad Waite, "Humilitainment? Lessons from 'The Apprentice': A reality television content analysis," Presented at the 17th Annual Convention of the American Psychological Society, Los Angeles, May 2005; Richard H. Smith, "Joy in another's shame: Humilitainment anyone?" *Psychology Today,* March 16, 2014, https://www.psychologytoday.com/us/blog/joy-and-pain/201403/joy-in-anothers-shame-humilitainment-anyone. See also Andy Lee Roth and Mickey Huff, eds, *Project Censored's State of the Free Press 2022* (Petaluma, CA: The Censored Press, 2021), chapter 3.

78 Mickey Huff and Peter Phillips, eds, *Censored 2011* (New York: Seven Stories Press, 2010), 165.

79 Ibid.

80   Gail Dines, Jean M. Humez, Bill Yousman, and Lori Bindig Yousman, *Gender, Race, and Class in Media: A Critical Reader*, 5th ed. (Thousand Oaks, CA: Sage Publications, 2018); Douglas Kellner and Jeff Share, *The Critical Media Literacy Guide: Engaging Media and Transforming Education* (Boston, MA: Brill, 2019).

81   Gillian Swanson, "Representation," in *The Media Studies Book: A Guide for Teachers*, ed. David Lusted (New York: Routledge Press, 1991), 123.

82   Dines, Humez, Yousman, and Bindig Yousman, *Gender, Race, and Class in Media.*

83   bell hooks, *Outlaw Culture: Resisting Representations* (New York: Routledge, 2006).

84   bell hooks, *Cultural Criticism and Transformation*, Media Education Foundation, 1997.

85   Stephanie Madon, "What do people believe about gay males? A study of stereotype content and strength," *Sex Roles* 37, no. 9 (1997): 666.

86   Brian Welk, "15 celebrities who have been accused of 'cultural appropriation'," *The Wrap*, July 9, 2018, https://www.thewrap.com/celebrities-who-have-been-accused-of-cultural-appropriation-photos/.

87   Ibid.

88   Ibid.

89   Ibid.

90   Ibid.

91   Ibid.

92   Ibid.

93   Zack Sharf, "'Isle of Dogs' critics slam the movie for 'ugly' cultural appropriation and whitewashing," *Business Insider,* March 23, 2018, https://www.businessinsider.com/isle-of-dogs-critics-slam-movie-for-ugly-cultural-appropriation-2018-3.

94   Jack Barth, "'Kill Bill' and cultural appropriation," *Jack Barth's Wordpress*, March 21, 2016, https://jackbarth.wordpress.com/2016/03/21/kill-bill-and-cultural-appropriation/; Tim Walker, "Quentin Tarantino accused of 'blaxploitation' by Spike Lee ... again," *Independent*, December 26, 2012, https://www.independent.co.uk/news/world/americas/quentin-tarantino-accused-of-blaxploitation-by-spike-lee-again-8431183.html.

95   Lionel Shriver, "Lionel Shriver's full speech: 'I hope the concept of cultural appropriation is a passing fad'," *The Guardian,* September 13, 2016, https://www.theguardian.com/commentisfree/2016/sep/13/lionel-shrivers-full-speech-i-hope-the-concept-of-cultural-appropriation-is-a-passing-fad.

96   Ibid.

97   "Examples of cultural appropriation and how to avoid it," *Your Dictionary*, https://examples.yourdictionary.com/cultural-appropriation-examples.html.

98   "7 myths about cultural appropriation debunked," *Critical Media Project*, https://criticalmediaproject.org/7-myths-about-cultural-appropriation-debunked-2/.

99   T.R. Reid, " Spanish at school translates to suspension," *Washington Post,* December 9, 2005, https://www.washingtonpost.com/archive/politics/2005/12/09/spanish-at-school-translates-to-suspension/8df9e017-f704-4a2b-af67-485d10316794/; "Student suspended for speaking native American language," *Indian Country Today*, February 8, 2012, https://indiancountrytoday.com/archive/student-suspended-for-speaking-native-american-language-f_5s-jHxAkuGfgKtnG_N-w#:~:text=After%20a%2012-year-old,past%20boarding%20school%20atrocities%20surfaced.

100 William A. Evans, "The interpretive turn in media research innovation, iteration, or illusion?" *Critical Studies in Media Communication* 7, no. 2 (1990): 147–168.

101 "Resistant reading," *Teaching Tolerance*, https://www.tolerance.org/classroom -resources/teaching-strategies/responding-to-the-readaloud-text/resistant-rea ding.

102 Tania Modleski, "Misogynist films: Teaching 'Top Gun'," *Cinema Journal* 47, no. 1 (2007): 101–105; Paul Burston, Paul Burston Nfa, and Colin Richardson, "Just a gigolo?: Narcissism, nellyism, and the 'new man' theme," in *A Queer Romance: Lesbians, Gay Men and Popular Culture*, eds Paul Burston and Colin Richardson (New York: Routledge, 2005), 131–143.

103 Maarten Overdijk and Wouter Van Diggelen, "Technology appropriation in face-to-face collaborative learning," in *Innovative Approaches for Learning and Knowledge Sharing, EC-TEL 2006 Workshops Proceedings*, pp. 89–96. 2006.

104 Nicole Constable, "The commodification of intimacy: Marriage, sex, and reproductive labor," *Annual Review of Anthropology* 38 (2009), 50.

105 Camille Paglia, "Madonna – finally, a real feminist," *New York Times*, December 14, 1990, https://www.nytimes.com/1990/12/14/opinion/ma donna-finally-a-real-feminist.html.

106 bell hooks, *Cultural Criticism and Transformation*, Media Education Foundation, 1997.

107 Joshua Hunt, "Colin Kaepernick, Nike, and the myth of good and bad companies: The brand's alignment with the embattled NFL star is nothing more than smart business," *The Atlantic*, September 5, 2018, https://www. theatlantic.com/business/archive/2018/09/nike-kaepernick/569371/.

Chapter 6

Critique Content
"Fake News" and Ethical Journalism

"Did you at the time believe that high-level Democrats and celebrities were worshipping Satan? Drinking the blood of children?" asked Anderson Cooper of CNN.[1] "Anderson, I thought you did that, and I would like to apologize for that right now. So, I apologize for thinking that you ate babies," responded Jitarth Jadeja.[2]

The 2021 CNN interview offered Jadeja an opportunity to apologize for believing the QAnon conspiracy. Sometimes referred to simply as "Q," it is a baseless conspiracy that posits there are a secret cabal of elite actors – which includes Satan-worshippers and a global child sex-trafficking ring of cannibalistic pedophiles – who colluded to undermine the presidency of Donald Trump while he was in office.[3]

> "You actually believed that I was drinking the blood of children?" Cooper asked.[4]
>
> "Yes, I did," Jadeja responded.[5]
>
> "Was it something about me that made you think that?" Cooper asked.[6]
>
> "It's because Q specifically mentioned you, and he mentioned you very early on, he mentioned you by name, and from there – he also talked about, like, for example, like, your family."[7]

The person named Q, who Jadeja was referencing, is a central actor in the conspiracy. Q communicates with believers through message boards on the social media website 4Chan.[8] Q, the name the persona uses on the message boards, purports to be a high-level federal government employee who is working tirelessly to expose the criminality of elites.[9] Q believers claimed that on March 4, 2021, Q would reveal themselves and expose the elite cabal and re-establish Trump as President.[10] The date came and went. Much like false prophesies of old, like the Millerites of the 1840s, or Heaven's Gate of the 1990s, or panic around Y2K, nothing prophesized occurred.

DOI: 10.4324/9781003250906-10

Although Jadeja eventually came to believe that the Q conspiracy was nonsense, many other users continue to consider Q's reporting to be legitimate news. When Cooper asked Jadeja if people still believe that Cooper is a blood drinking Satan-worshipper, Jadeja responded:

> "People still talk about that to this day …. There were posts about that just four days ago …. Some people thought you were a robot."[11]
> "You really believed this?" Cooper asked again. [12]
> "I didn't just believe that. I, at one stage, believed that QAnon was part of military intelligence, which is what he says, but, on top of that, that the people behind him were actually a group of fifth dimensional, interdimensional, extraterrestrial … aliens called blue avians," Jadeja said.

Part of the Q conspiracy claimed that Trump would declare a day of reckoning known as "the Storm."[13] On January 6, 2021, the U.S. Congress was scheduled to take part in the routine practice of certifying the 2020 presidential election results, which were in favor of Trump's rival, Joe Biden. Two weeks earlier, Trump tweeted "Statistically impossible to have lost the 2020 Election … Big protest in DC on January 6th. Be there, will be wild!"[14] On January 6, just a short distance from the U.S. Capitol building where Congress was slated to certify the election results, Trump spoke to a crowd of supporters stating, "We're going to walk down to the Capitol and we're going to cheer on our brave senators and Congressmen and women."[15] Moments later the crowd, which numbered in the thousands, headed toward the Capitol. Soon, an unknown, but substantial portion of the rally goers stormed the U.S. Capitol to stop the certification of Biden's election.[16] Some of them forced their way into the Capitol violently, while others were allowed in by the Capitol police.[17] Once inside, they made death threats, and clashed with authorities, causing 140 people to be injured and five others to die.[18] Reportedly, some attendees had planted bombs at the headquarters of the Democratic and Republican Party the night before in Washington D.C.[19] Almost four weeks after the events at the Capitol, in his interview with Cooper, Jadeja admitted "I was so far down in this conspiracy black hole that I was essentially picking and choosing whatever narrative that I wanted to believe in."

Jadeja's story stands in direct contradiction to the U.S. founders' contention that the existence of a free press would enable truth to penetrate falsehood. Although the founders were correct in asserting that a free press enables truth to enter the public sphere, they did not consider that a substantial portion of Americans may be unable to discern fact from fiction. Jadeja's story also stands in direct contradiction to those who conclude that certain people have become so unswerving in their commitment to falsehood that they can come to recognize truth. After all, just months earlier even Jadeja could not envisage rejecting Q and conversing civilly with Cooper. However, once equipped with critical thinking skills, people can attenuate the influence of misinformation and disinformation disguised as news. This chapter provides context for analyzing news content and information to determine its veracity.

The Free Press

In the U.S., the free press has great responsibility. Democracies view the press as an independent pillar of democracy that is "more important than they all" according to political theorist Edmund Burke.[20] The free press, which includes news organizations and outlets staffed by journalists, has five democratic functions:[21]

- **Marketplace of ideas:** The press offers a diverse set of facts, perspectives, and ideas for voters to consider when making their democratic decisions.
- **Agenda setter:** The press directs the public's focus on key issues and events.
- **Watchdog:** The press exposes corruption and holds the powerful accountable. In fact, the old adage is that "the job of the newspaper is to comfort the afflicted and afflict the comfortable"[22] is how fictional 19th century Mr. Dooley's assessment of newspapers is often remembered.[23]
- **Information disseminator:** The press has long acted as a tool of communication between the people and elected officials.
- **Public mobilization:** The press convinces the public about the policies and issues that are so important they require the public's involvement.

The functions of the press help them determine what news is worthy of their coverage, and by default, what is not. This is something that should be closely scrutinized by the public at large.

For their part, professional journalists aspire for **objectivity**, seeking to provide the public the facts, not opinion. Journalists collect information from their sources, whom they also protect. Those sources are then fact checked and vetted by editors before being presented to the public. Journalists use five criteria to determine if something is newsworthy:

- Is it new or timely?
- Is it unusual?
- Is it interesting to the target audience?
- Is it broadly significant?
- Does it have a human interest angle?

However, just because something is newsworthy does not make its publication inevitable.

Journalists, like many professions, have a code of ethics that helps them decide if it is ethical to publish a particular piece of content. With the professionalization of journalism in the mid-20th century, press outlets adopted codes of ethics for promoting responsible journalism. In fact, media scholar Alan Knight and his colleagues define a **journalist** as "anyone applying professional practices within recognized codes of ethics."[24] Journalists gather sources and transparently source them so the public can evaluate their reporting. They only report on what they have evidence for and they let the sources rather than their own bias guide their reporting. This is because journalists strive for objectivity, even if it is just an aspiration goal. It builds trust between them and the public in their reporting. They also have and dedicate their life to following a code of ethics. According to the Society of Professional Journalists, the practice of journalism is rooted in four main principles they call their Code of Ethics. Dating back to 1926, they have been adapted and modified over the years. These advise that ethical journalists ought to:

criteria for journalist

- **Seek truth and report it**: Ethical journalism should be accurate and fair. Journalists should be honest and courageous in gathering, reporting and interpreting information.
- **Minimize harm**: Ethical journalism treats sources, subjects, colleagues and members of the public as human beings deserving of respect.
- **Act independently**: The highest and primary obligation of ethical journalism is to serve the public.
- **Be accountable and transparent**: Ethical journalism means taking responsibility for one's work and explaining one's decisions to the public.[25]

Journalists are not the only people working at news outlets. Journalists often work with, and as a result are mistaken for, reporters, critics, and commentators. **Commentators and critics** are the individuals who comment on the news stories that someone else reported, such as Rachael Maddow of MSNBC, Sean Hannity of Fox News Channel, and Bakari Sellers of CNN. They are rarely onsite for the story, in real time or afterward. Rather than interview sources, critics and commentators talk to reporters or journalists who have interviewed sources. **Reporters** generally offer a timeline of events explaining the known and verified facts on a particular timeline. News anchors are sometimes accomplished journalists, but sometimes they are merely reading copy someone else has prepared. American media commentator George Snell explains reporters are well suited to provide the timeline of an event such as a plane crash, where a journalist goes beneath the reporting, providing investigative analysis and thoughtful commentary that contextualize the timeline.[26]

Media Manipulation

Although the press has an important role in a democracy, it is also crucial to understand that not all news is unvarnished truth. The process by which news is developed is a complex process that shapes the stories that are told. Journalists who work for news organizations such as the *New York Times, Washington Post,* and *Wall Street Journal* submit their reporting to editors who make a determination about the validity of the content, and whether or not it should be published. Editors can be a journalist's best friend, ensuring that their reporting is accurate, well supported, and following ethical guidelines. They can also be a source of frustration as they raise journalists' awareness about areas of weaknesses in their reporting.

In recent decades, the consolidation of media has caused concern about the manipulation of news content in the editorial process. In 2020, six corporations control roughly 90 percent of the news media in the U.S.[27] News media corporations almost monopolistic control of news editing in the U.S. gives them unmatched power to make determinations what news stories are published and which ones are ignored. The ways in which the larger institution shapes content is the subject of Edward Herman and Noam Chomsky, in their seminal 1988 book *Manufacturing Consent: The Political Economy of the Mass Media.* [28] They refer to this as the **propaganda model**. The propaganda model sets out to explain how the corporate press shapes the public's agenda to reflect more corporate and private sector interests. Herman and Chomsky argued that news content from these corporate outlets reflect a corporate and establishment agenda because they go through five filters: 1) ownership; 2) advertising; 3) sourcing (news makers/news shapers); 4) flak (criticism); 5) ideology (bias). The propaganda model contends that the interests of ownership, demands of advertisers, the bias of sources, the threat of flak or complaints from the audience, and the shared ideology of the news outlets results in narrow possibilities for how a story can be told.

In the first two filters, Herman and Chomsky contend that corporations avoid publishing content that is critical of the interests of ownership or advertisers because they want the public to have a positive view of both. It is hard to imagine that a news outlet such as the *Washington Post*, which is owned by Jeff Bezos, creator of Amazon and owner of the national supermarket chain Whole Foods, would want to publish content that is critical of Amazon, Whole Foods, or Bezos himself. Critical reporting could turn the audience against either or both companies which would result in lost revenues. Similarly, a company is not going to pay advertising fees to be on a news program that criticizes their product or service.

According to the third filter, sourcing, news media rely on people in positions of power as their sources, rather than average, everyday people. Journalists are especially likely to seek out sources who hold official positions in government agencies or corporate organizations. As a result, news stories often reflect the interests of powerful officials, rather than the majority of people. The fourth filter argues that news outlets make a determination about reporting based on whether or not they will get flak – which means criticism – for their reporting. This means sometimes avoiding fact-based stories because they may upset powerful people or organizations. As a result, the fifth filter explains that corporate news promotes the dominant ideology by highlighting potential threats – whether real, exaggerated, or imagined – and framing them in terms of "us" versus "them." Overall, Herman and Chomsky understand filtered news as a form of **propaganda**, which is defined as systematic and intentional form of persuasion that aims to influence the emotions, attitudes, opinions, and actions of a target audience for ideological, political, or commercial purposes. Propaganda works through controlled transmission of one-sided messages (which may or may not be factual) via mass and direct media channels. Filtered news is propaganda designed to persuade its audience to accept the views and interests of a ruling elite as their own.

Building upon the propaganda model, media watchdog Project Censored has argued that these filters amount to censorship as they limit reporting to content that does not threaten the economic incentives or power of major media organizations.[29] Members of the corporate press argue that these critiques derive from audiences misunderstanding about the press limited in time and space to cover stories. However, the founding director of Project Censored, Carl Jensen, countered that what they do cover, even when accurate, is not newsworthy, but worthless information he called "Junk Food News."[30] Tim Wu argues in *Attention Merchants* that the use of entertainment and sensational content at the expense of journalism is part of a historical pattern where profit and power in America derive from grabbing people's attention.[31] In fact, as media scholars Nolan Higdon and Mickey Huff noted in their book, *United States of Distraction: Media Manipulation in Post-Truth America (and what we can do about it)*, there have been four factors contributing to the increase of these practices, and public susceptibility to them, in the past half century. They refer to these as "four public vulnerabilities," which include 1) a pervasive commercial entertainment culture; 2) hyperpartisanship; 3) a fragmented media landscape; and 4) an ineffective educational system.[32]

In the decades since Herman and Chomsky's influential work, the target of media derision has changed. Prior to the 1990s, when the propaganda model was introduced, news media outlets sought to capture the largest audience possible, and as a result, they appealed to non-controversial and consensus issues. Their coverage focused on appealing to audiences' anti-communist sentiments, which dominated U.S. thinking after World War II. The advent of cable and the internet fragmented audiences, and the end of the Cold War in the 1990s quelled anti-communist sentiment. In response, news companies began to target a segment of the audience with news they wanted to hear.[33]

Programming research revealed that news audiences were more likely to tune in when their views were confirmed, and their political positions were treated as morally superior to the opposition.[34] In response, news outlets targeted smaller demographics based on political affiliation.[35] They abandoned the long quest for objectivity, and emphasized political bias, in turn building a brand and audience base.[36] **Bias** refers to an individual's preference or prejudice. The resulting content was hyper-partisan in nature, favoring one party and deriding the other. Indeed, scholars have noted that this led the *New York Times, Washington Post,* CNN, and MSNBC to become megaphones for the Democratic Party, and they faced off against Fox News, the *Wall Street Journal,* and *New York Post* for the Republican Party.[37]

News consumption patterns in the U.S. reveal a tribal mentality and a dearth of diversity in users' news diet. About 76 percent of U.S. adults visit the same news sources daily without drifting to another news outlet. This is crucial, considering that surveys reveal that individuals loyal to their news organizations check the news at a much higher rate than those willing to examine multiple news outlets.[38] More recently, the Pew Research Center's American News Pathways Project 2020 examined how the public navigated the news during the COVID-19 pandemic and tumultuous presidential election that year. They noted that "Americans inhabited different information environments, with wide gaps in how they viewed" key issues with "evidence pointing to media 'echo chambers' on the left and the right." The extensive study further concluded that "while Americans widely agree that misinformation is a major problem, they do not see eye to eye about what actually constitutes misinformation. In many cases, one person's truth is another's fiction."[39]

Many of the same techniques used to stoke fears of communism in the U.S. during the Cold War to demonize communism and the U.S.S.R. now have been operationalized on audiences to fear competing political parties and sow division domestically within the U.S. The political scientist Michael Parenti summed up some of these practices:

- Suppression by omission (censorship, passive or active);
- attacking and destroying the target (ad hominem);
- labeling (ad hominem/over generalization);
- pre-emptive assumption (stereotyping/status quo bias);

- face-value transmission (accept without questioning);
- slighting of content (limit information, but not all of it);
- false balancing (hearing from "both sides" when there are more views to consider); follow-up avoidance (don't ask further questions);
- framing (defining limits of information and perceptions allowed to be discussed).[40]

These practices enable news outlets to engage in spin. **Spin** refers to a twist put on a story so that it influences audience interpretation. Spin is such a problem that there are "spin rooms" at events such as campaign speeches and debates where public relations firms inform members of the press how a real fact or event confirms a journalist's or news outlet's political or economic ideology. Although the news media is supposed to "unspin" the content for the public, sometimes they report the spin as content. In addition to spin, news outlets slant their content to appeal to their target audience. **Slant** refers to the practice of how news outlets introduce a story in a narrow fashion that conforms to a certain organizational, institutional bias, often an accepted or popular interpretation about a topic so pervasive it is taken at face value without investigation. Veteran Journalist Sharyl Attkisson dedicated an entire bestseller to the topic, titled *Slanted: How the News Media Taught Us to Love Censorship and Hate Journalism*, she argued that such slant supports what she calls **The Narrative**:

> We in the media have, to a frightening degree, gotten on board with the efforts to convince the public that they do not need or deserve access to all information, only that which powerful interests see fit for them to have. Reporters are so aware of this that they have a name for it: The Narrative. The phrase is used to describe what we caught *others* doing to try to shape the news. Now we're doing it ourselves ... the point is that The Narrative is guiding what facts you get to learn about. Facts that serve The Narrative are deemed to be "news." Facts that don't are not news. Or they are obliterated.[41]

One of the most famous examples of a slant occurred with the following photo taken on January 18, 2019 in Washington, D.C.

Legacy media reported that Nick Sandmann, a 16-year-old Covington Catholic High School junior, was aggressively confronting Nathan Phillips, a Native American activist. They utilized a photo of Sandmann smirking while wearing Trump's signature Make America Great Again ball cap.[42] As it would later be revealed, he and his fellow students were involved in a confrontation, whose origins are unknown, with a group known as the Black Hebrew Israelites who reportedly accused the students of being products of incest and racists.[43] The teens began chanting back, with

Figure 6.1 Native American elder Nathan Phillips and Covington, Kentucky high-school junior Nick Sandmann at the Lincoln Memorial in Washington D.C. on January 18, 2019.

reportedly Catholic school songs, at which point they were approached by Native American elder and activist Nathan Phillips, on the right in the picture, on the steps of the Lincoln Memorial.[44] Phillips, who was there with other activists, claims he intervened because he heard some of the children yelling a phrase Trump popularized as part of his anti-immigration policy, "build that wall."[45] This was not verified by video.[46]

The press reports demonstrated the ways in which news media can frame a story to influence audiences' interpretation. **Framing** refers to "journalists' interpretation of an event in the context of larger concepts and theoretical perspectives."[47] For example, a journalist can frame a story about a hurricane as one about climate change or a story about government preparedness in how it responds to the hurricane. In the case of Sandmann, initial legacy media reports lacked context about the Black Hebrew Israelites or that it was Phillips who approached Sandmann, instead framing the story as racist, wealthy white children antagonizing Native Americans.[48] Yet, they reported as if their narrative was confirmed. For example, the *Detroit Free Press* described the video as depicting "Phillips peacefully drumming and singing, while surrounded by a hostile crowd;" NPR reported, without evidence, that it was the boys who antagonized Phillips by mocking him; Bakari Sellars agreed with a tweet from his fellow CNN pundit Reza Aslan that Sandmann had a "punchable" face; *BuzzFeed*'s Anne Petersen compared Sandmann's face to Supreme Court justice Brett Kavanaugh's; comedian Kathy Griffin expressed her hope that the high-school students would be doxed; and the *Huffington Post*'s Christopher Mathias analogized the students to violent segregationists.[49] The press reports were so egregious that within in a month Sandmann began a series of lawsuits against NBC Universal, ABC, CBS, USA Today, the *New York Times, Rolling Stone,* CNN, and the *Washington Post.*[50] The latter two settled out of court with Sandmann for an undisclosed amount and $250 million respectively in 2020.[51]

The Sandmann episode not only reveals the media's power to frame story, but to divide audiences along partisan lines. A generation ago civil rights and anti-war activists warned that the press not only framed key issues of the day, they engaged in a sort of information warfare to dissuade the general population from participating in movements that challenged the status quo. During the 1960s, at a speech in Harlem, civil rights leader Malcolm X spoke about these practices in dominant media (emphasis added):

> The press is so powerful in its image-making role, it can make the criminal look like he's the victim and make the victim look like he's the criminal. This is the press, an irresponsible press .... *If you aren't careful, the newspapers will have you hating the people who are being oppressed and loving the people who are doing the oppressing.*
>
> If you aren't careful, because I've seen some of you caught in that bag, you run away hating yourself and loving the man – while you're catching hell from the man. You let the man maneuver you into thinking that it's wrong to fight him when he's fighting you. He's fighting you in the morning, fighting you in the noon, fighting you at night and fighting you all in between, and you still think it's wrong to fight him back. Why? The press. The newspapers make you look wrong.[52]

Indeed, the 21st century resembles the hyper-partisanship dystopia that Malcolm X warned about.[53] A 2014 Pew Research study, "Political Polarization in the American Public," revealed that "partisan antipathy is deeper and more extensive" than ever before. Their survey of 10,000 people found that since the 1980s, liberals have been moving further left and conservatives further right. They found that "92 percent of Republicans are to the right of the median Democrat, and 94 percent of Democrats are to the left of the median Republican."[54] A 2016 Stanford University study confirmed that the partisan divide deepened quickly in the mid-1990s. Starting in the 1960s, people have generally believed that they may ultimately differ with members of the opposite party on policy, but they believed that they were similar to each other in terms of intellect and selfishness, a Stanford University study found. In the 1960s, approximately 20 percent of those polled felt that members of opposing parties were more selfish. However, by 2008, that number more than doubled, with nearly 50 percent of both Democratic and Republican respondents believing that members of the opposite party were more selfish.[55]

The failures of news media and their propensity to stoke bias and fear have not been lost on Americans. In fact, 2021 marked the first year that less than half of the American public, around 40 percent, showed faith in news media.[56] After the 2020 election, about 57 percent of Democrats and 18 percent of Republicans trusted news media.[57] This may help explain the recent trends that indicate audiences are abandoning legacy media for digital sources.[58] For example, following the inauguration of President Biden, ratings for cable news plummeted with outlets such as the *New York Times*, MSNBC, and CNN losing a fifth, fourth, and half of their audience respectively.[59] Meanwhile, the portion of Americans who rely on social media and YouTube for their news has surpassed newspapers.[60] This trend is also occurring among older generations.[61] Just as audiences are moving to digital spaces, scholars have noted that many of the same problems regarding news media manipulation are simply replicated in digital spaces.[62]

Fighting Fake News

It was digital news content, referred to as "fake news," that was blamed for misguiding voters in the so-called Brexit vote in the U.K., and the election of President Donald Trump.[63] After 2016, fears over fake news in the U.S. were heightened by Donald Trump's presidency; the proliferation of white nationalist and supremacist groups; and violent clashes such as those in Charlottesville, Virginia in 2017 and at the U.S. Capitol in 2021.[64] In fact, the World Health Organization (WHO), United Nations, UNESCO, and other global organizations warned that the proliferation of false information had become so ubiquitous that they were declaring a global "infodemic," which the WHO defined as "too much information including false or misleading information in digital and physical environments during a disease outbreak."[65]

Trump weaponized the "fake news" epithet to denounce any reporting he found inconveniently critical, problematic, or inaccurate.[66] However, Jennifer Allen and colleagues explain that fake news is "broadly defined as false or misleading information masquerading as legitimate news."[67] As Nolan Higdon notes in *The Anatomy of Fake News: A Critical News Literacy Education*, "fake news is anything but self-explanatory. It extends far beyond news itself and exists in numerous formats such as rumors, lies, hoaxes, bunk, satire, parody, misleading content, impostor content, fabricated content, and manipulated content."[68] The most effective fake news circumvents critical thinking by appealing to lower human emotions of hate and fear.[69] This includes legacy media. People are not powerless against the influence of news media. Critical news literacy users investigate the content and the process behind its production and dissemination. This begins with investigating who produces fake news.

The known producers of fake news include:

- **The legacy media:** They perpetuate false news stories that are as small as misattributing a quote or as large as long-running scandals such as the false stories that Iraq was procuring Weapons of Mass Destruction in 2003, which led to a full-scale invasion from the U.S.[70]
- **State-sponsored propaganda machines:** Governments, including the U.S., have long created and disseminated fake news at domestic and foreign populations. For example, the U.S. Government has worked with journalists to disseminate fake news in their mid-20th century program, Operation Mockingbird (part of what was referred more broadly in the CIA as their "Propaganda Assets Inventory," also known as "the Mighty Wurlitzer"). They had a hand in operating state-run media outlets such as *Voice of America* and television programs such as *Battle Report Washington.* More recently they have extended such agreements between legacy and digital media with the military and national security industrial complex. Other nations such as Russia ran Operation Infektion during the Cold War to shape international audiences, and more recently they have been involved in numerous attempts to shape overseas elections.[71]
- **Political party propaganda apparatuses:** A loose group of actors who work to shape electoral outcomes and policy debates through the use of content including fake news. These include public relations firms and members of the news media who work in tandem. For example, elements of the Republican Party and conservative media such as OAN and Fox News Channel worked in 2020 to normalize the "Stop the Steal" which argued that the Democrats had stolen the 2020 presidential election from Trump. Similarly, for four years during Trump's presidency, the Democratic Party perpetuated elements of the Russiagate scandal that proved to be false – such as the Russians hacked a Vermont power plant; infiltrated Bernie Sanders' 2020 campaign; hacked Democratic Party leaders' emails; put a bounty on U.S. soldiers' heads in Afghanistan; and repeatedly contacted Trump campaign adviser George Papadopoulos with damaging information about Hillary Clinton.[72]
- **Satirical fake news:** This refers to entertainment that lampoons dominant culture through a news media presentation. Examples include the *Daily Show, Colbert Report, Full Frontal,* and *The Onion.*

- **Self-interested actors:** People who create fake news to serve their own ends. For example, Jayson Blair reported fake news in thousands of stories at the *New York Times* and *Boston Globe* to further his journalistic career. He is hardly the only reporter to do so; others include Stephen Glass of *The New Republic*, Brian Williams of MSNBC, Bill O' Reilly of Fox News Channel, and American conservative political activist James O'Keefe of Project Veritas.[73]

Other self-interested actors create fake news to further white supremacy. One way to do this is through a race hoax, which occurs "when someone fabricates a crime and blames it on another person because of [their] race or when an actual crime has been committed and the perpetrator falsely blames someone because of [their] race."[74] These racial hoaxes have been used to justify the murder of Emmitt Till and imprisonment of the Scottsboro Boys.[75] Two of the most famous of the many racial hoaxes used to cover up crimes include Susan Smith in 1994 and Charles Stuart in 1989 who blamed a black man for the murder of their children and wife respectively. More recently in 2021, Katie Sorensen, a popular white Instagram influencer with 80,000 followers in California, was charged for filing false police reports after fabricating an elaborate thwarted stalking and kidnapping attempt in a shopping plaza parking lot. In the process, she accused a local couple, people of color who had been in the store she had visited, of being the culprits, and took to social media to tell the tale of her averted tragedy that garnered 4.5 million views and made national news. Unfortunately, the tragedy merely shifted to the innocent party she blamed, working parents who were outed in the media and who went to the police to clear their name. The police said no crime took place, other than the one perpetrated by Sorensen.[76] Hoaxes have also been used to draw attention to people such as actor Jussie Smollett, who hired people to beat him up and tie a noose around his neck, to feign a racist attack.[77] He is hardly alone as this has been copied by Yasmin Seweid, Khawlah Noman, and Amari Allen.[78]

Some self-interested actors seek to create media empires in online spaces. For example, since 1996, Alex Jones of *InfoWars* has amassed a highly lucrative media empire publishing content and selling items on the internet.[79] Much of his content sells the unsubstantiated theory that an elite group of powerful and influential politicians and business people, sometimes called the Illuminati, meet at places like Northern California's Bohemian Grove, with a goal of world domination.[80] His fake news stories have claimed that the world was ending in real time on January 1, 2000 (Y2K); the U.S. government uses "weather weapons" to create natural disasters in an effort to manufacture public support for a green economy; government aid locations for natural disasters are actually concentration camps; and school shootings like Sandy Hook are fake events, and those suffering in the images and videos are "crisis actors" hired by the federal government to legitimize plans to take away Americans' guns.[81] He is so influential he became one of the main sources of information for President Donald Trump.[82] At one time during his presidency, Trump himself was trusted more than the news media for 72 percent of Republicans.[83] This is concerning given that after two years in office, a team at the *Washington Post* tallied more than 10,000 false or misleading statements made by President Trump. By the time he was leaving office after one term, the *Post's* tally surpassed 22,000.[84] As critical media literacy scholars note, audiences are not beholden to fake news narratives.

Be a Model Media Citizen

People have the power to discern fact from fiction and reject the false and misleading content that is presented as legitimate news. Fake news content comes in spoken, written, print, broadcast, and digital forms. As Allison Butler of University of Massachusetts, Amherst, reminds us, critically news literate media users recast themselves not as "media consumers," but "media citizens because they want to identify truth to serve democracy not be confirmed in their beliefs.[85] Media does not use them, they use media. Critical news literacy asks media citizens to investigate each piece and type of content by asking the following questions:

- **Is the content journalism?** Media citizens determine whether the content from a journalist or another source such as critic, commentator, or reporter. This determination is made by investigating to see if the content serves the democratic function of the press, follows the criteria for determining if something is newsworthy, and is an organization or individual who follows a code of ethics.
- **Who is the publisher of this content?** Media citizens evaluate the publisher's validity. Evaluating the publisher of the content is a step taken easily and early for news evaluation. In the process, news users should consider the following questions: Does the publisher have a history of publishing journalism or slanted content? Does the publisher have any professional, personal, economic, and or political conflicts of interest? Do they have a history of retracting inaccurate reporting? This information can usually be found through examining the "About" page if it is a website and media analysis archives such as Project Censored and Fair and Accuracy in Reporting's archive.
- **Who is the author of this content?** Media citizens evaluate the author's validity. Evaluating the author of the content is also a crucial early step when encountering content. In the process, news users should consider the following questions: Who is the author? Does

the author have any professional, personal, and or political conflicts of interest? Do they have a history of having their stories retracted for inaccurate reporting? This information can usually be found through examining the "About" page if it is a website and media analysis archives such as Project Censored and Fairness and Accuracy in Reporting's archive.

- **Do I understand the content?** Media citizens slow down and carefully investigate content. It is not about virtue signaling that you can share more articles than anyone else, it is about finding truth and that takes time. So, spending more time with less content better positions media citizens to effectively evaluate content. This provides an opportunity to put critical thinking skills to work. In the process, news consumers should consider: What story is being told? Do the author's conclusions, assumptions, or connections make logical sense? Ask the Who, What, When, Where, Why, and How.

- **What is the evidence?** Media citizens identify, evaluate, and analyze the evidence. What is the evidence? Are there other views, sources, or evidence that you would expect to be included? Are the sources identified or unidentified sources? Journalists sometimes have to use anonymous sources to protect the identity of vulnerable individuals and whistleblowers. However, as John Christie notes from *Poynter*:

> That's one problem with anonymous sources: They often get it wrong because why make sure you [the journalist] have it right when you will not be held accountable for what you say. And even if it is accurate, readers cannot judge the value of the material for themselves if they don't know the source. Many sources hide behind anonymity to take cheap shots without anyone knowing they have an axe to grind or a dog in the fight. And even more importantly, the frequent and often unnecessary use of anonymous sources reinforces the mistrust readers already have for journalists.[86]

As Christie's critique points out, it is a good idea to be skeptical or anonymous sources.

- **What is missing from the content?** Media citizens analyze news media not just for what is there, but for what is missing. What ideologies and viewpoints are missing? What identity groups both as sources and as journalists are missing? How do these missing elements strengthen others? What does that reveal about the validity and purpose of the content?

- **What is the bias?** All content will have some bias. In addition to the political bias discussed in this chapter, AllSides points out that there are ideological biases beyond left versus right, which include:[87]

- **Authoritarian vs libertarian:** This bias appears in discourses about policy positions that revolve around a trade-off between authority and liberty such as abortion, gun control, and plastic bag bans.
- **Individualist vs collectivist:** This bias appears in discourses about policy positions that a trade-off between what is good for the individual versus the collective such as environmentalism and redistribution of wealth.
- **Secular vs religious:** This bias appears in discourses about question the role of religious morality in social policies such as abortion or same-sex marriage.
- **Traditionalist vs progressive:** This bias appears in discourses about policy positions regarding if structures should respect tradition or seek new and different approaches in issues regarding gender roles, the role of government, and monetary policy.
- **Elitist vs populist:** This bias appears in media representations that either adhere to the elites as the vanguards of democracy – such as the political, economic, cultural, or media establishment ("the elite") – or portray them as self-serving, corrupt, powerful figures who disregard or act in opposition to the concerns of everyday people as populists would describe them.
- **Rural vs urban:** This bias is in regards to the geographical impact of views on policy positions such as utility of gun ownership and the size of government.
- **Nationalist/localist vs globalist:** This bias appears in discourses that seek to address he conflict between national and global needs over issues such as health resource allocation, and peace.

Media literate citizens set themselves apart because they engage with content ready to ask questions and investigate rather than be passively informed.

Conclusion: The Harm and Hope in Fake News

The fact that Jitarth Jadeja was able to engage in civil dialogue with Anderson Cooper, months if not days after believing Cooper was Satan incarnate, illustrates two things.[88] First, it demonstrates that fake news can be an influential force that drives otherwise good people to do terrible things. Take the examples of Pizzagate, where a 34-year-old father of two shot up a pizza restaurant based on false information that it housed a democratic party pedophilia ring, or Ashli Babbitt, an Air Force veteran who falsely believed the 2020 election was stolen and was shot and killed while storming the Capitol to stop the election certification process on

January 6, 2021. In both cases, had the information that the two had used been factual, which it was not, they would have been heroes for saving children and the democratic process. This reveals that it was not their values – beliefs in democracy and the protection of children – that made them act in a horrific manner, but their misinformed ideas fed by a poor and toxic media diet.

That is why we must remember the second lesson from the interview: People who believe and act upon fake news are not necessarily innately bad people. Jadeja demonstrates that they are lost and manipulated people who not only can be saved, but like any other person are worth saving. Facts do matter, context matters, critical thinking matters. In our democratic discourse, news, no matter who reports it, plays a crucial role in shaping our attitudes and behaviors as they relate to policies, parties, and politicians. The democratic process is strongest when the electorate is debating differing views and policies on a foundation of fact-based stories rather than false or misleading content. Dialogue is a way to penetrate falsehood and critical thinking is a process for marginalizing its pernicious influence on human behaviors and attitudes.

This chapter has introduced the ways in which we can better identify, analyze, and evaluate news sources. However, our conception of the world is more complicated than ever thanks to the internet, which simultaneously promises yet hinders constructive discourse. The next chapter investigates the internet's potential and weaknesses to foster constructive dialogue.

Notes

1 Aris Folley, "Former QAnon supporter apologizes to Anderson Cooper," *The Hill*, January 31, 2021, https://thehill.com/homenews/media/536682-form er-qanon-supporter-apologizes-to-anderson-cooper.
2 Ibid.
3 David Neiwert, "Conspiracy meta-theory 'The Storm' pushes the 'alternative' envelope yet again," Southern Poverty Law Center, January 17, 2018, https:// www.splcenter.org/hatewatch/2018/01/17/conspiracy-meta-theory-storm-push es-alternative-envelope-yet-again; Associated Press, "QAnon supporters sharing 'deep state' satanic sex trafficking ring/cannibalism theories at Trump rallies," *Fox*, February 9, 2020, https://www.fox32chicago.com/news/qanon-supporters-sharing-deep-state-satanic-sex-trafficking-ring-cannibalism-theorie s-at-trump-rallies; Vox Staff, "QAnon: The conspiracy theory embraced by Trump, several politicians, and some American moms," *Vox*, October 9, 2020, https://www.vox.com/2020/10/9/21504910/qanon-conspiracy-theory-fa cebook-ban-trump; Kevin Roose, "What is QAnon, the viral Pro-Trump conspiracy theory?" *New York Times*, August 28, 2020, https://www.nytimes. com/article/what-is-qanon.html.
4 Aris Folley, "Former QAnon supporter apologizes to Anderson Cooper," *The Hill*, January 31, 2021, https://thehill.com/homenews/media/536682-form er-qanon-supporter-apologizes-to-anderson-cooper.

5 Ibid.
6 Ibid.
7 Ibid.
8 Paris Martineau, "The Storm is the new Pizzagate – only worse," *New York Magazine*, December 19, 2017, https://nymag.com/intelligencer/2017/12/qa non-4chan-the-storm-conspiracy-explained.html.
9 Andrew Griffin, "What is QAnon? The origins of the bizarre conspiracy theory spreading online," *The Independent*, London, August 24, 2020, https://www.indep endent.co.uk/life-style/gadgets-and-tech/news/what-is-qanon-b1790868.html.
10 David Gilbert, "QAnon thinks Trump will become President again on March 4," Vice, January 25, 2021, https://www.vice.com/en/article/88akpx/qanon-thinks-trump-will-become-president-again-on-march-4.
11 Aris Folley, "Former QAnon supporter apologizes to Anderson Cooper," *The Hill*, January 31, 2021, https://thehill.com/homenews/media/536682-form er-qanon-supporter-apologizes-to-anderson-cooper.
12 Ibid.
13 David Neiwert, "Conspiracy meta-theory 'The Storm' pushes the 'alternative' envelope yet again," Southern Poverty Law Center, January 17, 2018, https:// www.splcenter.org/hatewatch/2018/01/17/conspiracy-meta-theory-storm-push es-alternative-envelope-yet-again.
14 Adam Shaw, "Trump promises 'wild' protest in Washington DC on Jan. 6, claims it's 'impossible' he lost Trump's campaign has filed a number of unsuc-cessful lawsuits challenging the election results," *Fox News*, December 19, 2020, https://www.foxnews.com/politics/trump-wild-protest-washington-dc-jan-6.
15 Brian Naylor, "Read Trump's Jan. 6 Speech, a key part of impeachment trial," *NPR*, February 10, 2021, https://www.npr.org/2021/02/10/96639684 8/read-trumps-jan-6-speech-a-key-part-of-impeachment-trial.
16 The Capitol siege: The arrested and their stories," *NPR*, February 12, 2021, https://www.npr.org/2021/02/09/965472049/the-capitol-siege-the-arrested-a nd-their-stories; Marisa Peñaloza, "Trump supporters clash with Capitol police at protest," *NPR*, January 6, 2021, https://www.npr.org/sections/con gress-electoral-college-tally-live-updates/2021/01/06/953616207/diehard-tru mp-supporters-gather-in-the-nations-capital-to-protest-election-Resul.
17 Minyvonne Burke, "Former Capitol police chief shares thoughts on why offi-cers appeared to let rioters in: 'Sometimes when you don't have enough per-sonnel, you can't stand and fight a large crowd like that,' Gainer said. / Former Capitol police chief: 'They needed more personnel' to control rioters," *NBC News*, January 7, 2021, https://www.nbcnews.com/news/us-news/form er-capitol-police-chief-shares-thoughts-why-officers-appeared-let-n1253273; Samantha Putterman, "Ask PolitiFact: Did Capitol police let mob of Trump supporters in?" *PolitiFact*, January 7, 2021, https://www.politifact.com/a rticle/2021/jan/07/ask-politifact-did-capitol-police-let-mob-trump-su/.
18 Kenya Evelyn, "Capitol attack: The five people who died," *The Guardian*, January 9, 2021, https://www.theguardian.com/us-news/2021/jan/08/capitol-a ttack-police-officer-five-deaths.
19 Katie Benner, Maggie Haberman, and Michael S. Schmidt, "An explosive device is found at the R.N.C., and the D.N.C. is evacuated," *New York Times*, January 6, 2021, https://www.nytimes.com/live/2021/01/06/us/electoral-vote #pipe-bomb-rnc.
20 Nolan Higdon and Mickey Huff, *United States of Distraction: Media Manip-ulation in Post-truth America (and what we can do about it)* (San Francisco, CA: City Lights Books, 2019), 22.

21 Nolan Higdon, *The Anatomy of Fake News: A Critical News Literacy Education* (Oakland, CA: University of California Press, 2020).

22 David Shedden, "Today in media history: Mr. Dooley: 'The job of the newspaper is to comfort the afflicted and afflict the comfortable'," *Poynter,* October 7, 2014, https://www.poynter.org/reporting-editing/2014/today-in-media-history-mr-dooley-the-job-of-the-newspaper-is-to-comfort-the-afflicted-and-afflict-the-comfortable/.

23 Ibid.

24 Alan Knight, Cherian Geuze, and Alex Gerlis, "Who is a journalist," *Journalism Studies* 9, no. 1 (2008): 117–131.

25 Society of Professional Journalists, *Code of Ethics*, online at https://www.spj.org/ethicscode.asp.

26 Ibid.

27 Rich Buchler and Staff, "Six corporations Own 90% of news media – truth!," *Truth or Fiction,* https://www.truthorfiction.com/six-corporations-own-90-percent-of-news-media/; Ashley Lutz, "These 6 corporations control 90% of the media In America," *Business Insider,* June 14, 2012, www.businessinsider.com/these-6-corporations-control-90-of-the-media-in-america-2012-6.

28 Edward Herman and Noam Chomsky, *Manufacturing Consent: The Political Economy of the Mass Media* (New York: Pantheon Books, 1988).

29 Mickey Huff and Andy Lee Roth, eds, *Censored 2017: 40th Anniversary Edition* (New York: Seven Stories Press, 2016).

30 Ibid.

31 Tim Wu, *The Attention Merchants: The Epic Scramble to Get Inside Our Heads* (New York: Vintage Books, 2016).

32 Nolan Higdon and Mickey Huff, *United States of Distraction: Media Manipulation in Post-Truth America (and what we can do about it)* (San Francisco: City Lights Books, 2019), 52–74.

33 Matt Taibbi, *Hate Inc: Why Today's Media Makes Us Despise One Another* (New York: OR Books, 2019).

34 Ibid.

35 Ibid.

36 Ibid.

37 Nolan Higdon, *The Anatomy of Fake News: A Critical News Literacy Education* (Oakland, CA: University of California Press, 2020).

38 Michael Barthel et al., "Pathways to news," *Pew Research Center,* July 7, 2016, www.journalism.org/2016/07/07/pathways-to-news/.

39 Amy Mitchell, Mare Jurkowitz, J. Baxter Oliphant, and Elisa Shearer, "How Americans navigated the news in 2020: A tumultuous year in review," *Pew Research Center,* February 2021, https://www.journalism.org/2021/02/22/how-americans-navigated-the-news-in-2020-a-tumultuous-year-in-review/. See the full study online at https://www.pewresearch.org/topic/news-habits-media/media-society/american-news-pathways-2020-project/.

40 Michael Parenti, "Monopoly media manipulation," *MichaelParenti.org,* May 2001, http://www.michaelparenti.org/MonopolyMedia.html.

41 Sharyl Attkisson, *Slanted: How the News Media Taught Us to Love Censorship and Hate Journalism* (New York: Harper Collins, 2020), 2–3.

42 Eun Kyung Kim, "Nick Sandmann on encounter with Nathan Phillips: 'I wish I would've walked away'," *NBC Today,* January 23, 2019, https://www.today.com/news/nick-sandmann-interview-today-show-s-savannah-guthrie-encounter-native-t147242.

43 Ibid.

44 Ibid.
45 Ibid.
46 Brian Planalp, "Motions to dismiss denied in Sandmann suits against media companies," WLBT, October 1, 2020, https://www.wlbt.com/2020/10/01/m otions-dismiss-denied-sandmann-suits-against-media-companies/.
47 Nolan Higdon, *The Anatomy of Fake News: A Critical News Literacy Education* (Oakland, CA: University of California Press, 2020), 22.
48 Ibid.
49 Robby Soave, "A year ago, the media mangled the Covington Catholic story. What happened next was even worse," *Reason,* January 21, 2020, https://rea son.com/2020/01/21/covington-catholic-media-nick-sandmann-lincoln-memo rial/.
50 Eun Kyung Kim, "Nick Sandmann on encounter with Nathan Phillips: 'I wish I would've walked away'," *NBC Today*, January 23, 2019, https://www.today.com/news/nick-sandmann-interview-today-show-s-savannah-guthrie-enc ounter-native-t147242.
51 Oliver Darcy, "CNN settles lawsuit with Nick Sandmann stemming from viral video controversy," *CNN*, January 7, 2020, https://www.cnn.com/2020/01/07/media/cnn-settles-lawsuit-viral-video/index.html; Steve Rogers, "Covington teen settles defamation suit with the Washington Post," *WTVQ,* July 24, 2020, https://www.wtvq.com/2020/07/24/covington-teen-settles-defama tion-suit-with-the-washington-post/.
52 Malcolm X, speech at the Audubon Ballroom in Harlem, NY, December 13, 1964, later published in *Malcolm X Speaks: Selected Speeches and Statements*, ed. George Breitman (New York: Grove Press), 93.
53 Nolan Higdon and Mickey Huff, *United States of Distraction: Media Manipulation in Post-truth America (and what we can do about it)* (San Francisco, CA: City Lights Books, 2019); Nolan Higdon, *The Anatomy of Fake News: A Critical News Literacy Education* (Oakland, CA: University of California Press, 2020).
54 Staff, "Political polarization in the American public: How increasing ideological uniformity and partisan antipathy affect politics, compromise and everyday life," *People Press,* June 12, 2014, www.people-press.org/2014/06/12/political-polarization-in-the-american-public/.
55 Matthew Gentzkow, "Polarization in 2016," Stanford University, 2016, www.web.stanford.edu/~gentzkow/research/PolarizationIn2016.pdf.
56 Felix Salmon, "Economy & business media trust hits new low," *Axios*, January 21, 2021, https://www.axios.com/media-trust-crisis-2bf0ec1c-00c0-4901-906 9-e26b21c283a9.html.
57 Christian Fuchs, "Propaganda 2.0: Herman and Chomsky's propaganda model in the age of the internet, big data and social media," in *The Propaganda Model Today: Filtering Perception and Awareness,* eds Joan Pedro-Carañana, Daniel Broudy, and Jeffery Klaehn (London: University of Westminster Press, 2018): 86.
58 Jeffrey Gottfried and Elisa Shearer, "Americans' online news use is closing in on TV news use," *Pew Research Center,* September 6, 2017, https://www.pewresearch.org/facttank/2017/09/07/americansonline-news-use-vs-tv-news-u se/; Elisa Shearer, "Social media outpaces print newspapers in the U.S. as a news source," *Pew Research Center*, December 10, 2018, https://www.pewresea rch.org/fact-tank/2018/12/10/social-media-outpacesprint-newspapers-in-the-u -s-as-a-news-source/; Galen Stocking, Patrick Van Kessel, Michael Barthel, Katerina Eva Matsa, and Maya Khuzam," Many Americans get news on

YouTube, where news organizations and independent producers thrive side by side," *Pew Research Center,* September 28, 2020, https://www.journalism.org/2020/09/28/many-americans-get-news-on-youtube-where-news-organizations-and-independent-producers-thrive-side-by-side/.

59 Gavin Bridge, "Cable news ratings begin to suffer Trump slump," *Variety,* March 10, 2021, https://variety.com/vip/cable-news-ratings-begin-to-suffer-trump-slump-1234926617/; Joshua Zitser, "CNN ratings are dramatically down since Trump left office," *Business Insider,* March 20, 2021, https://www.businessinsider.com/cnn-ratings-have-crashed-since-donald-trump-left-the-white-house-2021-3.

60 Elisa Shearer, "Social media outpaces print newspapers in the U.S. as a news source," *Pew Research Center,* December 10, 2018, https://www.pewresearch.org/fact-tank/2018/12/10/social-media-outpacesprint-newspapers-in-the-u-s-as-a-news-source/; The Pew Research Center, *State of the News Media 2015,* April 29, 2015, https://assets.pewresearch.org/wp-content/uploads/sites/13/2017/05/30142603/state-of-the-newsmedia-report-2015-final.pdf.

61 Jeffrey Gottfried and Elisa Shearer, "Americans' online news use is closing in on TV news use," *Pew Research Center,* September 6, 2017, https://www.pewresearch.org/facttank/2017/09/07/americansonline-news-use-vs-tv-news-use/.

62 Christian Fuchs, "Propaganda 2.0: Herman and Chomsky's propaganda model in the age of the internet, big data and social media," in *The Propaganda Model Today: Filtering Perception and Awareness,* eds Joan Pedro-Carañana, Daniel Broudy, and Jeffery Klaehn (London: University of Westminster Press, 2018): 86; Nolan Higdon, *The Anatomy of Fake News: A Critical News Literacy Education* (Oakland, CA: University of California Press, 2020).

63 Nolan Higdon, *The Anatomy of Fake News: A Critical News Literacy Education* (Oakland, CA: University of California Press, 2020).

64 Nolan Higdon and Mickey Huff, *United States of Distraction: Media Manipulation in Post-truth America (and what we can do about it)* (San Francisco, CA: City Lights Books, 2019); Daniel Hellinger, *Conspiracies and Conspiracy Theories in the Age of Trump* (Cham, Switzerland: Palgrave Macmillan, 2018); Staff, "The year in hate 2019: White nationalist groups rise for a second year in a row – up 55% since 2017," *Southern Poverty Law Center,* March 18, 2020, https://www.splcenter.org/presscenter/year-hate-2019-white-nationalist-groups-rise-second-year-row-55-2017; Alexander Laban Hinton, *It Can Happen Here: White Power and the Rising Threat of Genocide in the US* (New York: New York University Press, 2021).

65 WHO, UN, UNICEF, UNDP, UNESCO, UNAIDS, ITU, UN Global Pulse, "Managing the COVID-19 infodemic: Promoting healthy behaviours and mitigating the harm from misinformation and disinformation. Joint statement by WHO, UN, UNICEF, UNDP, UNESCO, UNAIDS, ITU, UN Global Pulse, and IFRC," World Health Organization, September, 23, 2020, https://www.who.int/news/item/23-09-2020-managing-the-covid-19-infodemic-promoting-healthy-behaviours-and-mitigating-the-harm-from-misinformation-and-disinformation.

66 Ibid.

67 Jennifer Allen, Baird Howland, Markus Mobius, David Rothschild, and Duncan J. Watts, "Evaluating the fake news problem at the scale of the information ecosystem," *Science Advances* 6, no. 14 (2020): eaay3539. DOI: 10.1126/sciadv.aay3539, https://advances.sciencemag.org/content/6/14/eaay3539.

68 Nolan Higdon, *The Anatomy of Fake News: A Critical News Literacy Education* (Oakland, CA: University of California Press, 2020), 5.

69 Ibid.

70 Higdon, *The Anatomy of Fake News*.

71 Ibid. For more on a history of CIA media manipulation, see Brian Covert's "Played by the Mighty Wurlitzer: The press, the CIA, and the subversion of truth," in *Censored 2017: 40th Anniversary Edition*, eds Mickey Huff and Andy Lee Roth (New York: Seven Stories Press, 2016), Chapter 6.

72 Matt Taibbi, "It's official: Russiagate is this generation's WMD. The Iraq war faceplant damaged the reputation of the press. Russiagate just destroyed it," *Substack*, March 23, 2019, https://taibbi.substack.com/p/russiagate-is-wmd-times-a-million; "Was a Vermont power grid infiltrated by Russian hackers? *The Washington Post* was heavily criticized for jumping the gun and suggesting a Vermont power company had been targeted for disruption by Russian hackers," *Snopes*, https://www.snopes.com/fact-check/report-vermont-power-grid-infiltrated-by-russian-hackers/; Luis Martinez, "Top Pentagon officials say Russian bounty program not corroborated. Secretary Esper and Gen. Milley said the reports are still being looked at," *ABC News*, July 9, 2020, https://abcnews.go.com/Politics/top-pentagon-officials-russian-bounty-program-corroborated/story?id=71694167; Aaron Maté, "The failed Russiagate playbook can't stop Bernie Sanders: A politics rooted in real issues and real people is far more powerful than the cynical methods that brought us Russiagate," *The Nation*, February 25, 2020, https://www.thenation.com/article/politics/bernie-sanders-russiagate/; "Bombshell: Crowdstrike admits 'no evidence' Russia stole emails from DNC server," *The Greyzone*, May 11, 2020, https://thegrayzone.com/2020/05/11/bombshell-crowdstrike-admits-no-evidence-russia-stole-emails-from-dnc-server/; Interview of: Shawn Henry, December 5, 2017, Executive Session Permanent Select Committee on Intelligence, U.S. House of Representatives, Washington, D.C., https://intelligence.house.gov/uploadedfiles/sh21.pdf, 32; Aaron Maté, "Mueller and Weissmann op-eds greatly at odds with their report and evidence," *RealClearInvestigations*, July 16, 2020, https://www.realclearinvestigations.com/articles/2020/07/16/mueller_and_weissmann_op-eds_greatly_at_odds_with_their_report_and_evidence_124483.html.

73 Nolan Higdon, *The Anatomy of Fake News: A Critical News Literacy Education* (Oakland, CA: University of California Press, 2020).

74 Katheryn Russell-Brown, *The Color of Crime: Racial Hoaxes, White Fear, Black Protectionism, Police Harassment and Other Macroaggressions* (New York: New York University Press, 1998), 70.

75 Jeremi Duru, "The Central Park Five, the Scottsboro Boys, and the myth of the bestial black man," *Cardozo L. Rev.* 25 (2003): 1315; Timothy B. Tyson, *The Blood of Emmett Till* (New York: Simon and Schuster, 2017).

76 Marouf Hasian Jr and Lisa A. Flores, "Mass mediated representations of the Susan Smith trial," *Howard Journal of Communication* 11, no. 3 (2000): 163–178; Thomas W. Cooper, "Racism, hoaxes, epistemology, and news as a form of knowledge: The Stuart case as fraud or norm?" *Howard Journal of Communications* 7, no. 1 (1996): 75–95; Schultz, Benjamin, "'They're moving North': Milwaukee, the media, and the murder of Barbara Anderson," in *2020 Harrison Symposium Lawrence University*, p. 176; "Hunters charged in Texas shooting had blamed immigrants," *Associated Press*, February 17, 2017, https://apnews.com/article/6cb4c81139024035af7bc406447e716f; Susan Spencer, "Millbury police officer's wife admits to filing false burglary report," *Telegram & Gazette*, June 7, 2017, https://www.telegram.com/news/20170607/millbury-police-officers-wife-admits-to-filing-false-burglary-report; Caitlin O'Kane, "Influencer who detailed alleged kidnapping attempt on Instagram charged with giving false information to police," *CBS News*, May 3, 2021, https://www.cbsnews.com/news/katie-sorensen-false-information-alleged-kidnapping/.

77 "Jussie Smollett: Actor charged again over alleged hoax attack," *The Guardian*, February 11, 2020, https://www.theguardian.com/us-news/2020/feb/11/jussie-smollett-hoax-attack-allegation-charges-chicago-police.

78 "'My family did not want this': Yasmin Seweid's sister says sending her to jail for lying would be 'violent and abhorrent,' accuses NYPD of leaking private info," *NBC*, December 15, 2016, https://www.nbcnewyork.com/news/local/yasmin-seweids-sister-says-sending-her-to-jail-for-lying-would-be-violent-and-abhorrent-accuses-nypd-of-leaking-private-info/2102126/; Karma Allen, "6th-grader lied about white students attacking her and cutting hair, family admits," *ABC News*, September 30, 2019, https://abcnews.go.com/US/virginia-6th-grader-falsely-accused-white-students-forcefully/story?id=65959500; "Toronto family apologises for bogus hijab attack claim," *BBC News*, January 18, 2018, https://www.bbc.co.uk/news/world-us-canada-42736525.

79 Wealthy Gorilla Staff, "Alex Jones net worth," *Wealthy Gorilla*, 2019, https://wealthygorilla.com/alex-jones-net-worth/.

80 Nolan Higdon, "Disinfo Wars: Alex Jones' war on your mind," *Project Censored*, September 26, 2013, https://www.projectcensored.org/disinfo-wars-alex-jones-war-mind/.

81 Ibid.; Laura Bradley, "Watch the opposition shout down Alex Jones – or was it a crisis actor?," *Vanity Fair*, April 13, 2018, https://www.vanityfair.com/hollywood/2018/04/the-opposition-alex-jones-defamation-crisis-actor; Eric Killelea, "Alex Jones' mis-infowars: 7 bat-sh*t conspiracy theories," *Rolling Stone*, February 21, 2017, https://www.rollingstone.com/culture/culture-lists/alex-jones-mis-infowars-7-bat-sht-conspiracy-theories-195468/the-government-is-controlling-the-weather-118190/.

82 Tim Murphy, "How Donald Trump became conspiracy theorist in chief: He's made the paranoid style of American politics go mainstream," *Mother Jones*, November/December 2016 Issue, https://www.motherjones.com/politics/2016/10/trump-infowars-alex-jones-clinton-conspiracy-theories/.

83 Tal Axelrod, "Poll: More voters trust media to tell the truth than Trump," *The Hill*, September 12, 2018, https://thehill.com/homenews/administration/406221-poll-more-voters-trust-media-than-trump.

84 Glenn Kessler, Salvador Rizzo, and Meg Kelly, "President Trump has made more than 10,000 false or misleading claims, *Washington Post*, April 29, 2019, www.washingtonpost.com/politics/2019/04/29/president-trump-has-made-more-than-false-or-misleading-claims/?utm_term=.856ebcacc61a; for previous ongoing tallies, see "In 745 days, President Trump has made 8,459 false or misleading claims," *Washington Post*, February 3, 2019, www.washingtonpost.com/graphics/politics/trump-claims-database/?utm_term=.411bcfb4d239; Glenn Kessler, "Fact checking in a post-Trump era, *Washington Post*, November 9, 2020, https://www.washingtonpost.com/politics/2020/11/09/fact-checking-post-trump-era/.

85 Nolan Higdon and Allison Butler, "Episode 19 – 5 ways to be a more media literate citizen," *Along The Line*, March 12, 2019, https://www.youtube.com/watch?v=KwfccwGNJE&list=PLefnCMJ5W_iILomqv3wJKyKLyY0lWtebw&index=21&t=3s.

86 John Christie, "Anonymous sources: Leaving journalism's false god behind," *Poynter*, April 23, 2014, https://www.poynter.org/reporting-editing/2014/anonymous-sources-leaving-journalisms-false-god-behind/.

87 Julie Mastrine, "Beyond left vs right: 14 types of ideological bias," *AllSides*, February 27, 2020, https://www.allsides.com/blog/beyond-left-vs-right-14-types-ideological-bias.

88 Aris Folley, "Former QAnon supporter apologizes to Anderson Cooper," *The Hill*, January 31, 2021, https://thehill.com/homenews/media/536682-former-qanon-supporter-apologizes-to-anderson-cooper.

Chapter 7

Assess and Analyze Digital Media Use and Abuse

"Giving grace ... means being able to hear someone say something that can be hurtful, and trying to think about how to have a real conversation and connect with them," explains Vivian Topping, a participant in the successful 2018 Massachusetts canvassing campaign to protect transgender rights. The operation saw LGBTQIA (Lesbian, Gay, Bisexual, Transgender, Queer and/or Questioning, Intersex, and Asexual and/or Ally) activists and allies going door-to-door to foster dialogue with voters about transgender rights.[1] Topping explained to *Vox* the difficulty of "giving them grace" when "them" are transphobic voters: "I came out two years ago now, and one of the hardest things for me has been talking with folks who don't understand [gender identity], and not immediately writing someone off because they don't immediately get it."[2]

The persuasive influence of dialogue on transphobic voters is not just anecdotal. A 2016 study in *Science Magazine* titled "Durably reducing transphobia: A field experiment on door-to-door canvassing," found that "a single approximately 10-minute conversation encouraging actively taking the perspective of others can markedly reduce prejudice..."[3] The study saw canvassers go door-to-door to engage 501 Miami, Florida voters into dialogue about transgender rights. The study found that these ten-minute conversations were effective in convincing voters to shift from opposing to supporting transgender rights.[4]

As that study was being released, Hillary Clinton's presidential campaign had already decided to go against its findings and abate the age-old practice of door-to-door campaigning in key states. Instead, they decided to rely upon digital communication to expand their voter base.[5] Some argue that the decision cost Clinton the Electoral College victories in Michigan and Missouri.[6] These critics were not alone. From the Arab Spring to the January 6 failed insurrection attempt at the Capitol building in Washington D.C., scholars have questioned the ability of digital tools to produce constructive democratic dialogue.[7] Regardless of these concerns, and long before the shelter in place during the COVID-19 pandemic forced many communications to move to digital spaces,

DOI: 10.4324/9781003250906-11

communication was trending away from face-to-face and toward digital media.

Studies continue to reveal that young people are spending the majority of their day with their smartphone, in part because of their "fear of missing out," also known as FOMO, on important events. This leads them to sleep with their phone, which studies show contributes to unhealthy sleep patterns. Worse, studies show that prolonged screen time is associated with depression and unhappiness among users. Indeed, suicide among young people has skyrocketed. Young people are 35 percent more likely to attempt suicide if their smartphone use is three or more hours a day.[8] Despite the mass use of so-called "social" media, young people report feeling isolated. Data reveal that there has been a 40 percent decline in teen sex since 1991.[9] There have been similar drops in physical time spent with friends, teens who get their driver's license, and dating. These patterns have led some to declare that we are in the midst of the "worst mental-health crisis" in history.[10] As University of Westminster Director of the Communication and Media Research Institute (CAMRI) Professor Christian Fuchs notes, part of the problem is that it is not clear what is *social* about *social media*. He explains that there are four forms of sociality: Information cognition, communication, community, and collaboration and cooperative work. What passes for social media, according to Fuchs, does not achieve a broad sense of sociality as we are accustomed to understanding it.[11] Indeed, by privileging information that appeals to lower human emotions and false and misleading information, the economic model of most internet platforms hinders critical thinking and exacerbates destructive dialogue.

These concerns were amplified by the wildly popular 2020 Netflix documentary *The Social Dilemma*. The film documented how the interworking of big-tech was shaping tools in a way that resulted in harmful effects on users such as screen addiction and depression. It was a succinct argument, targeted largely at parents, about the pernicious influence of digital media. However, the film portrayed users as helpless victims, who had no choice but to succumb to the will of big-tech. This thinking is anathema to critical scholars because they contend that users have the autonomy to negotiate their relationship to media. This chapter takes a critical approach to digital media literacy. Scholars have often defined digital literacy as a process of decoding, meaning making, and using and analyzing digital content.[12] **Critical digital literacy** seeks to strengthen democratic practices by engendering autonomy among digital media users through an analysis of the political and socioeconomic costs and benefits that shape digital communication.[13]

Political Economy in a Digital Era

The pathology of social media's power is rooted in the political economy of digital media. University of Birmingham's Gianfranco Polizzi argues that critical digital literacy "incorporate[s] political economy reflections on how advertising and ownership, for instance, shape how online content is consumed and created, and with what implications."[14] Harvard Business School Professor Shoshanna Zuboff explains that the political economy of the internet is best understood as a form of surveillance capitalism. Surveillance capitalism is an economic order that utilizes hidden practices of commercial extraction to collect online information, known as data, and convert it into valuable commodities.[15] **Data** refers to the digital records of every action taken by an internet user.[16] The commercial aspects of the internet were dramatically transformed by the economic recession in 2000 and the terrorist attacks of September 11, 2001. Since their inception, technology companies have always collected users' data.[17] Initially, tech companies viewed data analysis as a limited, but necessary process to improve the design of their platform to serve customers. Any extra or unrelated data, known as **behavior surplus data**, was determined to be useless.[18] That all changed in 2000 when a recession brought about by internet speculation weakened the U.S. economy.[19] Struggling tech companies soon found a lucrative savior in the federal government. After the events of September 11, 2001, the federal government offered massive contracts to tech companies to practice domestic and international surveillance for the purposes of preventing a future terrorist attack.[20] Soon, the federal government became one of the technology industries' biggest clients, offering lucrative contracts for massive data collection.[21]

In response, tech companies built an infrastructure that collected data on users 24 hours a day, for the purpose of understanding and manipulating users' behaviors and attitudes.[22] This constant surveillance of users produced a seemingly endless stream of data from cellphones, smart televisions and remotes, in home assistances such as Amazon's Alexa, facial recognition security cameras, DNA samples from ancestry websites, video calls such as on Zoom, and educational software and platforms.[23] Indeed, **digital algorithms** – which are sets of rules for computer codes that make calculations or solve problems based on data – have the ability to analyze large swaths of data to promote psychographic profiles of individuals that reveal their behaviors and attitudes. In 2018, *Forbes* reported that humans create 2.5 quintillion bytes of data daily, with over 90 percent of that data generated in the previous two years alone.[24] To maximize their data collection, companies such as Facebook, Amazon, Apple, Microsoft, Netflix, Spotify, and Yahoo share their data with each other.[25]

Marketing insiders claim that their machine intelligence capabilities enabled them to create algorithms that could anticipate what a user will do at a particular moment, soon thereafter, and even much later.[26] Algorithmic-based predictive analytic products are lucrative features because they enable effective micro-targeting.[27] Gutenberg University research associate Simon Kruschinski and University of Bamberg researcher Andre Haller describe **micro-targeting** as "a commercial direct marketing practice and refers to the process of making strategic decisions at the individual level about which customer to target with what campaign message."[28] **Predictive analytic products** operationalize data in order for companies to micro-target a particular individual or group with effective messaging. Predictive analytic products have proven so successful to the advertising industry that social media advertisement revenue jumped from $11 billion 2015 to $23.5 billion in 2018.[29]

Predictive analytic products can serve various functions for various industries: Health insurers would like to know what ailments their patients have searched for on Google and how active they are in order to calculate their patients' health insurance fees; car insurance companies seek Global Positioning System (GPS) data to analyze their customers' driving speed and frequency in order to calculate their customers' insurance premiums; law enforcement agencies seek DNA data from genealogy websites in order to solve crimes; and advertisers seek customers' data to create effective advertisements.[30] In addition, micro-targeting has been used to influence electoral outcomes. By customizing information – regardless of its veracity – micro-targeting represents a threat to critical thinking and democracy.[31]

More recently, technology companies have begun experimenting with a more promising and thus more lucrative way to exploit behavioral surplus data: An economy of action.[32] In an **action economy**, companies operationalize users' data to direct rather than predict their behavior. Data offer a window into users' thoughts and cognitive processes. Those with access to these data can construct content and situations where a user will act in a desired fashion. This redirection of behavior can be as subtle as a phrase found in a user's Facebook news feed or the particular timing and placement of a purchase button on a website.[33] Zuboff concludes that technology companies' long-term goal is to triangulate data in an effort to direct every human action.[34] The user mistakenly assumes that the search engine, market place, app store, or search engine is free. In fact, it is not. The payment comes from users' labor. While users toil away posting, searching, producing, sharing, and more, their labor is being commodified and their privacy is being erased.[35]

Digital Power

Due to their accumulation of massive wealth, tech corporations have garnered immense influence and power. Scott Galloway refers to the most powerful and wealthy media companies – Amazon, Apple, Facebook, and Google – as "the four."[36] By 2021, Amazon was responsible for somewhere between 40 and 50 percent of all e-commerce; Apple controls the iPhone app store and extracts wealth from all app developers; Facebook accounted for nearly 71.8 percent of all social media site visits in the US; and Google dominated 92 percent of the search engine market.[37] These companies sometimes work together, such as Apple's longstanding agreement to make Google the default search engine on its products.[38] In 2020, the U.S. Government accused these companies of engaging in anti-competitive practices such as purchasing potential competitors before they threaten their market share.[39] For example, Facebook purchased Instagram for $1 billion and WhatsApp for $19 billion in 2012 and 2014 respectively.[40] The threat of government regulation aims to curtail big-tech's power. Previously, the government has largely served to protect tech companies' financial interests. Most famously, big-tech has been protected from traditional media regulations thanks to section 230 of the 1996 Communication Decency Act.[41] Section 230 effectively gives big-tech companies immunity from prosecution, a protection that pre-digital media was not afforded, regarding the content published on their platform.[42]

Government protections and lacking regulations have enabled big-tech to consolidate its power and influence. Tech companies' profits have afforded them massive political power as demonstrated by their ability to deplatform a sitting president, Donald Trump, in 2021.[43] Market dominance affords big-tech with tremendous power over users. In 2021, Facebook removed news content for an entire nation, Australia, in response to that country's effort to spread the digital wealth more equally.[44] It illuminated the incredible influence and power that Facebook has over sovereign nations and their people.

The Australia debacle illustrates the ways in which big-tech serves as one of the most influential gatekeepers of information for 21st century media users. For example, the editor of the American Association of University Professors' Academe Blog, John K. Wilson, cataloged Zoom's censorship of events that featured speakers critical of the Israeli occupation of Palestine at San Francisco State University. In other words, the digital medium (Zoom) becomes the message, deciding what is and is not permissible even at a public institution of higher education. Similarly, the associate director of media watchdog Project Censored, Andy Lee Roth, has noted the impact of algorithmic censorship on the LGBTQIA community and even academic critical media literacy channels on platforms like YouTube. Roth refers to these algorithms, and their creators, as the new gatekeepers.[45] Big-tech companies and their algorithms are the new content curators and censors even over activities at public institutions, which could be interpreted as a violation by proxy of First Amendment protections as noted earlier in this text. Critical digital literacy is not only about understanding the power and political economy of digital media, but how their ideology shapes their platforms and users' access to information.

Algorithms

A platform's algorithm has awesome power for shaping users' perceptions of the world. A platform algorithm decides what content users see and do not see on social media feeds, search engine results, and any other digital internet experience. As Jillian York notes in *Silicon Values: The Future of Free Speech Under Surveillance Capitalism,* big-tech shapes society's values through algorithms that decide which speech, ideologies, nudity, sex, and spelling is appropriate for users.[46] The ways in which algorithms reflect the biases of their creators is an expression of big-tech's power. Algorithmic biases have been found to reinforce dominant ideologies under the veneer of objectivity. For example, Safiya Umoja Noble, Associate Professor at the University of California, Los Angeles (UCLA) in the Department of Information Studies, in her 2018 *Algorithms of Oppression: How Search Engines Reinforce Racism*[47] found that Google searches for images of African Americans reinforce white supremacist ideology by producing pictures of monkeys, a long-used racist trope against blacks in America. Similarly, Emily Chang in *Brotopia: Breaking up the Boys' Club of Silicon Valley*, notes that Silicon Valley products are shaped by and serve patriarchal ideologies dating back to the famous picture of Lena Sodenberg (real name) from Playboy, which University of Southern California engineers used to perfect communication and scanners.[48]

Big-tech biases are not only revealed in the content displayed on a particular platform, but the interpretation of data as well. Polizzi explains that critical digital literacy requires "an understanding of socio-economic issues underpinning how information is accessed, used and produced in the digital age."[49] **Socio-economics** refers to "a wide range of inter-related and diverse aspects relating to or involving a combination of social and economic features."[50] Scholars such as mathematician and data scientist, Cathy O'Neil, and New York University data journalism professor, Meredith Broussard, have noted that the efforts to use big-tech algorithms to produce equity in educational outcomes actually worsened the education of students from lower socio-economic status.[51] Similarly, rather than mitigate fraud in the public sector as they promised to do, Professor in the Department of Women's Studies at the University at Albany, Virginia Eubanks, points out that 40 years of data collection and algorithmic systems has actually cut social services to those who depend upon them most.[52] Lastly, rather than deliver worker autonomy or an opportunity to increase their revenue stream, Assistant Professor of Sociology at University of North Carolina at Chapel Hill, Alexandrea Ravenelle, points out in *Hustle and Gig, Struggling and Surviving in the*

Sharing Economy, that the gig or shared economy is predicated on max-imizing wealth for the tech company while keeping working people on call 24 hours a day, for declining wages.[53] Technology ethnographer, Alex Rosenblat, goes further, referring to the promises of the shared economy to be "fool's gold."[54]

Platforms

The ways in which tech companies design their platforms serve as a reflection of their power. After all, they decide what is possible and impossible. For example, Facebook allowed a "like button," but not a "dislike button," and Twitter sets character limits on posts. They also decide which types of information users are able to access. Every user's search results and social media feed differs because algorithms seek to give users content that will keep them engaged with their platform by filtering out content that is likely to make users uninterested in the platform. This is known as the **filter bubble**. [55] The result is a custo-mized experience based on what tech companies think users want to access. The content that they privilege appeals to lower human emotions both positive (admiration, appreciation, amusement, romance, satisfac-tion, sympathy, triumph) and negative (anxiety, awkwardness, boredom, confusion, craving, disgust, envy, fear, horror, sadness) because that is the content that best garners users' attention and engagement.[56]

Since the profitability depends upon collecting and analyzing data derived from prolonged media use, this is the content that is most bene-ficial to their company. These big-tech firms are not peddling in the social, they are data mining, surveilling, and collecting information to sell to other companies, while devising more ways to manipulate users, keeping them online in the process. These social media companies are using the users, not the other way around, which is why these platforms are "free" as these are the hidden costs. As media scholar Siva Vaidhya-nathan, Director for the Center for Media and Citizenship at the Uni-versity of Virginia, wrote in *Anti-Social Media: How Facebook Disconnects Us and Undermines Democracy,* companies like Facebook operate more like casinos than some social club. He writes:

> Facebook, like snack foods, cigarettes, and gambling machines, is designed for 'stickiness.' Unlike these other things, Facebook is designed for 'social stickiness.' Every acquisition that Facebook has made has been in the interest of keeping more people interacting with Facebook services in different ways to generate more data.[57]

Vaidhyanathan argues that their economic model is based on the gam-bling model, which seeks to get people addicted or in the habit of using social media by having users conflate repetition with pleasure. It is based on psychologist B.F. Skinner's concept of providing an individual with a reward or rewarding feeling in exchange for that individual exhibiting a desired behavior.[58] They will continue to do the desired behavior in search of a reward even if one is not attained. In the digital realm, rewards are the carefully placed and constructed notifications, alerts, and requests that direct users' attention to their screens.[59] Effectively, the user thinks they are using the technology to access information, but again, and this bears repeating, they are actually the ones *being used by* social media companies, often for data harvesting.

One of the most egregious examples of this is the social media platform Snapchat. It successfully keeps teenagers addicted to their phones through a system that offers rewards, such as emojis, for people who have long Snapchat streaks, typically 100 days. A streak is measured by the back-and-forth communication between two participants; the less time with communication, the shorter the streak.[60] As critical scholars have noted, users have the power to determine if the benefits of social media are worth the costs, but only if they are educated and reminded of what is transpiring in their interactions with various digital platforms.

User Power

Critical theory and thinking recognizes the power of big-tech, but also the power of users to determine and negotiate their relationship with digital media. One way, that this can be achieved is by doing a cost–benefit analysis. That is when users list the benefits and costs associated with media use to determine if the benefits are worth the cost. To get users started, here is an introductory list of some of the most commonly cited costs and benefits:

Costs

- **Cyber-bullying:** Refers to "an aggressive, intentional act carried out by a group or an individual, using electronic forms of contact, repeatedly and over time against a victim who cannot easily defend him or herself".[61] Scholars contend that when it comes to young people, those who identify as young girls are often more likely to be the victim of cyber-bullying than young boys.[62]
- **Off-screen violence:** The destructive conflicts in digital spaces have gone offline. For example, in 2014, a group of anonymous internet users organized on websites such as 4chan, Internet Relay Chat, Twitter, and Reddit to devise and execute a doxing scheme and a series of threats of rape and murder against women suspected of making feminist video games known as Gamergate.[63] The users'

anger was sparked by a fake news story, posted online, by a game creator's former boyfriend that alleged the game creator had received a favorable review for her video game by having sex with a reviewer.[64] In actuality the reviewer named in the story had never reviewed the game, something the former boyfriend later acknowledged. The episode would be part of a much larger violent campaign against women fostered on the internet.[65]

- **Polarization:** Despite studies revealing that users on the far extremes are more similar than different, a hateful division persists due to the perception cultivated through social media.[66] Researchers contend that social media platforms are designed in a way that deepens polarization in the U.S.[67] The polarization online runs counter to constructive dialogue, as it comes at the expense of healthy relationships among loved ones offline.[68] Indeed, Anne Applebaum uses the example of how friends she had 20 years earlier no longer speak to her due to polarization.[69] Consider your own friends from 5, 10, 15, 20, 25 years ago. How many do you not talk to because of something on social media?

- **Legitimization of false content:** Social media threatens critical thinking and constructive dialogue because it reinforces things that people believe even if they are false. Nolan Higdon notes that it is no coincidence that the fears of fake news center on social media because fake news appeals to the very lower emotions that tech companies privilege. Others, such as Chief Technologist at the Center for Social Media Responsibility, Aviv Ovadya, warns that it has led to an "Infocalypse," which he defines as a crisis of misinformation that risks destabilizing the key institutions of what constitutes civilization as we know it.[70] Much of the problem is owed to new technologies which allow the production of convincing content such as deepfakes, which are videos which appear to be actual film, but in fact are fabricated. Similarly, political grifters such as Steve Bannon, who reportedly collected millions of dollars in revenue from a false wall project, and Alex Jones, a self-professed performance artist who made millions peddling baseless conspiracies, have cashed in on the new opportunities.

- **Health problems:** There are a series of health problems associated with media use including mental health issues that bring about depression, feeling of isolation, and suicide.[71] Similarly, social media use has been associated with body dysmorphia and eating disorders.[72] Digital communication has brought upon physical health problems known as screen addiction and fatigue.[73]

- **Privacy:** Dating back to the Cold War up through the War on Terror era revelations of Edward Snowden, which revealed that big-tech was aiding the federal government in domestic surveillance, big-tech has been emaciating user privacy.[74] Currently, data is collected from microphones, cameras, GPS, and other tools placed in computers, tablets, laptops, kindles, Alexa, phones, cars, televisions, and pretty much any item with the word "smart" attached to it. This includes children's toys.[75]

- **Threats to personal security:** These costs refer to internet frauds and scams.
- **Keyboard courage of screen bravery:** Refers to the practice of individuals communicating messages that they would be reticent to communicate face-to-face. Former professional boxer Mike Tyson summed up this phenomenon by humorously noting "Social media made y'all way too comfortable with disrespecting people and not getting punched in the face for it."[76]
- Slacktivism: An ineffective form of activism where users conflate their communication of policy preferences and politicians with actual transformative change.

Benefits

- **Reach a large audience:** Whether it be building more awareness of a cause or a brand, social media has allowed humans to reach audiences previously thought impossible.
- **Economic growth:** As danah boyd notes, the scholarship concerning the benefits of social media has highlighted the ways in which "social media helped engineers, entrepreneurs, and everyday people reimagine the role that technology could play in information dissemination, community development, and communication."[77]
- **Participatory culture:** Refers to "a culture in which large numbers of people from all walks of life have the capacity to produce and share media with each other."[78] The benefit here is that people from around the world are able to communicate and collaborate thanks to digital tools.

Based on the cost-benefit analysis, users can determine how, if at all, to use the devices moving forward.

One way of structuring digital media use is known as digital minimalism. Coined by Cal Newport, digital minimalism is "a philosophy of technology use in which you focus your online time on a small number of carefully selected and optimized activities that strongly support things you value, and then happily miss out on everything else."[79] Newport argues that digital tools were introduced as an added bonus to our lives but by making every task seem perfunctory, they use the user. Newport contends that users can achieve digital minimalism by adopting a philosophy known as **digital declutter**. The process is to step away from optional online activities for 30 days in order to undermine many of the cycles of addiction that digital tools instill.[80] Even the pioneering founder of virtual reality, technology critic Jaron Lanier, has addressed the problematic spike in online and social media use in his book *Ten Arguments for Deleting Your Social Media Accounts Right Now.* [81] Lanier "compares the problem to past crusades against 'mass addictions' like smoking or drunk driving, arguing that hearing more voices from people who are outside of the addiction may be the most helpful way to turn the tide."[82] Others, like Tiffany Shlain, founder of the online Webby Awards and author of *24/6: Giving up Screens One Day a Week to Get More Time, Creativity, and Connection,* talks about the importance of giving up devices and social media even one day a week, what her family calls a Technology Shabbat, and offers suggestions to reconnect with nature and engage in nondigital activities.[83]

Cal Newport further argues that smartphones play a key role in creating solitude deprivation. **Solitude deprivation** refers to "a state in which you spend close to zero time alone with your own thoughts and free from input from other minds."[84] Solitude deprivation pushes people to extremes where they miss out on positive things, are unable to clarify their problems, regulate emotions, or strengthen relationships, and lack moral courage. Solitude is a critical part of digital minimalism because it enables unhurried self-reflection that people like Martin Luther King and Abraham Lincoln relied upon to make some of their most crucial decisions. The three benefits of solitude are new ideas, an understanding of the self, and a closeness to others. Newport, and others like Shlain, recommend that users consider leaving their phone at home when they go out, take long walks or hikes, and even engage with themselves by writing letters to themselves. Shlain's website offers a multitude of resources for how to take control of your digital life and use technology more mindfully rather than permit it to use you.[85]

Finally, Newport argues that rather than low-quality leisure, such as social media, folks use high-quality leisure which includes joyful activities that make life worth living. In our leisure time we should privilege strenuous activities that favor action over more traditional ideas of relaxation because strenuous activities do not cost much money, provide physical exercise, and are good for mental health. In addition, they are quite virtuous. Users should prioritize demanding activity over passive consumption, employ skills to produce valuable things in the physical world, and seek activities require real-world structured interactions.

Users are also empowered when they accept that humans are smart, machines are not. Franklin Foer points out in that the philosophy of Silicon Valley assumed that their goal was to advance technology to a point where machines could create a more efficient society by replacing human intelligence with machine intelligence.[86] However, decades ago serious engineers and computer scientists abandoned the concept of an autonomous artificial intelligence that would surpass human intellect.[87] As a result, we must resist the urge toward **technochauvenism**, which is "the belief that tech is always the solution" to every problem.[88] In fact, the stories of Elizabeth Holmes of Theranos and Mark Zuckerberg of Facebook demonstrate the lofty unattained promises of Silicon Valley.[89] Holmes promised that an entire lab, staff, and waiting process for blood analysis would be replaced with a box she called Edison.[90] It turned out to be a physical impossibility that lost billions of dollars in funding.[91] Similarly, Zuckerberg promised his Facebook platform could deliver democracy to the world, but instead has been fingered as being responsible for divisive discourse that is unraveling the democratic process across the world.[92] In fact, today, many of the work performed by algorithms actually relies on humans to intervene and complete the job. Scholars have noted that algorithms often fail to adequately perform functions such as facial recognition or content moderation, and when these failures occur the content in question is sent to a human to evaluate.[93]

Data feminists like Catherine D'Ignazio and Lauren Klein remind users that they have to the power to examine and challenge the power invested in media. They argue that users' understanding of the world is influenced by data collection and analysis practices that reflect current social inequities. One example is "big dick data," which they define as

> big data projects that are characterized by patriarchal, cis-masculinist, totalizing fantasies of world domination as enacted through data capture and analysis. Big Dick data projects ignore context, fetishize, and inflate their technical and scientific capabilities.[94]

An example is the Global Database of Events, Language and Tone (GDelt), which falsely reported to have collected massive amounts of data that were used in news reports, such as *FiveThirtyEight's* exaggerated coverage of the kidnappings in Nigeria, that later were retracted when the data was shown to be inaccurate.[95] Ruha Benjamin points out another example of how power-dynamics shape data collection and analysis processes known as the New Jim Code. It refers to the ways in which data collection and analysis processes reinforce racist ideologies.[96] Data feminists argue that in response to big dick data projects, the New Jim Code, and other colonial data practices, users must investigate the ways in which data are collected to reveal the power-dynamics that shape what is able to collect data. Rather than accept the findings of data analysis – such as the output of an algorithm – data feminists call upon users to audit how power shapes the ways in which data are analyzed. In addition, data feminists ask that users imagine what a more liberatory internet – one that is shaped by fair and equitable data practices – would look like.

They further call upon users to engage and empower the next generation of data feminists through teaching about the power-dynamics that shape data collection and analysis.[97]

Lastly, users can utilize their power by joining the attention resistance. Newport argues that we can defeat the attention economy by deleting social media from our phones, turning our devices into single-use computers, using social media only as a professional, embracing more slow media, and dumbing down our smartphone. Rather than depend upon the empty promises of big-tech, overthrow this digital master. Digital devices control user behavior through notification and invade privacy with surveillance mechanisms with little consideration. In the process, they make profits from selling your data and weaponizing it to nudge or direct users to make a purchase or related decision. Users should turn off all notifications and check their devices when they choose to, not when their device tells them to. Similarly, rather than give a device access to microphones, photos, contacts, and cameras, all the time, users should turn them off until they are ready to use them. By forcing themselves to turn on a device's feature for use, users create opportunities to reflect upon the necessity of using their device: Is it worth turning on the features and turning them off again to take this picture? Or should I just eat the food and enjoy the moment? By re-framing their relationship with technology in this way, users control the technology not the other way around.

Conclusion

"Once you have dialogue starting, you know you can break down prejudice," remarked the gay rights activist and politician Harvey Milk in his 1978 "The Hope Speech."[98] As a South Florida study and subsequent canvassing in Massachusetts revealed, those words were as true in 1978 when Milk spoke them as they are now. Despite the affordances offered by social media they have yet to demonstrate a similar effectiveness at challenging prejudice. Rather they have been associated with anti-democratic patterns such as the proliferation of deep divisions that threaten constructive dialogue, the proliferation of falsehoods that threaten critical thinking, and the spread hateful ideologies over the last few decades.[99] This is not to say that all digital communication is useless; rather, it is to say that users must be cognizant of the ways in which the political economy of the internet reinforces these ideologies and puts limits on the liberatory potential of digital communication. Critical thinkers and communicators are aware of the limits and potential for digital information gathering and communication, and seek to maximize digital benefits and minimize digital costs and damages. The next and concluding chapter outlines best practices for utilizing digital spaces for the purposes of furthering constructive dialogue and democratic culture more specifically.

Notes

1 Brian Resnick, "How to talk someone out of bigotry: These scientists keep proving that reducing prejudice is possible, It's just not easy," *Vox*, January 29, 2020, https://www.vox.com/2020/1/29/21065620/broockman-kalla-deep-canvassing.

2 Ibid.

3 David Broockman and Joshua Kalla, "Durably reducing transphobia: A field experiment on door-to-door canvassing," *Science* 352, no. 6282 (2016): 220–224.

4 Ibid.

5 Jonathan Allen and Amie Parnes, *Shattered: Inside Hillary Clinton's Doomed Campaign* (New York: Random House, 2017).

6 Edward-Isacc Dovere, "How Clinton lost Michigan – and blew the election," *Politico*, December 14, 2016, https://www.politico.com/story/2016/12/michigan-hillary-clinton-trump-232547; Joshua Darr, "The incredible shrinking Democratic ground game: The Clinton campaign staffed far fewer field offices than Obama's campaigns did," *Vox*, November 16, 2017, https://www.vox.com/mischiefs-of-faction/2017/11/16/16665756/shrinking-democratic-ground-game.

7 Christian Fuchs, *Social Media: A Critical Introduction* (Los Angeles, CA: Sage, 2017); Adam Smidi and Saif Shahin, "Social media and social mobilisation in the Middle East: A survey of research on the Arab spring," *India Quarterly* 73, no. 2 (2017): 196–209.

8 Jean M. Twenge, "Have smartphones destroyed a generation? More comfortable online than out partying, post-millennials are safer, physically, than adolescents have ever been. But they're on the brink of a mental-health crisis," September 2017, https://www.theatlantic.com/magazine/archive/2017/09/has-the-smartphone-destroyed-a-generation/534198/.

9 Ibid.

10 Ibid.

11 Oil Mould, *Against Creativity* (Brooklyn, NY: Verso Books, 2018).

12 Juliet Hinrichsen and Antony Coombs, "The five resources of critical digital literacy: A framework for curriculum integration," *Research in Learning Technology* 21 (2013).

13 Gianfranco Polizzi, "Information literacy in the digital age: Why critical digital literacy matters for democracy," in *Informed Societies: Why Information Literacy Matters for Citizenship, Participation and Democracy*, ed. Stéphane Goldstein (London: Facet Publishing, 2020), 1–23.

14 Ibid.

15 Shoshana Zuboff, *The Age of Surveillance Capitalism: The Fight for the Future at the New Frontier of Power* (New York: Public Affairs, 2019).

16 Xing Zhang, Zhenglei Yi, Zhi Yan, Geyong Min, Wenbo Wang, Ahmed Elmokashfi, Sabita Maharjan, and Yan Zhang, "Social computing for mobile big data," *Computer* 49, no. 9 (2016): 86–90.

17 Zuboff, *The Age of Surveillance Capitalism*.

18 Ibid.

19 Guido Buenstorf and Dirk Fornahl, "B2C – bubble to cluster: The dot-com boom, spin-off entrepreneurship, and regional agglomeration," *Journal of Evolutionary Economics* 19, no. 3 (2009): 349–378.

20 Yasha Levine, *Surveillance Valley: The Secret Military History of the Internet* (New York: Hachette Books, 2018).

21 Ibid.

22 Ibid.

23 Zuboff, *The Age of Surveillance Capitalism*; Nolan Higdon and Mickey Huff, "Zooming past equity in higher education: Technocratic pedagogy fails social justice test guest blogger," *Academe Blog*, May 22, 2020, https://academeblog. org/2020/05/22/zooming-past-equity-in-higher-education-technocratic-pedag ogy-fails-social-justice-test/.

24 Bernard Marr, "How much data do we create every day? The mind-blowing stats everyone should read," *Forbes*, May 21, 2018, https://www.forbes.com/ sites/bernardmarr/2018/05/21/how-much-data-do-we-create-every-day-the-mi nd-blowing-stats-everyone-should-read/#635d904a60ba.

25 Aaron Mak, "The industry: How Facebook made those eerie 'people you may know' suggestions," *Slate*, December 19, 2018, https://slate.com/technology/ 2018/12/facebook-friend-suggestions-creepy-people-you-may-know-feature.ht ml?__twitter_impression=true.

26 Ibid.

27 Ibid.

28 Simon Kruschinski and Andre Haller, "Restrictions on data-driven political micro-targeting in Germany," *Internet Policy Review* 6, no. 4 (2017).

29 "Social network advertising revenues in the United States from 2015 to 2018 (in billion U.S. dollars)," Statista, https://www.statista.com/statistics/271259/ advertising-revenue-of-social-networks-in-the-us/.

30 Bianca Bosker, "The binge breaker: Tristan Harris believes Silicon Valley is addicting U.S. to our phones. He's determined to make it stop," *The Atlantic*, November, 2016, https://www.theatlantic.com/magazine/archive/2016/11/ the-binge-breaker/501122/; Eoin O'Carroll, "Are the trackers really voluntary?" *Chrisitan Science Monitor*, March 15, 2018, https://www.csmonitor.com/ Technology/2018/0315/Can-your-boss-make-you-wear-a-Fitbit; Megan Molteni, "The creepy genetics behind the Golden State killer case," *Wired*, April 27, 2018, https://www.wired.com/story/detectives-cracked-the-golden-state-k iller-case-using-genetics/; Tina Hesman Saey, "Crime solvers embraced genetic genealogy: The Golden State killer case was just the beginning," *Science News*, December 17, 2018, https://www.sciencenews.org/article/genet ic-genealogy-forensics-top-science-stories-2018-yir.

31 Meta S. Brown, "Big Data Analytics And The Next President: How Microtargeting Drives Today's Campaigns," Forbes, May 29, 2016, https://www. forbes.com/sites/metabrown/2016/05/29/big-data-analytics-and-the-next-presi dent-how-microtargeting-drives-todays-campaigns/?sh=2df8f46d6c42; Isobel Asher Hamilton, "Easily overblown, little-understood, and dangerous: Why we need to understand political microtargeting," Business Insider, October 4, 2020, https://www.businessinsider.com/microtargeting-efficacy-overblown-stil l-dangerous-2020-10.

32 Shoshana Zuboff, *The Age of Surveillance Capitalism: The Fight for the Future at the New Frontier of Power* (New York: Public Affairs, 2019).

33 Ibid.

34 Ibid.

35 Christian Fuchs, *Social Media: A Critical Introduction* (Los Angeles, CA: Sage, 2017).

36 Scott Galloway, *The Four: The Hidden DNA of Amazon, Apple, Facebook, and Google* (New York: Random House, 2017).

37 Lauren_Feiner, "House Democrats say Facebook, Amazon, Alphabet, Apple enjoy 'monopoly power' and recommend big changes," *CNBC*, October 6, 2020, https://www.cnbc.com/2020/10/06/house-democrats-say-facebook-ama zon-alphabet-apple-enjoy-monopoly-power.html; H. Tankovska, "U.S. market

share of leading social media websites 2021," *Statista,* June 17, 2021, https://
www.statista.com/statistics/265773/market-share-of-the-most-popular-social-
media-websites-in-the-us/#:~:text=U.S.%20market%20share%20of%20leadi
ng%20social%20media%20websites%202021&text=In%20May%202021%
2C%20Facebook%20accounted,social%20media%20website%20by%20far;
Joseph Johnson, "Global market share of search engines 2010–2021," *Statista,*
July 8, 2021, https://www.statista.com/statistics/216573/worldwide-market-
share-of-search-engines/; Blake Droesch, "Amazon dominates US ecommerce,
though its market share varies by category," *eMarketer,* Apr 27, 2021, https://
www.emarketer.com/content/amazon-dominates-us-ecommerce-though-its-ma
rket-share-varies-by-category.

38 Daisuke Wakabayashi and Jack Nicash, "Apple, Google and a deal that controls the internet: In a landmark antitrust complaint, the Justice Department
is targeting a secretive partnership that is worth billions of dollars to both
companies," *New York Times,* October 25, 2020, https://www.nytimes.com/
2020/10/25/technology/apple-google-search-antitrust.html.

39 Feiner, "House Democrats say Facebook, Amazon, Alphabet, Apple enjoy
'monopoly power' and recommend big changes."

40 Jean M. Twenge, "Have smartphones destroyed a generation? More comfortable online than out partying, post-Millennials are safer, physically, than
adolescents have ever been. But they're on the brink of a mental-health
crisis," September 2017, https://www.theatlantic.com/magazine/archive/2017/
09/has-the-smartphone-destroyed-a-generation/534198/.

41 Shoshana Zuboff, *The Age of Surveillance Capitalism: The Fight for the Future at
the New Frontier of Power* (New York: Public Affairs, 2019); Nolan Higdon,
The Anatomy of Fake News: A Critical News Education (Oakland, CA: University
of California Press, 2020).

42 Higdon, *The Anatomy of Fake News.*

43 Sam Shead, "Facebook owns the four most downloaded apps of the decade,"
BBC, December 18, 2019, https://www.bbc.com/news/technology-50838013
#:~:text=Facebook%20bought%20Instagram%20in%202012,than%20a%20
billion%20users%20each.

44 Josh Taylor, "Facebook's botched Australia news ban hits health departments,
charities and its own pages: Social media company's ban on sharing news has
also affected dozens of government, not-for-profit and community pages," *The
Guardian,* February 17, 2021, https://www.theguardian.com/technology/
2021/feb/18/facebook-blocks-health-departments-charities-and-its-own-pages-
in-botched-australia-news-ban.

45 Andy Lee Roth, "The new gatekeepers: How proprietary algorithms increasingly
determine the news we see," *The Markaz Review,* March 15, 2021, https://thema
rkaz.org/magazine/the-new-gatekeepers-andy-lee-roth; John K. Wilson, Zoom,
"YouTube, and Facebook censor event at SF State," *Academe Blog,* September 23,
2020, https://academeblog.org/2020/09/23/zoom-youtube-and-facebook-censor-
event-at-sf-state/.

46 Jillian York, *Silicon Values: The Future of Free Speech Under Surveillance Capitalism* (New York: Verso Books, 2021).

47 Safiya Umoja Noble, *Algorithms of Oppression: How Search Engines Reinforce
Racism* (New York: New York University Press, 2018).

48 Emily Chang, *Brotopia: Breaking up the Boys' Club of Silicon Valley* (New York:
Portfolio/Penguin, 2018).

49 Gianfranco Polizzi, "Information literacy in the digital age: Why critical digital
literacy matters for democracy," in *Informed Societies: Why Information Literacy*

Matters for Citizenship, Participation and Democracy, ed. Stéphane Goldstein (London: Facet Publishing, 2020), 1–23; see also David Buckingham, Shakuntala Banaji, Diane Carr, Susan Cranmer, and Rebekah Willett, "The media literacy of children and young people: A review of the research literature," Ofcom, 2005, http://discovery.ucl.ac.uk/10000145; David Buckingham, "Digital media literacies: Rethinking media education in the age of the internet," *Research in Comparative and International Education* 2, no. 1 (2007): 43–55.

50 Jyoti Kumari, Ritu Dubey, Dipak Kumar Bose, and Vandana Gupta, "A study on socio-economic condition of Tharu tribes in Bahraich district of Uttar Pradesh in India," *Journal of Applied and Natural Science* 10, no. 3 (2018): 939–944.

51 Cathy O'Neil, *Weapons of Math Destruction: How Big Data Increases Inequality and Threatens Democracy* (New York: Broadway Books, 2016, 2017); Meredith Broussard, *Artificial Unintelligence: How Computers Misunderstand the World* (Cambridge, MA: MIT Press, 2019).

52 Virginia Eubanks, *Automating Inequality: How High Tech Tools Profile, Police, and Punish the Poor* (New York: St. Martin's Press, 2017).

53 Alexandrea Ravenelle, *Hustle and Gig, Struggling and Surviving in the Sharing Economy* (Oakland, CA: University of California Press, 2019).

54 Alex Rosenblat, *Uberland: How Algorithms Are Rewriting the Rules of Work* (Oakland, CA: University of California Press, 2018).

55 Eli Pariser, *The Filter Bubble: How the New Personalized Web is Changing What We Read and How We Think* (New York: Penguin, 2011).

56 Siva Vaidhyanathan, *Anti-Social Media: How Facebook Disconnects Us and Undermines Democracy* (New York: Oxford University Press, 2018); Alan S. Cowen and Dacher Keltner, "Self-report captures 27 distinct categories of emotion bridged by continuous gradients," *Proceedings of the National Academy of Sciences* 114, no. 38 (2017): E7900-E7909, https://doi.org/10.1073/pnas.1702247114.

57 Vaidhyanathan, *Anti-Social Media*, 38–39.

58 Julie Bort, "An early investor in Facebook and Google has slammed them for 'aggressive brain hacking'," *Business Insider,* August 8, 2017, www.businessinsider.com/famous-facebook-and-google-investor-condemns-brain-hacking-2017-8; B.F. Skinner, *The Behavior of Organisms: An Experimental Analysis of Behavior* (New York: Appleton-Century-Crofts, 1938).

59 Tim Wu, *The Attention Merchants: The Epic Scramble to Get Inside Our Heads* (New York: Vintage Books, 2016).

60 Taylor Lorenz, "Teens explain the world of Snapchat's addictive streaks, where friendships live or die," *Business Insider,* April 14, 2017, https://www.businessinsider.com/teens-explain-Snapchat-streaks-why-theyre-so-addictive-and-important-to-friendships-2017-4.

61 Peter K. Smith, Jess Mahdavi, Manuel Carvalho, Sonja Fisher, Shanette Russell, and Neil Tippett, "Cyberbullying: Its nature and impact in secondary school pupils," *Journal of Child Psychology and Psychiatry* 49, no. 4 (2008): 376–385.

62 Jean M. Twenge, "Have smartphones destroyed a generation? More comfortable online than out partying, post-Millennials are safer, physically, than adolescents have ever been. But they're on the brink of a mental-health crisis," *The Atlantic,* September 9, 2017, https://www.theatlantic.com/magazine/archive/2017/09/has-the-smartphone-destroyed-a-generation/534198/.

63 Emma A. Jane, *Misogyny Online: A Short (and Brutish) History* (London: Sage, 2016).

64 Chandra Steele, "Everything you never wanted to know about GamerGate," *PC Magazine,* October 21, 2014, https://www.pcmag.com/article2/0,2817,2470723,00.asp.

65   Jane, *Misogyny Online.*

66   Zaid Jilani, "The woke Left v. the Alt-Right: A new study shows they're more alike than either side realizes," *Quillette*, August 3, 2020, https://quill ette.com/2020/08/03/the-woke-left-v-the-alt-right-a-new-study-shows-theyre-more-alike-than-either-side-realizes/.

67   Nolan Higdon, *The Anatomy of Fake News: A Critical News Education* (Oakland, CA: University of California Press, 2020); Ezra Klein, *Why We're Polarized* (New York: Simon & Schuster, 2020); Mike Wendling, *Alt-Right from 4chan to the White House* (London, Pluto Books, 2018).

68   Jesselyn Cook, "'I miss my mom': Children of QAnon believers are desperately trying to deradicalize their own parents," *HuffPost*, February 11, 2021, https://www.huffpost.com/entry/children-of-qanon-believers_n_601078e9c5b 6c5586aa49077.

69   Anne Applebaum, *Twilight of Democracy, the Seductive Lure of Authoritarianism* (New York: Double Day Press, 2020).

70   Charlie Warzel, "He predicted the 2016 fake news crisis. Now he's worried about an information apocalypse," *BuzzFeed News,* February 11, 2018, https://www.buzzfeednews.com/article/charliewarzel/the-terrifying-future-of-fake-news.

71   Jean M. Twenge, "Have smartphones destroyed a generation? More comfortable online than out partying, post-Millennials are safer, physically, than adolescents have ever been. But they're on the brink of a mental-health crisis," *The Atlantic*, September 9, 2017, https://www.theatlantic.com/maga zine/archive/2017/09/has-the-smartphone-destroyed-a-generation/534198/.

72   Avneet Kaur Himanshu, Ashishjot Kaur, and Gaurav Singla, "Rising dysmorphia among adolescents: A cause for concern," *Journal of Family Medicine and Primary Care* 9, no. 2 (2020): 567.

73   Vignesh Ramachandran, "Stanford researchers identify four causes for 'Zoom fatigue' and their simple fixes: It's not just Zoom," *Stanford*, February 23, 2021, https://news.stanford.edu/2021/02/23/four-causes-zoom-fatigue-solutions/.

74   Yasha Levine, *Surveillance Valley: The Secret Military History of the Internet* (New York: Hachette Books, 2018).

75   Christian Hetrick, "Business beware the holiday 'smart toys' that spy on your kids. Many new toys are equipped with cameras and are linked to the internet, raising concerns that they are collecting information on children without permission," *The Inquirer*, December 4, 2018, https://www.inquirer.com/news/smart-toy-spy-hack-cayla-bear-amazon-fire-20181204.html.

76   Kyle Dalton, "Mike Tyson confronts cyberbullying and warns potential keyboard warriors," *Sportscasting*, July 7, 2020, https://www.google.com/amp/s/www.sportscasting.com/mike-tyson-confronts-cyberbullying-and-warns-poten tial-keyboard-warriors/%3famp.

77   danah boyd, "Social media: A phenomenon to be analyzed," *Social Media + Society* 1, no. 1 (2015): 2056305115580148, 1.

78   Henry Jenkins, *Participatory Culture: Interviews* (Medford, MA: John Wiley & Sons, 2019), 3.

79   Ibid. 28.

80   Ibid.

81   Jaron Lanier, *Ten Arguments for Deleting Your Social Media Accounts Right Now* (New York: Henry Holt and Co., 2018).

82   Ibid.; Eric Johnson, "If you can quit social media, but don't, then you're part of the problem, Jaron Lanier says," *Vox-Recode*, July 27, 2018, https://www.vox.com/2018/7/27/17618756/jaron-lanier-deleting-social-media-book-kara-s wisher-too-embarrassed-podcast.

83 Tiffany Shlain, *24/6: Giving up Screens One Day a Week to Get More Time, Creativity, and Connection* (New York: Gallery Books, 2019), online at https://www.24sixlife.com.

84 Henry Jenkins, *Participatory Culture: Interviews* (Medford, MA: John Wiley & Sons, 2019), 103.

85 Shlain, additional resources online at https://www.24sixlife.com/resources.

86 Franklin Foer, *World Without Mind: The Extensional Threat of Big Tech* (New York: Penguin, 2017).

87 Meredith Broussard, *Artificial Unintelligence: How Computers Misunderstand the World* (Cambridge, MA: MIT Press, 2019).

88 Ibid., 7–8.

89 Karl J. Lackner and Mario Plebani, "The Theranos saga and the consequences," *Clinical Chemistry and Laboratory Medicine (CCLM)* 56, no. 9 (2018): 1395–1396.

90 Ibid.

91 Ibid.

92 Mike Isaac, "Facebook unveils redesign as it tries to move past privacy scandals," *The New York Times*, April 30, 2019, https://www.nytimes.com/2019/04/30/technology/facebook-private-communication-groups.html; Siva Vaidhyanathan, *Anti-Social Media, How Facebook Disconnects Us and Undermines Democracy* (New York: Oxford University Press, 2018).

93 Sarah Roberts, *Behind the Screen: Content Moderation in The Shadows of Social Media* (New Haven, CT: Yale University Press, 2019); Mary L. Gray and Siddhartha Suri, *Ghost Work: How to Stop Silicon Valley From Building a New Global Underclass* (Boston, MA: Houghton Mifflin Court, 2019).

94 Catherine D'Ignazio and Lauren Klein, *Data Feminism* (Cambridge, MA: MIT Press, 2020), 151.

95 Ibid., 149–152.

96 Ruha Benjamin, *Race After Technology* (Medford, MA: Polity Press, 2019).

97 D'Ignazio and Klein, *Data Feminism*.

98 Harvey Milk, "The Hope Speech," June 25, 1978, at https://almeida.co.uk/index.php?option=com_docman&view=download&alias=733-hope-speech-teaching-resource&category_slug=participate&Itemid=133.

99 Mike Wendling, *Alt-Right from 4chan to the White House* (London: Pluto Books, 2018).

Part IV

Lead by Example: Democracy is Not a Spectator Sport

From the outset of this text, we have shared what we have found to be the best practices for enhancing and supporting critical thinking, compassionate listening, and mental independence. Knowing constructive ways to handle conflicts and navigate differences can be quite utilitarian in disarming volatile parties and even build bridges where once there were disparate and yawning gaps. We hope readers find the information shared in this text self-empowering, and that it helps build confidence in peoples' ability to effectively argue, not fight. We hope it works to improve interpersonal and public communication as well as understanding, eschewing obfuscation for clarity and transparency while building trust between potentially disparate groups. When we suggest that it is possible to "agree to disagree," we do not imply that people should be doormats, accept abuse, or tolerate racism, sexism, classism, or other harmful forms of hierarchical control. Nor do we believe that people should take our intention to create more critical and compassionate citizens as a sign of weakness or fear of confrontation. On the contrary, we think that if we follow the many guidelines and suggestions in this book, people can go a long way to start hard conversations and keep them going, leaving open the possibility not only for change and growth, but for democracy to thrive and fulfill its historic and theoretical promise.

In this final chapter, we outline and recap these best practices for critical thinking and communication and hope this distillation is something that can be shared widely, especially for those who are not formal students or educators, because at the end of day, we all are in one way or another. We are always learning, teaching, sharing, and evolving, all of us.

Here's to implementing the materials in this final chapter into our lives in the hopes of creating a better, more inclusive, thoughtful, just, and equitable world. The choice is ours.

Let's get C.R.I.T.I.C.A.L.!

DOI: 10.4324/9781003250906-12

1   C – Create constructive dialogue;
2   R – Reflect on communication practices;
3   I – Inquire: Be a critical thinker;
4   T – Test theory and spot ideology;
5   I – Investigate and evaluate mass media;
6   C – Critique content: "Fake news" and ethical journalism;
7   A – Assess, analyze, and evaluate digital media use and abuse;
8   L – Lead by example: Democracy is not a spectator sport.

Chapter 8

Conclusion
Let's Get C.R.I.T.I.C.A.L.

Jerry Taylor recalls:

> From 1991 through 2000, I was a pretty good warrior on that front. I was absolutely convinced of the case for skepticism with regard to climate science and of the excessive costs of doing much about it even if it were a problem. I used to write skeptic talking points for a living.[1]

By the end of the 20th century, Taylor had become a well-known skeptic of climate change.

Two decades later, Taylor has transformed from skeptic to climate activist. In fact, Taylor currently serves as head of the Niskanen Center, a Washington, D.C. think-tank that among another things advocates for environmentalism.[2] In 2017, Taylor was asked to recall his transition from a climate change skeptic to climate justice activist, he responded:

> It started in the early 2000s. I was one of the climate skeptics who do battle on TV and I was doing a show with Joe Romm. On air, I said that, back in 1988, when climate scientist James Hansen testified in front of the Senate, he predicted we'd see a tremendous amount of warming. I argued it'd been more than a decade and we could now see by looking at the temperature record that he wasn't accurate. After we got done with the program and were back in green room, getting the makeup taken off, Joe said to me, 'Did you even read that testimony you've just talked about?' And when I told him it had been a while, he said 'I'm daring you to go back and double check this.' He told me that some of Hansen's projections were spot on. So I went back to my office and I re-read Hansen's testimony. And Joe was correct. So I then I talked to the climate skeptics who had made this argument to me, and it turns out they had done so with full knowledge they were being misleading.[3]

DOI: 10.4324/9781003250906-13

Taylor's transformation rested upon constructive communication and critical thinking. The dialogical process forced Taylor to confront uncomfortable realities that highlighted the flimsy and non-existent evidence his claims were based upon. Taylor refers to these as "blows":

> The first blow in that argument was offered by my friend Jonathan Adler, who was at the Competitive Enterprise Institute. Jon wrote a very interesting paper in which he argued that even if the skeptic narratives are correct, the old narratives I was telling wasn't an argument against climate action. Just because the costs and the benefits are more or less going to be a wash, he said, that doesn't mean that the losers in climate change are just going to have to suck it up so Exxon and Koch Industries can make a good chunk of money. The final blow against my position, which caused me to crumble, was from a fellow named Bob Litterman, who had been the head of risk management at Goldman Sachs. Bob said, "The climate risks aren't any different from financial risks I had to deal with at Goldman. We don't know what's going to happen in any given year in the market. There's a distribution of possible outcomes. You have to consider the entire distribution of possible outcomes when you make decisions like this." After he left my office, I said "there's nothing but rubble here."[4]

Each of these "blows" deepened Taylor's doubts about his assumptions, which resulted in a long arduous process of reformulating his conclusions about climate change.

The case of Taylor is also instructive because it reminds us that critical thinking is a process that takes time. Indeed, Taylor explains that his position was not changed immediately:

> It was more gradual. After that, I began to do more of that due diligence, and the more I did, the more I found that variations on this story kept arising again and again. Either the explanations for findings were dodgy, sketchy or misleading or the underlying science didn't hold up. Eventually, I tried to get out of the science narratives that I had been trafficking in and just fell back on the economics. Because you can very well accept that climate change exists and still find arguments against climate action because the costs of doing something are so great.[5]

Taylor's story illustrates that critical thinking through dialogue can plant seeds that produce truths. Thus, those seeking to engage in constructive dialogue must consider meeting people where they are at, and working to understand the evidence that supports their position and vice a versa.

Research has shown that providing evidence of how climate change impacts someone's community – such as down the street or in their state – is more powerful than discussing a natural disaster in another state or nation.[6] Essentially, the closer to home the example, the more likely it is to convince.

As this text has noted, when it comes to constructive dialogue, the content is as pivotal as the participants' behaviors and attitudes. How we communicate is just as important as what we think we are communicating. In fact, often *how* people interpret the message is more consequential than the message itself. This is particularly important given that we do not always get second chances to make first impressions in arguments. Although the evidence for climate change is sound, the proposed solutions may threaten a person's way of life. For example, if someone works in the fossil fuel industry, a green economy sounds like disruptive change to their existence rather than environmental progress. As a result, participants must consider that sometimes it is the implications of arguments, not the soundness of the arguments themselves, that lead people to reject them. This is true in climate change as well. A 2014 study revealed that climate change denial is not always rooted in a rejection of its existence, but skepticism over the proposed solutions.[7] Those seeking to convince others that climate change is real should account for solutions aversion in their analysis.[8]

Taylor's tale is also a cautionary one: Participants would be wise to limit their critique of other people, and keep their minds open to the possibility that it is their position that suffers from weak or non-existent evidence. Rather than engage in dialogue for the sole purpose of "winning," "being right," or even changing minds, we hope you will consider the value in agreeing to disagree. We can learn from each other, we can be transformed by one another, and we can share all that we have to offer in effort to attain a higher state of enlightenment. It is important to acknowledge that even here in the conclusion of this text, conclusions are often temporary. This chapter collates key findings from each chapter into a series of takeaways for best practices. The readers can be leaders in furthering democratic behaviors and attitudes based on critical thinking. Here are eight steps to help on the path to getting critical.

Let's Get C.R.I.T.I.C.A.L.

1: C – Create Constructive Dialogue

In a democracy, it is not a question of how to avoid or eradicate conflict, but how to manage it constructively. Where destructive conflict seeks to eradicate or dismiss the possibility of relationships, constructive conflict seeks to "balance the interests of both parties to maximize opportunities for mutual gains."[9] Of course there are often more than two parties or views, but as participants experience conflict, they might work to develop trust by displaying acts of respect, decency, integrity, credibility, humility, reciprocity, sympathy, and empathy. Some examples of actions participants can take to achieve these goals are:

- **Avoid defense posture:** Seek to avoid physical demeanor, facial expressions, and body language that makes you appear as anything, but magnanimous, urbane, and engaged.
- **Come together:** Strive to build unity, by seeking a possible conclusion both parties could partially embrace. This is also an opportunity to find common values to sort where a divergence of views took place.
- **Give the benefit of the doubt:** If you receive a nasty or curt message from someone, be charitable. Remember that they too are human, and they are being influenced by the divisive and reactionary nature of the internet. If possible, try to explain to them what you found problematic about their message in a respectful way.
- **Have emotional clarity:** Reactionary responses are not conducive to constructive dialogue. Instead, you should slow down and think. However, as noted, the internet is designed to create an emotional and quick response. So, if you feel the need, write the angry post or email. Say every terrible thing you want to say and are feeling. Then save it as a draft, if possible, go to bed, and check to see if you still want to hit send in the morning. A few hours will allow for some emotional clarity to better determine if sending the message is a good idea.
- **Inquire:** Consider what evidence would change one's mind.
- **Monitor your performance:** Monitor your performance throughout rather than at the end of a task. Ask yourself if you are being critical. Are you being respectful?
- **Practice active listening:** Try to avoid turgid behavior and assert humility and interest by listening and considering what the other person has to say. This includes reiterating their argument and asking questions to make sure you understand and that they know you want to understand their argument and perspective.
- **Seek out feedback and then use it:** Ask others for feedback and suggestions, and spend time integrating it into your approach to the task at hand.
- **Treat the arguments as construction zones,** not combat zones (we are learners, not warriors).
- **Treat others how you want to be treated:** Decorum and respect online seem impossible unless you see it in action. So take action. Demonstrate the importance of kind message greetings and

conclusions. Avoid name calling, labeling, cancelling, and blocking people. Instead, engage in conversation; try to mitigate the influence of harmful words and messages by answering them with love and critical thinking.

- **Use qualifiers:** Avoid speaking about groups as monoliths.

In addition to individual behaviors and attitudes, there is a lot that participants can do together.

Structured approaches to conflict can be useful for facilitating a shared experience that is both collaborative and inclusive. However, as communications expert Fred Jantd noted, a collaborative approach is much more labor intensive than simply creating structural rules and procedures.[10] When approaching dialogue, we encourage users to use the problematization process. As critical pedagogy scholar Paulo Freire's teaching emphasized, the problem-posing approach to dialogue is more equitable in that it illustrates that knowledge is not passed on from one person to another, but instead is formulated through dialogue.[11] We echo Freire's approach, which begins with the posing of a problem, and could result in a structured approach to dialogue, such as viewing the dialogue as a process of the following steps:

Step 1. Define the problem: Ensure that the group is focused on the same goal.

Step 2. Analyze the problem: Strive for consensus about the factors that contribute to or enable the problem.

Step 3. Generate possible solutions: Introduce possible solutions to the problem.

Step 4. Evaluate solutions: Consider how well each solution addresses the factors discussed in Step 2.

Step 5. Implement and assess the solution: Devise the best strategy to implement and assess the effectiveness of the solution.[12]

When it comes to difficult conversations, effective communicators utilize all the tools at their disposal. This includes proposing and adhering to a set of agreements:

- Stay engaged
- Experience discomfort
- Make space/take space
- Speak your truth
- Talk in first person
- Expect and accept non-closure
- Maintain confidentiality
- Listen with the intent to learn
- Suspend judgment

In addition to agreements, effective communicators use strategic questions to:[13]

- Reflect back for clarity and understanding
- Reflect back to validate
- Affirm for the purpose of making inclusive space
- Offer alternative positions
- Respond if feeling hurt or offended
- Make time and space for themselves
- Connect for realizable solutions or connections with the other participant(s)

2: R – Reflect on Communication Practices and Censorship

Given that constructive conflict management rests upon participants engaging in collaborative dialogue, it is crucial to have a shared space for diverse ideas and debate. Despite the use of seemingly new language such as "cancel culture" and "deplatforming" it is our contention that these practices reflect long-term anti-dialogical practices that have acted in opposition to the free and open debate that defines a functioning democracy. We recommend, no matter how difficult it may seem, that participants defend the principles of freedom of speech and oppose censorship. At the same time, they should be conscious of the power dynamics that shape speech, and as a result they should be cognizant of the duality of communication styles such as humor.

We operate from the assumption that Americans are not unwilling to engage in dialogue, but simply lack the spaces and tools to do so. As a result, we encourage participants to avoid the pitfalls that spur destructive conflict management:

- **Conflating searching with knowing or investigating:** Especially in our 21st century environment, dialogue and debate will see someone turn to their digital device and quickly search for a fact or piece of evidence to settle or inform the discussion. However, be wary of a quick search followed by an even quicker explanation. Did they investigate? Is the source credible? Is the search engine confirming what they already believe? It is better to spend some time searching, investigating, and analyzing before proceeding with the dialogue.
- **Discuss, but do not dismiss morality:** Social psychologist Jonathan Haidt argues that all human thought goes through a person's moral filter.[14] The implication of Haidt's contention is that if we insult or dismiss someone's morality in dialogue we have wasted an opportunity to engage in constructive dialogue with them. It is better to discuss these matters rather than dismiss or disregard them.

- **Othersidism:** When a conversation about politics, race, gender, or any other possible dichotomous topic is in focus it provides an opportunity to distract from the actor or group in focus and examine *the other side!* If the focus is the group or actor at hand, othersidism distracts from them. If it is the behavior or attitude of the actor or group, then focusing on all sides is more effective than othersidism. Either way, the "what about the other side" commentary is ineffective, illogical, and thus destructive.

- **Talking past one another:** Refers to communication where participants are discussing different aspects and not recognizing or comprehending what the other person is communicating.[15] This is sometimes due to competing definitions and perception of concepts that go unrecognized. After the racially charged discourses following the arrest and beating of Rodney King and the trial of his police abusers, Professor of Sociology at University of California, Berkeley, Bob Blauner, noticed that his black and white students were talking past each other. He explains that:

Whites locate racism in color consciousness and its absence in color blindness. They regard it as a kind of racism when students of color insistently underscore their sense of difference, their affirmation of ethnic and racial membership, which minority students have increasingly asserted. Many black, and increasingly also Latino and Asian, students cannot understand this reaction. It seems to them misinformed, even ignorant. They in turn sense a kind of racism in the whites' assumption that minorities must assimilate to mainstream values and styles. Then African-Americans will posit an idea that many whites find preposterous: Black people, they argue, cannot be racist, because racism is a system of power, and black people as a group do not have power.[16]

- **Talking to the unicorn:** Often in dialogue, baseless context is provided that shapes the conversation. Examples of these unicorns include: "Some people say"; "All through history"; and "Many people say." If you encounter these, it is critical to ask for the studies and data to confirm. If they cannot provide it, it is time to investigate the claims.

3: I – Inquire: Be a Critical Thinker

Critical thinking is among the best tools citizens have at our disposal to make sense of an increasingly complex and contentious world. With our 21st century technologically ubiquitous communication and media-saturated culture, these skills are needed perhaps more than any other time in our history. How else are humans expected to make sense of the world, contribute to the growth of knowledge and understanding, and be situated to make intelligent, well-informed decisions about key elements of their lives as individuals and as a society? We noted that critical thinkers seek knowledge, make and analyze arguments, evaluate and seek evidence, recognize bias, and strive for objectivity. As scholars M. Neil Browne and Stuart M. Keeley note in *Asking the Right Questions*, cited earlier in this book, critical thinkers have four primary values: 1) autonomy; 2) curiosity; 3) humility; and 4) respect.

In order to hone one's critical thinking skills, we suggest that citizens:

- **Avoid joining the herd for the herd's sake:** It feels nice to engage with what is trending, but remember, these algorithms can shape a view that feels pervasive. Instead, investigate the view and be brave in following the evidence regardless of which side it impacts.
- **Broaden their information base:** Internet content reinforces rather than challenges your views. Consider using search engines that do not collect or operationalize data, like DuckDuckGo. This will allow a more diverse set of search results rather than ones that confirm your view. If you are going to continue using corporate programs, clear your search history and sign out of your account to receive more diverse results.
- **Evaluate and analyze content/arguments:** Rather than just pick the content that confirms your view or that you sought to find and then use or share, evaluate it. Critically think about the author, publishers, evidence, and argument that the content makes. Consider if it is responsible to share or comment with the information you have.
- **Investigate their image:** Consider spending a fair amount of time analyzing how you are perceived online. How do your pictures, posts, and messages introduce you to the world? Sure, it is an online environment and that may not be how you perceive yourself, but in many cases this is all people have to formulate an opinion of you. What can you do to make your online persona more in line with how you want to or should be perceived?
- **Keep a diary:** A diary is helpful tool in assessing and reflecting on your performance before, during, and after a task. This can illuminate crucial insights into your metacognition.[17] Rather than assume others are stupid or wrong, scholars encourage the practice of metacognition, which put simply is thinking about how we think to plan, monitor, and assess one's understanding and performance.[18] We encourage you to utilize your critical thinking skills as you approach and engage with dialogue.

- **Privilege quality over quantity:** Whether it be browsing websites, or the reading or sending of emails, posts, or similar content, privilege quality over quantity. Spend more time doing fewer things in digital spaces to improve the quality.

- **Seeking out dissenting views:** In political ideology, race, gender, class, sexuality, and more there are differences in how we see the world in terms of policy, events, statements, and more. In your digital environment, consider finding views that differ from your own. Analyze their evidence. Determine their rationale and consider changing your own view or asking more questions about how they arrived at their view.

- **Slow down:** Engage with content, rather than react; consider listening to the Director Media Literacy Certificate Program in the Department of Communication at the University of Massachusetts, Amherst Allison Butler, who reminds us to "slow down."[19] Social media content is designed to get us to react without considering or investigating the content. It is better to slow down and investigate content carefully.

- **Work on concentration:** As researchers have noted, concentration is a skill that comes from practice and training. Boredom helps foster concentration. This is achieved by avoiding distractions such as social media and scheduling breaks, especially if you have a job or lifestyle that requires prolonged screen time. This will help require your brain to be comfortable with resisting distracting stimuli. Users can improve their memory through such easy games as memorizing a deck of cards.[20]

4: T – Test Theory and Spot Ideology

Although critical thinking in the traditional sense remains hugely important, we argue that a combination of critical thinking and theory are necessary for developing a democracy grounded in truth. Critical thinking requires an analysis of the social meaning given to that knowledge.[21] That is where critical theory comes in. In addition to acquiring knowledge, critical thinkers examine the social construction of knowledge and its fusion with ideology. As a result, when analyzing evidence, we encourage people to:

- **Test critical theory:** Citizens should analyze evidence and argument through a critical lens (class, race, gender, sexuality, and ability).

- **Spot ideology:** This means recognizing the power-dynamics that shape knowledge and looking for the ideologies that frame and perpetuate hegemonic and colonial mentalities.

- **Recognize co-optation:** The deliberate appropriation of a concept or movement for means contrary to the original intention, often in maintenance of those in power to control opposition and dissent.

Further, these critical frameworks are also useful for producing constructive dialogue. When participants enter dialogue, they are encouraged to:

- **Account for power inequities:** Those with privilege (such as white heterosexual males) typically speak more often, and interrupt rather than listening and waiting to speak. Make it clear from the beginning that all parties should be heard, and that they should all practice active listening.
- **Avoid the oppression olympics:** Critical frameworks are most useful when they help participants understand they are destructive when used for a contest to decide which group has it worse.
- **Work on cultural competence:** Examine and consider multiple perspectives, recognize the importance and utility of culture, and build cultural bridges. This involves being aware of the power-dynamics shaping the dialogue. Treat other people's knowledge, experience, and values respectfully.

5: I – Investigate and Evaluate Mass Media

We cannot begin to engage in dialogue without a shared understanding of evidence. This process relies on one's ability to verify the veracity of available information, to tell apart fact from fiction. Ascertaining informational integrity of mass media messages is a democratic survival skill in the 21st century, as the establishment media frame, influence, produce, and promote the basis for much of what constitutes much societal dialogue. As a result, it is more important than ever that we investigate media content and we all become more critically media literate. We explained that rather than engage in a protectionist, arts and education, or media literacy education approach to media, we encourage citizens to be aware of and utilize the tenets of critical media literacy education:

- **Active audience:** We are always analyzing, evaluating, and reflecting on media, not merely passively accepting it at face value.
- **Citizenship not consumerism:** Allison Butler, co-president of the national critical media literacy organization Action Coalition for Media Literacy Education (ACME), argues that, as citizens in a democracy, we must recast ourselves as media citizens rather than media consumers.[22]

- **Critical awareness of media:** Scholars Douglas Kellner and Jeff Share note a "critical awareness in critical media literacy involves identifying, analyzing, and challenging media that promote representations or narratives involving racism, sexism, classism, homophobia and other forms of discrimination a further marginalized targeted social groups."[23]
- **Understanding the message:** Media communicate, and critical media literate citizens identify and analyze messages being communicated.
- **The politics of representation:** Although ideologies are invisible, representations in media help make them visible. Thus, media citizens analyze these representations and their implications, and are aware of how stereotypes are used to distort how various groups' representations can be distorted, co-opted, or commodified via media programming.

6: C – Critique Content: "Fake News" and Ethical Journalism

Increasingly, news media seem to shape dialogue and thinking in destructive ways. Although the founders were correct in asserting that a free press enables truth to enter the public sphere, they did not consider that a substantial portion of Americans may be unable to discern fact from fiction. As a result, we encourage citizens to uphold the principles of the free press while remaining aware of:

- **Journalistic ethics:** Every news outlet should have and adhere to a set of ethics, the most basic of which are: Truth and accuracy; independence; fairness and impartiality; humanity; transparency; and accountability.
- **Media manipulation:** Refers to the use of spin, bias, slant, and framing.
- **Propaganda model:** Noam Chomsky and Edward Herman's propaganda model explains the five filters through which information must pass in corporate news media: Ownership; advertising; official sources; flak; and marginalizing dissent.
- **Fake news:** This comes in many forms, including misinformation and disinformation. It is any content that is introduced as legitimate news, but is false or misleading.[24]
- **Fake news producers and their motives:** The producers of fake news include the legacy media, state-sponsored propaganda machines, political party propaganda apparatuses, satirists, and self-interested actors.[25] When encountering content presented or perceived as journalism, media consumers should not be passive; rather, they should carefully engage the material and ask the following basic questions:

- Is the content journalism?
- Who is the publisher of this content?
- Who is the author of this content?
- Do I understand the content?
- What is the evidence supporting this article?
- What is missing from the content?

In addition to avoiding false or misleading content, it is incumbent upon citizens to *be the media*. Democracies depend upon the free flow of information, and every story has the potential to change the trajectory of the democratic experiment. We increasingly hear about news deserts, areas without any news media coverage. These trends are inimical to the democratic process. Readers should consider serving their democracy by developing news media for their local region to share vital information about what is happening in their communities.

7: A – Assess and Analyze Digital Media Use and Abuse

The wildly popular 2020 Netflix documentary *The Social Dilemma* portrayed users as helpless victims of big-tech. This thinking is anathema to critical scholars because they contend that users have the autonomy to negotiate their relationship to media. This is what it means to be a critically literate digital media citizen. Critical digital literacy seeks to strengthen democratic practices by engendering autonomy among digital media users through an analysis of the political economy, and the socio-economic, benefits, and costs that shape digital communication.[26] This means being aware of how surveillance capitalism and filter bubbles shape the possibilities and limits of digital media in the 21st century.

Critically literate digital media users:

- **Agree on standards of expectation:** Engage in dialogue with your coworkers, classroom, family, and loved ones about rules and expectations regarding screen use at events, meals, and conversation. Try to make the focus less on the screen and more on the experience at hand. One example is **netiquette,** a term used to describe the preferred or accepted way to communicate in digital spaces.
- **Are mindful of digital limits:** Every medium has limitations such as the amount of characters, to availability of non-verbal cues, and more. Rather than blindly engage in dialogue on social media, consider if the truncated communication allows for the lack of depth necessary for the topic of discussion. Pay the topic and the other person the respect they deserve and only use the medium if it is conducive to the constructive discourse required.

- **Avoid solitude deprivation:** Refers to "a state in which you spend close to zero time alone with your own thoughts and free from input from other minds."[27] Solitude deprivation pushes people to extremes where they miss out on positive things, are unable to clarify their problems, regulate emotions, or strengthen relationships, and lack moral courage.

- **Avoid technochauvenism:** The "belief that tech is always the solution" to every problem.[28]

- **Avoid trolls and trolling:** Rather than signal that you find someone to be wrong through name calling, labeling, or cancellation, consider asking questions about their evidence to see if they know something you do not or if they will find that a lack of evidence explains their problematic conclusion. Similarly, consider taking the conversation/debate to a platform more conducive to constructive dialogue.

- **Negotiate terms of use with big-tech:** Citizens have the power to negotiate if and when they use digital media. We recommend starting that negotiation with an analysis of the costs and benefits derived from using digital media, and branch into attempts at digital minimalism.

- **Join the attention resistance:** Cal Newport argues that we can defeat the attention economy by deleting social media from our phones, turning our devices into single-use computers, using social media only as a professional, embracing more slow media, and dumbing down our smartphones.[29]

- **Practice digital declutter:** This process involves stepping away from optional online activities for 30 days in order to undermine many of the cycles of addiction that digital tools instill. If that seems drastic, some, like pioneering computer scientist Jaron Lanier, advocate for cancelling social media usage entirely. Others have more balanced approaches, like bestselling author Tiffany Shlain, who encourages what she calls a Technology Shabbat in her book *24/6: Giving up Screens One Day a Week to Get More Time, Creativity, and Connection.* Both Lanier and Shlain offer well-proven ways to implement such practices, even in our busy and increasingly digital lives.[30]

- **Overthrow the digital masters:** Digital devices can control or influence our frequency of use and behavior through algorithms, by constantly interrupting us with notifications, as well as invade privacy with a variety of surveillance mechanisms with little notice by the user. In the process, they make profits from selling your data and weaponizing it to nudge or direct you to make a purchase or related decision. Users should turn off all notifications and check their devices when they want. Similarly, rather than give your device access to microphones, photos, contacts, and cameras, all the time, turn them all off. Then, you will have to turn on a feature to use it rather than have it always available. This creates an extra step for considering if the action you are seeking to engage is worth it. Do you need to take a picture? Or can you just eat the food and enjoy the moment? In other words, who is controlling whom? Do we use these devices or do they use us? Remember, we need to decide, not the machines.

The internet in general, and the most popular platforms in particular, do not necessarily have to be for profit or surveillance driven. Decades of law and policy are responsible for this narrow interpretation of the internet. However, the open-software movement, championed by activists like the late Aaron Swartz, which supports voluntarily writing and exchanging programming code for the purposes of software development, and encryption software, which utilizes cryptography to protect the privacy of digital information on computers and over the internet, are powerful reminders that individuals, such as you the reader, can create and access media in a way that better serves the public and democratic process.

8: L – Lead by Example: Democracy is Not a Spectator Sport

Long-time consumer rights advocate, lawyer, and presidential candidate Ralph Nader reminds us that "democracy is not a spectator sport." Citizens not only can engage in dialogue with the people they disagree with, it is essential for our democracy that they do so. It is naïve to think that we can force others to behave or think in a certain way, but it is a lot easier to convince them to consider alternative behaviors and attitudes when the suggestion derives from someone who not only says it, but lives it. We encourage the reader to allot time for self-reflection on how they contribute to irrational thinking, engage in media illiterate practices, and foster destructive dialogue. In an effort to inspire others, we encourage the reader to act as a leader and engage in critical thinking and constructive dialogue even when it is difficult. The daily behaviors and attitudes that the readers display can be as instructive as they are inspiring.

A Critical Conclusion for a Constructive Future Revisited

From the outset of this book, we've argued that critical thinking and constructive dialogue take real effort because being civically engaged in a democratic society is a major responsibility. We call for a robust civic education, more critical pedagogy in classrooms, and critical awareness of media and its role in society. We have tied these concepts directly to community engagement and cultural competency, including increased civility and empathy towards those different from ourselves. Empathy is a critical concept for community engagement and cultural competency.[31] Psychologist Alfred Adler explains that "empathy is seeing with the eyes of another, listening with the ears of another and feeling with the heart of another."[32] Empathy refers to an individual's ability to put themselves, cognitively, in the position of another person to better understand their perspective.[33] This is how we achieve civility. Author and social critic Os Guinness warned that such conduct threatens the very foundations of American democracy, noting: "

> Civility must truly be restored. It is not to be confused with niceness and mere etiquette or dismissed as squeamishness about differences. It is a tough, robust, substitutive concept that is a republican virtue, critical to both democracy and civil society, and a manner of conduct that will be decisive for the future of the American Republic.[34]

Civility rests upon empathy for others. Without empathy, increased social alienation and hyper-polarization is ensured. Empathy "bridges divides by elevating the role of listening over attacking, providing space to consider others' stories, experiences, and grievances. Empathy provides a path for appreciating diversity and advancing solidarity across differences of culture, race, gender, age, and location."[35]

Indeed, a constructive future is possible even as we find ourselves in contentious times. The 21st century in America kicked off with the historic and controversial election of President George W. Bush and the tragic events of September 11, 2001, and is turning out to be as turbulent as other past eras, as we noted in the introduction of this volume, in 1968, with the words of Black Panther Eldridge Cleaver, from Folsom Prison, who noted:

> The destiny of the entire human race depends on what is going on in America today. This is a staggering reality to the rest of the world; they must feel like passengers in a supersonic jetliner who are forced to watch helplessly while a passel of drunks, hypes, freaks, and madmen fight for the controls and the pilot's seat.[36]

We are nearly a quarter of the way into the 21st century as we write this, and while the world has changed in many ways, certain power dynamics remain, and many see the U.S. as more divided than any time since its Civil War, struggling with seemingly irreconcilable differences domestically, and increasingly precarious situations internationally. That said, we wrote this text because not all is lost, and there is much we can do in the present to mitigate our differences and transcend tendentious trajectories. Our future living together on this planet, with its volatile environment, climatically as well as socially, politically, and economically, depends on how well we can make logical sense of the world around us, understand each other in truly holistic ways, and even learn how to build bridges and work together where we can, even if we agree to disagree.

Notes

1 Sharon Lerner, "How a professional climate change denier discovered the lies and decided to fight for science," *The Intercept*, April 28 2017, https://thein tercept.com/2017/04/28/how-a-professional-climate-change-denier-discovered -the-lies-and-decided-to-fight-for-science/.

2 Jonathan H. Adler, "Confessions of a former climate skeptic: Jerry Taylor on why he now considers climate change a serious problem," *Reason*, June 3, 2019, https://reason.com/volokh/2019/06/03/confessions-of-a-former-climate-s keptic/.

3 Lerner, "How a professional climate change denier discovered the lies and decided to fight for science."

4 Ibid.

5 Ibid.

6 Rohan Kundargi, Sucharita Gopal, and Mina Tsay-Vogel, "Understanding the perception of global climate change: Research into the role of media," in *AGU Fall Meeting Abstracts*, vol. 2016, pp. ED51C-0815.

7 Troy H. Campbell and Aaron C. Kay, "Solution aversion: On the relation between ideology and motivated disbelief," *Journal of Personality and Social Psychology* 107, no. 5 (2014): 809.

8 Andrea Morris, "The science behind getting people to believe climate science," *Forbes*, February 28, 2019, https://www.forbes.com/sites/andreamorris/ 2019/02/28/the-science-behind-getting-people-to-believe-climate-science/?sh =23e2477c7329.

9 Ibid., 238.

10 Fred E. Jandt, *Conflict Communication* (Thousand Oaks, CA: Sage Publications, 2017).

11 Paulo Freire, *Pedagogy of the Oppressed* (New York: Bloomsbury Publishing, 1970, 2018).

12 "14.3 Problem solving and decision making in groups," *Communication in the Real World*, University of Minnesota, https://open.lib.umn.edu/communica tion/chapter/14-3-problem-solving-and-decision-making-in-groups/.

13 Lee Mun Wah, "Mindful Facilitation Training for the Workplace," 2018, http s://bhdp.sccgov.org/sites/g/files/exjcpb716/files/lp-mindfully-resolving-conflict s-for-diversity-issues-handout-04-02-18.pdf.

14 Jonathan Haidt, *The Righteous Mind: Why Good People Are Divided by Politics and Religion* (New York: Vintage Books, 2012).

15 Jeffrey Goodman, "A critical discussion of talking past one another," *Philosophy & Rhetoric* 40, no. 3 (2007): 311–325.

16 Bob Blauner, "Talking past each other: Black and white languages of race," *American Prospect* 10 (1992): 55–64.

17 "8 ways to develop metacognitive skills," *Inner Drive*, https://blog.innerdrive. co.uk/eight-ways-to-develop-metacognitive-skills.

18 Pablo Briñol and Kenneth G. DeMarree, eds, *Social Metacognition* (New York: Psychology Press, 2012).

19 Nolan Higdon and Allison Butler, "Episode 19–5 ways to be a more media literate citizen," *Along The Line*, March 12, 2019, https://www.youtube.com/watch?v=Kwfcc2wGNJE&list=PLefnCMJ5W_iILomqv3wJKyKLyY0lWtebw&index=21&t=3s.

20 Cal Newport, *Deep Work, Rules for Focused Success in a Distracted World* (New York: Grand Central Publishing, 2016).

21 Ozlem Sensoy and Robin DiAngelo, *Is Everyone Really Equal?: An Introduction to Key Concepts in Social Justice Education* (New York: Teachers College Press, 2017).

22 Nolan Higdon and Allison Butler, "Episode 19 – 5 ways to be a more media literate citizen," *Along The Line*, March 12, 2019, https://www.youtube.com/watch?v=Kwfcc2wGNJE&list=PLefnCMJ5W_iILomqv3wJKyKLyY0lWtebw&index=21&t=3s.

23 Douglas Kellner and Jeff Share, *The Critical Media Literacy Guide, Engaging Media and Transforming Education* (Boston, MA: Brill Sense, 2019), xiii.

24 Nolan Higdon, *The Anatomy of Fake News: A Critical News Literacy Education* (Oakland, CA: University of California Press, 2020).

25 Ibid.

26 Gianfranco Polizzi, "Information literacy in the digital age: Why critical digital literacy matters for democracy," in *Informed Societies: Why Information Literacy Matters for Citizenship, Participation and Democracy*, ed. Stéphane Goldstein (London: Facet Publishing, 2020), 1–23.

27 Ibid., 103.

28 Meredith Broussard, *Artificial Unintelligence: How Computers Misunderstand the World* (Cambridge, MA: MIT Press, 2019), 7–8.

29 Cal Newport, *Deep Work, Rules for Focused Success in a Distracted World* (New York: Grand Central Publishing, 2016).

30 Ibid.; see also Jaron Lanier, *Ten Arguments for Deleting Your Social Media Accounts Right Now* (New York: Henry Holt and Co., 2018); and Tiffany Shlain, *24/6: Giving up Screens One Day a Week to Get More Time, Creativity, and Connection* (New York: Gallery Books, 2019), online at https://www.24sixlife.com.

31 Katharine E. Scott and James A. Graham, "Service-learning: Implications for empathy and community engagement in elementary school children," *Journal of Experiential Education* 38, no. 4 (2015): 354–372.

32 Helen Demetriou, *Empathy, Emotion and Education* (Cambridge, UK: Springer, 2018).

33 Michael E. Morrell, *Empathy and Democracy: Feeling, Thinking, and Deliberation* (University Park, PA: Penn State Press, 2010).

34 Ibid., p. 3.

35 Nolan Higdon and Mickey Huff, *United States of Distraction: Media Manipulation in Post-Truth America (and what we can do about it)* (San Francisco: City Lights Books, 2019), 160–161. For more on what we can do about these situations, see the concluding chapter in that volume, "Make America Think Again."

36 "America in 1968: An overview in 17 quotes – we take a quick look at the major events and pop culture highlights in a pivotal year in American history," *Saturday Evening Post*, January 18, 2018, https://www.saturdayeveningpost.com/2018/01/america-1968-overview-17-quotes/.

Index